NATIONALISM AND THE CLASS STRUGGLE

BER BOROCHOV
(1881-1917)

NATIONALISM
and the
CLASS STRUGGLE

A MARXIAN APPROACH TO
THE JEWISH PROBLEM

SELECTED WRITINGS

by

BER BOROCHOV

Introduction by ABRAHAM G. DUKER

GREENWOOD PRESS, PUBLISHERS
WESTPORT, CONNECTICUT

The Library of Congress has catalogued this publication as follows:

Library of Congress Cataloging in Publication Data

Borochov, Ber, 1881-1917.
  Nationalism and the class struggle.

  Reprint of the 1937 ed.
  1. Jewish question. 2. Jews--Political and
social conditions. 3. Zionism. I. Title.
DS141.B68   1972   320.5'4'095694   70-97268
ISBN 0-8371-2590-1

Originally published in 1937
by Poale Zion-Zeire Zion of America and
Young Poale Zion Alliance of America, New York

First Greenwood Reprinting 1972

Library of Congress Catalogue Card Number 70-97268

ISBN 0-8371-2590-1

Printed in the United States of America

LIBRARY
University of Texas
At San Antonio

CONTENTS

EDITOR'S PREFACE

THIS volume has been prepared to help fill a need that has grown with the development of a Socialist Zionist youth movement in America.

The English-reading public which wants to make a closer acquaintance with Socialist Zionist[1] ideology finds very little material available in English—only scattered bits of interpretation. But the serious student cannot be satisfied with a mere exegesis of the fundamental literature; he is interested in perusing the source material for himself. And especially in the case of Borochov's writings is this important; for many of the so-called interpretations of Borochov are in reality flagrant *mis*interpretations. The English rendering of the writings of one of the leading exponents of Socialist Zionist thought is intended to make some of this source material accessible and to enable the student to arrive at his own conclusions.

The selections included in this work are drawn chiefly from the two Yiddish volumes published by the Poale Zion Party of America (1920) and the Jewish National Workers' Alliance of America (1928). Only the more important essays are included, particularly those dealing with various phases of the Jewish problem. The criteria for the selection of an article were (1) its contribution toward an understanding of the problems of Socialist Zionism, (2) its significance to the American reader, and (3) its historical value.

The essays fall into three sections. Section One includes selections most of which were written during the World War. They concern themselves with the economic position of the Jews, the various proposed solutions to the Jewish problem, the opposition to Zionism, the attitude of socialists toward nationalism, and finally

---

[1]The terms Socialist Zionism, Labor Zionism, proletarian Zionism, and Poale Zionism are used interchangeably.

the re-definition of Socialist Zionism in the light of contemporary events. "The Jewish Terrorist and the *Shomer*" perhaps gives the best insight into the human Borochov.

Section Two consists of the lengthy essay, "The National Question and the Class Struggle", a work dating back to 1905. This was one of the first attempts to refute the vulgarized "Marxian" concept of cosmopolitanism with its resultant indifference and opposition to nationalism. Borochov's analysis remains a classic in Marxian socialist literature.

The third section includes several essays portraying the development of the Poale Zion movement and its ideology. "Our Platform" was the theoretical program of the Russian Poale Zion. No doubt the editor will be accused of having given preference to Borochov's later and shorter articles and for having reduced the corner-stone, as some call it, of Borochovism—"Our Platform"— to a mere document. However, when one bears in mind that the document was written when Borochov was a youth of but twenty-four years, and that he himself later expressed the opinion that it should be revised to conform with new conditions in Jewish life, one will understand what motivated the editor to make this arrangement. Those who point to "Our Platform" as the basis of Borochov's ideology shut their eyes to his later metamorphosis.

The only liberties taken by the editor have been to omit various parenthetical portions throughout the text and various polemics that would be of little interest to the reader. Since many of the essays were written under pressure of time for the Jewish daily press, they required slight revisions for their inclusion in book form.

Borochov's own footnotes are indicated by an asterisk. A number of explanatory notes have been added by the editor, indicated by Arabic numerals. In many cases the editor has drawn comparisons with modern Jewish life. Full use has been made of the notes and introductory remarks of Berl Locker, editor of the second Yiddish volume of the selected works of Borochov, and full acknowledgement is hereby made.

The title, "A Marxian Approach to the Jewish Problem", is used advisedly. Lest it be misinterpreted, we bring a quotation from Borochov which clearly indicates his attitude toward Marxism. In it Borochov mercilessly attacks those who seek to canonize and vulgarize Marx:

Historic necessity will deliver us into the promised land of socialism—this Marx conceived, and this Engels popularized. Have we need to think any more? Are not all questions solved now?

True, that which Marx said some seventy years ago may have been correct then, but has not the world changed and grown older?

But there is no God but Allah, and Mohammed is His only prophet. Similarly there is no God other than "scientific socialism", and Karl Marx is its only prophet. A prophet may foresee fifty, seventy, or a thousand years hence. That accounts for Caliph Omar's command that all the libraries in Alexandria be destroyed. If the secular books contained that which is in the Koran, of what use were they? If they contained something not in the Koran, then they were surely heretical and must be destroyed. The "modern" Marxists are sufficiently tolerant not to burn the books of their opponents, and for that they should certainly be congratulated.

I can envision Marx arising from his grave. Upon seeing his present disciples, he motions them away and utters, "I—God forbid—I am no Marxist!"

Marx was undoubtedly the greatest thinker of the nineteenth century. None has better analyzed the complex problems of our social organization. But because Marx is dead and because new problems have arisen, we must think independently and arrive at our own solutions; we must accustom the world to utilize its own mental faculties. ("The Old Karl Marx and His Disciples", *Die Warheit,* March 20, 1915.)

This translation of Borochov's writings was initiated by the Young Poale Zion Alliance, in cooperation with the Poale Zion-Zeire Zion Party. The entire staff of the Young Poale Zion Alliance has contributed its share to the preparation and publication of this volume—it is truly a cooperative venture.

The original drafts of the translation of "The National Question and the Class Struggle" were prepared by Jacob Katzman, "Our Platform" by Ben Yitzhaki, "The Tenth Jubilee of the Poale Zion" and "Reminiscences" by Harry Steiner. In all cases the editor and his associates took the liberty of making changes in line with the scope and aim of this volume. The editor is indebted to Solomon Katz and Ben Halpern for valuable revisions in "Our Platform" and to Isaac Frank for revision of "The Economic Development of the Jewish People". Most useful suggestions have been made by Ben Zion Applebaum, Saadia Gelb, Shlomo Grodzensky, Louis Guttman, and Nathan Guttman. The editor is also indebted to Abraham G. Duker for his very valuable introduction to this volume.

New York, N. Y.

August, 1937.

MOSHE COHEN

BER BOROCHOV

A BIOGRAPHICAL SKETCH

BER BOROCHOV was born June 21, 1881 (seventh of Tammuz), in the town of Zolotonoshi in Ukraine. The constant pogroms and attacks in the small towns and villages forced many Jews to move to the larger cities. Two months after his birth Borochov's parents settled in the capital city of Poltava.

Poltava was by no means a large city. It had no factories to speak of, and the Jews gained their livelihood mainly from trading with the neighboring cities and villages. For some unknown reason, the Russian government chose to exile revolutionists to Poltava, and some of the outstanding intellectuals of that time were sent there. They exerted a profound influence on the youth of that city.

Poltava was also one of the first Zionist centers. A branch of the "Lovers of Zion" was established there. Borochov's father, Moses Aaron, was among its active members. The practical work for Zion evoked an interest in Jewish culture, schools, and libraries, and enriched Jewish life.

The ideological components of Socialist Zionism thus found their way into Poltava. These currents of thought operated independently of each other. Both of them, no doubt, impressed Borochov, who later integrated socialism with Zionism.

Ber Borochov's parents were cultured people. His father (now living in New York), a Hebrew teacher, had to work long hours to eke out his living and therefore could devote little time to the education of his son. His mother, Rachel, possessing a love for learning, spared no effort to educate Borochov. With

11

her help, at the age of three he could already read Russian; and listening to his father's classes, he also learned Hebrew. Reading was his hobby. Young as he was, he never put away a book without making sure that he understood it. Even in his early childhood, his Jewish and non-Jewish comrades recognized him as their leader, although some of them were much older than he. He could tell them stories and help them with their lessons.

Though Borochov read everything he could lay his hands on, his favorites were travel stories. Inspired by these stories and by the Zionist atmosphere of his home and town, Borochov (at the age of ten) and a playmate decided to "leave" for Palestine. Secretly, they sneaked away from home early one morning, but were brought back late at night by strangers who found the "travelers" on the outskirts of the city.

At the age of eleven, Borochov entered the *Gymnasium*. At that time he knew Russian well, for his parents had conversed in Russian with him since he was three years old. They did that because the school authorities did not tolerate "a Jewish accent". Thus he was called Bori, and only later did he adopt the Jewish name Ber.

Though an excellent pupil, his interests lay outside his textbooks. The study of philosophy and languages attracted him greatly. Even before he was graduated (in 1900) he already had a good command of Greek, Latin, Sanskrit, philosophy, and economics. His instructors acknowledged his scholarship but resented his lack of discipline. Once, having escaped punishment in school, he decided for the second time to leave for Palestine. He had earned enough money from his tutoring for a day's travel. Having reached Nicolayev penniless, he turned to the local rabbi. He told the rabbi of his noble mission and asked him for assistance. The rabbi explained to young Bori the unfeasibility of the plan and convinced him to return home, assuring him that his parents would not punish him.

Social problems attracted Borochov very soon. Because his father was a government-licensed teacher, he was not suspected of harboring revolutionists or illegal literature. When the occasion arose, therefore, Borochov's father offered a safe haven. In this way, Borochov came in contact with illegal literature. He became interested in the lives of conspirators and learned that one of their holiest vows is not to disclose the names of fellow members. Once his mother noticed a wound on his hand. Upon inquiry, he told her that he had wanted to test his endurance. He had held his hand over the flame of a candle until he was convinced that he would not betray his comrades no matter how brutally the police should treat him.

Borochov was a candidate for the gold medal offered by the *Gymnasium* to the most outstanding student. Because of the anti-Semitism prevailing in the *Gymnasium* he failed to receive it. He therefore refused to enter the university, lest he meet in the higher schools of enlightenment and learning the same anti-Semitic ire. From then on his political life begins.

In 1900 Borochov affiliated with the Social-Democratic Party and for a time served as an organizer and propagandist. An independent thinker, searching for a solution to the problem of nationalism which the party ignored, Borochov's doubts led to his expulsion from the party in May, 1901. He then organized a labor club with Socialist Zionist leanings. He was a travelling lecturer for the General Zionist organization, addressing himself to the Jewish worker. Then he made his first attempts to integrate Zionism with Marxism. At the close of 1903 he made his literary debut—in an essay dealing with "The Nature of the Jewish Intellect".

Officially Borochov joined the Poale Zion Party in November, 1905, after the Sixth Zionist Congress, when the burning issue was Zion versus Uganda. His opposition to any other territory than Palestine found expression in his famous essay "To the Question: Zion and Territory". At the Poltava conference (November, 1905), Borochov helped to formulate the Poale Zion program. The young Party could not unite all the elements because of the various current ideologies (described at length in his "Reminiscences", pp. 179-182). Only in the December of 1906, after numerous splits, did the first convention of the pro-Palestine Poale Zion take place; and its adopted program guided the party till the Bolshevik Revolution. At that time Borochov published his "Our Platform", the result of a three-week discussion of the committee which was delegated to draft a program. During 1905-06, Borochov edited the Russian Party organ, *Yevreskaya Rabotochaya Chronika* ("Jewish Labor Chronicle"). He also wrote then "The National Question and the Class Struggle".

On June 3, 1906, the Czarist government disbanded the *Duma* (Parliament), and on the same night Borochov was arrested. Among the prisoners he founded a "People's University". There were many Ukrainians there who fell under the spell of Borochov's theories of nationalism. Later, a number of Social-Democratic Ukrainian groups even called themselves "Borochovists", and many of his theories of nationalism were adopted. He soon escaped from prison and settled for a time in Minsk. There in 1907 he first began to write in Yiddish. Constantly spied on by the police, Borochov was forced to leave Russia; and in the latter part of 1907 he left for Crakow and thence to the Hague.

From that time on Borochov's life became that of a wanderer. In the summer of 1907 Borochov helped found the World Confederation of Poale Zion. He became a member of its administration and for a time was also its secretary.

He went to Vienna to edit the Party organ, *Das Freie Wort* ("The Free Word"), from 1907 to 1910. Up to the World War Borochov travelled continually. He visited England, France, Belgium, Holland, and Switzerland; and everywhere he shared his time between literary work and Party activities. He was a correspondent for a number of European and American Jewish papers, and collaborated in the writing of the Russian Jewish Encyclopedia (which contain his articles on Vienna, Jewish professions, and the Yiddish language). In 1913, he published in the *Pincas* ("The Record") two monumental works: "The Tasks of Yiddish Philology" and the "Library of the Yiddish Philologist", which to this very day are the basis for this branch of Jewish science.

During this period he also attempted to form a union among all Jewish socialist and labor parties, but without success.

With the outbreak of the World War, Borochov was forced to leave Austria, and he came to America. Here too he divided his time between Party work and literary work. A gifted orator and writer, Borochov enriched the Party during his stay in America. He edited for a while *Der Yiddisher Kaempfer* ("The Jewish Militant"). He became one of the outstanding proponents of a democratically organized American and World Jewish Congress. He edited the publication, *Der Yiddisher Congress.* His profound analysis of the minority problem and of the question of minority rights is contained in the book, *In The Struggle For Jewish Rights.* In his fight for democracy within Jewish life he spared no one. He disclosed the timid psychology of the wealthy assimilationist and the cosmopolitan Jewish socialist. That American Jewry was finally represented at the Peace Conference in Paris is in no small measure due to Borochov's activities.

More than once his views conflicted with those of the majority in the Party. He was against the pro-Allies sentiment which dominated the Party during the World War. He also criticized severely the Party's orientation on bourgeois Zionism, asserting that in its attempts to bring socialism into the ranks of General Zionism, it estranges itself from the Jewish labor movement. In spite of these differences and also his opposition to participation in the Zionist Congress, he knew that this period of *Sturm und Drang* was not the time for debates.

His literary activities were none the less abundant. He was on the staff of the Yiddish daily, *Die Warheit,* writing articles and editorials. He continued with his research work in the Yiddish language and literature and completed—a yet unpublished work— "A History of the Yiddish Language and Literature". He also introduced a new Yiddish orthography which, with but slight revisions, is now in standard use.

The March Revolution broke out in Russia in 1917, and Borochov could no longer bear to remain in exile. The Russian

Party, too, demanded his immediate return. His wife, Luba, and their five-year-old daughter (now in Palestine) at first pleaded with Borochov not to return to Russia. His wife was again an expectant mother, but even this did not influence Borochov's course. "I am a soldier—I must answer the call!" was his reply.

On his way to Russia, Borochov stopped in Stockholm and helped to prepare the memorandum containing the Poale Zion demands before the Holland-Scandinavian Socialist Conference, to which he was also a delegate. From there he proceeded to Russia to attend the Third All-Russian Poale Zion Convention.

S. Har, who met Borochov in Petrograd and accompanied him to Kiev, relates that among other things Borochov announced his plans to issue a revised edition of "Our Platform" to take account of present Jewish and Palestinian realities. (His speeches at the Conference and the impressions will be found on pp. 124-132.)

The Party selected him as one of its delegates to the Conference of Nationalities, and there he delivered two addresses: "The Federation of Nationalities in the New Russia" and "The Language Problem". His proficiency in the problem of nationalism resulted in his selection as a delegate to the Constitutional Convention of the Russian Republic. In the course of the Party's preparation for these responsible tasks, Borochov travelled day and night as its emissary. On one of those trips he caught a cold which later developed into an inflammation of the lungs; and after a brief illness he died in Kiev on December 17, 1917 (second of Tebet)—at the age of 36.

INTRODUCTION

THE THEORIES OF BER BOROCHOV AND THEIR PLACE IN
THE HISTORY OF THE JEWISH LABOR MOVEMENT

by ABRAHAM G. DUKER

TODAY SOCIALISTS and communists have come to the realization that Jewish group survival may be feasible, desirable, or justifiable even from their respective points of view. The example of the Soviet Union setting up a separate territory for Jewish settlement in Biro-Bidjan, whether it be merely a means of defending the Soviet Far-East from a Japanese invasion or an *Ahad Ha'amist* attempt to establish a cultural center for Yiddish speaking Jewry, is an open recognition of the right of the Jews to survival as a national group. The recent admission of the "cosmopolite" anti-nationalist Leon Trotsky that the Jewish problem must be solved through territorial concentration follows the same principle, although he would postpone this task until the world revolution had taken place. The socialist schools of the Second International recognized this right during and immediately after the World War. Their leadership is very sympathetic and active on behalf of the idea of Labor Palestine. The smaller revolutionary socialist groups as well as some of the communist Trotskyite groups of all varieties have recognized this principle. Even the most extreme among them are not averse to the admission on an equal basis of the representatives of the Zionist revolutionary parties, like the *Hashomer Hatzair* and the Left Poale Zion, to their conferences and deliberations. One cannot say that all socialists and communists are favorably inclined to the idea of Jewish survival, which to a socialist must imply territorial concentra-

17

tion of the Jews in a given locality. There are still many who cling to the idea of the assimilation of the Jewish masses, even under the present order. Assimilation and the resulting indifference to the plight of the Jewish masses are especially very popular among the adherents of various left-wing ideologies who happen to be of Jewish descent. Most of it can be explained on the basis of the inferiority complexes of minorities and *Juedisches Selbsthass* (self-hate). There is no doubt, however, that the hostility of the socialists and communists to Jewish group survival has lessened considerably. The upbuilding of a strong Jewish labor movement in Palestine, the national policy of the Soviet Union, and especially the example of Nazi Germany and Poland, have been the prime factors in exposing the impracticability of assimilation under capitalism and, to a lesser degree, its undesirability under socialism. Differences of opinion exist concerning the place, the time, and the method for territorial settlement. Some would have it only in Palestine; others would have it in any other place but Palestine. Some advocate its immediate realization; others would postpone it until after the social revolution or limit it to Biro-Bidjan. Many insist on the Yiddish language as the only distinguishing trait of the Jewish proletarian nation of the future. Others advocate Hebrew and a set of certain religio-national cultural traditions. It can be said with certainty, however, that no socialist or communist will today deny the right of the Jewish proletariat to national self-determination at some time and under certain circumstances. Even the Jewish official communists will grant it, if "they, the Jewish masses, express their desire for it".

This increasingly realistic approach to the Jewish problem is in direct opposition to the opinions of the founders and leading lights of the pre-war socialism of all schools. Karl Marx never repudiated his youthful views on the Jewish religion which he expressed so vehemently in his dispute with the Hegelian Bruno Bauer. To him "the basis for the Jewish religion was practical need"; "the worldly ground of the Jews" was "practical need, avarice". "What is their worldly God? Money." "Money is the jealous God of Israel above whom there cannot be any other God." Judaism and the Jewish caste which confesses it would disappear with the disappearance of the capitalistic order. The definition by Marx of the Jews as a caste was based on complete ignorance of both the history and economic circumstances of the Jewish people in his own times, even in the then relatively industrialized Germany. His opinions of Judaism are too strikingly parallel to those expressed by Feuerbach to admit their originality. Besides, these opinions were the common stock of the "enlightened" world of his day. To Marx goes the credit of approaching the Jewish problem from an economic point of view rather than from the theological-moralistic one which was so prevalent in his day. One cannot say that Marx was an anti-Semite. Yet there is no doubt that in spite of the fact that "it has often been said that Marx both embodied and intensified the dialectical powers of the Jewish spirit", the founder of socialism was emotionally blocked on the Jewish problem. His later utterances about it are too few and far-between to indicate definitely his process of reasoning, but most of them are unkind and hostile. His silence in the face of the beginnings of the socialist movement among the Jews in the 1870's, the series of Russian pogroms in 1881, and the subsequent mass migrations cannot be explained in any other way.

This attitude of Marx gave the socialist thinkers the easiest way out—to ignore or to minimize the Jewish problem. It gave Jewish-born socialists a good excuse for assimilating and for neglecting the interests of their brethren in the Ghetto. Moses Hess, the "communist Rabbi", was an object of contempt in socialist circles when he published his *Rome and Jerusalem* in 1862. This is not the place to trace in detail the influence of Marx on the attitudes of the leading pre-war socialists to the Jewish problem. A few illustrations will suffice. Franz Mehring referred to Marx's study about the Jews with: "These few pages are of greater value than the huge pile of literature on the Jewish problem which appeared since that time." Kautsky maintained even later that the Jews were a caste and not a nation in the Middle Ages and that they still constituted one in Eastern Europe. Lenin, who relied largely upon Kautsky and Bauer as experts on the Jewish problem, still maintained in 1913 that the "Jews in the civilized world are not a nation; they have become most assimilated . . . The Jews in

Galicia and Russia are not a nation; they unfortunately . . . are still a *caste*." He said continually that the solution of the Jewish problem in Russia should take the same course which it followed in Western Europe, namely, "a doubtless progress of their assimilation with the surrounding population". "The Jewish question," he stated in 1903, "stands now as follows: assimilation or isolation? And the idea of a Jewish 'nationality' has a definitely reactionary character, not only among its consequential followers (the Zionists), but also among those who attempt to combine it with the ideas of Social-Democracy (the *Bundists*) . . . The idea of a Jewish nationality is a denial of the interests of the Jewish proletariat, introducing within it directly or indirectly a feeling which is hostile to assimilation, a Ghetto feeling." He quoted with enthusiastic approval Kautsky's idea that the complete assimilation of minorities "is the only possible solution to the Jewish problem, and we have to support everything which will aid to remove Jewish isolation". For this reason Lenin was opposed even to Yiddish schools for Jewish children in Russia. Stalin too followed the policies of Marx and Lenin in his pre-war treatment of the Jewish problem. Brachman, an outstanding Soviet scholar in the field, agreed as late as 1936 with Marx that "the special caste situation of the Jews" was *"taken from life"*. The presentation of the Jews as the "nationality of the merchant and money man was not an invention of the Jew haters."

It is not within the space of this essay to trace the evolution of the change of opinion of socialist leadership today. In Russia, it took place because of the realization after the Bolshevik revolution that the Jews could be converted to communism only through the medium of the Yiddish language, and that unless some recognition of national rights be given to the Jews in the Soviet Union, Zionism would constitute a permanent menace to the spread of the communistic ideology among them. The declassment and poverty of the majority of the Jewish masses in Russia, which took on a very sharp form during the period of Military Communism and a somewhat milder form during the NEP (New Economic Policy) period, also were important factors, since the proposed land settlement of Russian Jewry could not take place on an individual basis.

The introduction of the "national policy" by the Communist Party of the Soviet Union gave the stamp of approval to the idea of solving the problem of Jewish unemployment through concentrated territorial settlement, and gave rise to a series of plans in this direction. The most important among these are the now forgotten "Jewish Republic" in Crimea which was widely publicized as the solution of the Jewish problem in its own times and the more recent establishment of the autonomous region in Biro-Bidjan.

Among the socialists in Western Europe, it can be said, the recognition of the special interest of the Jews as a national group and of their right to survive was brought about almost entirely through the efforts of the Socialist Zionist movements, especially the Poale Zion Party, during and after the World War.

The earliest attempts to conduct socialist propaganda among Jews were mainly of the assimilationist cosmopolitan variety. The earliest Jewish socialist circle, which was organized in the Government Rabbinical Seminary at Vilna about 1875, had as its only purpose "to mingle with the people". Its founders, except Lieberman, were not interested in propaganda among the Jews. In 1880, a group of Jewish socialists in Switzerland, who intended to conduct socialist propaganda in the Yiddish, stressed the fact that they were not interested in any Jewish questions, their only purpose being "to preach the ideas of social revolution among the Jewish masses. In order to do this successfully, the masses must be approached in the language which they understand". The first Yiddish socialist newspaper, *Die Arbeiter Zeitung* (1881), had no specific Jewish aims. The early Hebrew and Yiddish publications of Morris Vintchevsky, who continued Lieberman's work in London in the 1880's, were typically cosmopolitan. He even raised a doubt as to the possibility of the continued existence of the Jewish people. The *Narodnik* movement counted many Jews among its members and teachers.

The pogroms of 1881 came as a rude shock to all the Jewish intelligentsia of Russia. The revolutionaries particularly were faced by the recognition of the pogroms on the part of their

Russian contemporaries as a progressive revolutionary tendency. In 1881, the executive committee of the *Narodnaya Volya* issued a proclamation calling upon the Ukrainian peasants to continue their pogrom activities because the Jews were guilty of all their sufferings. In 1882 this proclamation was further popularized The official organ of the movement stated that "we have no right to be negative or even indifferent to a pure folk movement", and that it was impossible to avoid the fact that the revolution would begin with the beating up of the Jews. The attitude of the leaders of this movement changed later, but the bitter taste remained in the mouths of many of the Jewish revolutionaries.

These reactions of the Jewish revolutionaries were varied. Some abandoned their socialism and became Jewish nationalists. Others justified the interpretations of the role of pogroms. Some remained indifferent and even for years after continued to maintain that "there were no Jewish people, no Jewish language, and no Jewish workers". Some awakened to the realization that socialists ought to pay some attention to the Jewish problem. P. B. Axelrod, for instance, in his brochure, *About the Tasks of the Jewish Socialist Intelligentsia,* criticized them for their neglect of the Jewish masses. He pointed out the mistake of ignoring the fact that "the Jews as a nation occupy in Russia an exceptional position" and that the population of the country was far from having the cosmopolitan views of international solidarity among the poorer classes. He speculated about directing the pogroms "if not against all the centers of exploitation", at least exclusively against the wealthy Jewish classes. He seriously thought of Palestine as a place of immigration for Russian Jewry. The opinion of a noted geographer that Palestine was not fit for mass settlement dissuaded him from further action in this direction. Most characteristic was the attitude of complete bewilderment such as was expressed by Leo Deutch, a leading revolutionary, in a letter to P. Lavrov. "It is impossible for a revolutionary to solve the Jewish problem in a practical way. What can be done by revolutionaries in places where the Jews are attacked? To defend them would mean to arouse the hostility of the peasants against the revolutionaries. It it bad enough that they killed the Czar; yet in addition they are defending the *Zhids*. The revolutionaries are faced with two contradictions. It is simply a situation without an escape, both for the Jews and for the revolutionaries . . . Do not think that I was not embittered and faced by a dilemma. Nevertheless I shall always remain a member of the Russian Revolutionary Party and will not leave it even for one day, because this contradiction, the same as many others, was not created by the Party."

At the time when cosmopolitan socialism made its beginnings among the Jews in Russia, there arose a national tendency as well. Aaron Lieberman, who organized the first "Society of Hebrew Socialists" (London, 1876), never speculated about definitions of Jewry. He took its national existence for granted, at least on a cultural basis. He always referred to the Jews as a nation. He was too much a product of his own generation of cosmopolitan socialists to become an adherent of the nebulous Zionism of his period. He was, however, a lover of the Hebrew language, and his last public appearance in New York was at a meeting of a Hebrew speaking society. He insisted on the observance of the Ninth of Ab as a national holiday and looked upon his earlier propaganda work in Russia "not only as a means of gaining recruits for the Russian revolutionary army, but also as a means of heightening the national consciousness of the Jews". But his influence among the contemporary Jewish socialists was nil.

The next effort at the introduction of specific Jewish issues into the revolutionary movement came strangely enough from the Ukrainian, M. Dragomanov, who in his theory of the free union of peoples (promulgated in the early 1880's) promised autonomy to the Jewish cities. His follower, the Jewish revolutionary, Rodin, issued a proclamation calling on Jews to join the revolutionary movement and to demand cultural autonomy with Yiddish as their language.

The most significant effort of this early period to bring the Jewish needs to the attention of active socialists was made by Chaim Zhitlovsky, who was one of the founders and leading spirits of the Socialist Revolutionary Party. Beginning with the publication of an essay in 1887, which dealt with the Essenes from an economic point of view, this thinker developed his interpretation of Jewish life and socialism which so greatly influenced the Jewish labor movement at a much later stage. Zhitlovsky maintained that "scientific" Marxism was not a scientific system, but merely a metaphysical theory. He denied the need and utility of the theory of economic materialism for the socialist movement. His approach to socialism was of the agrarian ethical variety. From this point of view he denied the "iron laws" of Marxism about the disappearance of the Jewish people. He maintained that the Jewish people had always fought for its national existence and that religion was merely a means for this struggle. He saw the need for a Jewish progressive renaissance, the aim of which he visualized in the establishment of a secular, Yiddish speaking, mainly agricultural, group life. The main obstacle in the way was assimilation, which to him was at the same time the main cause of anti-Semitism. Under capitalistic Russia, the Jewish bourgeoisie was bound to increase in number and to become Russianized. The Jews thus would be identified by the masses with reaction. Assimilationist socialism took away the best elements of the Jewish nation and forced them to work for their ideals among the non-Jews, whereas they could have done this same work among their own people. The return of the Jewish intelligentsia to Jewish nationalism would, in his opinion, revive agriculture and the Yiddish language among the Jews, and would eliminate the artificial religious factor in their survival. The best way of fitting this scheme into the frame of the Galut was the orientation of the *Narodnik* movement, which was based on agricultural Russia, and later of the Socialist Revolutionary movement which had the most liberal nationality policy. Zhitlovsky's earlier efforts at organization and propaganda failed to bring any direct results within the Jewish labor movement. He is known better for his later contributions.

The early workers' mutual aid societies and study circles among the Jews in Russia and Poland, which later developed into trade unions and gave rise to the *Bund,* also began without any specific Jewish aim. When at their beginnings in the 1880's they were very small, they served as educational and Russianizing agencies.

Later, the increase in the number of members and the maturity of the leadership caused them to utilize the Yiddish language in their propaganda, which remained of the purely *Narodnik* or Social-Democratic variety. At the earliest celebration of May First by the Jewish workers in Russia, held in Vilna in 1892, one of the speakers discussed the question as to whether the Jewish workers ought to join the socialist movement or follow those who advise the Jews to go to Palestine and to settle there the Jewish and social problems. He condemned the idea of the existence of a "separate Jewish nationality" and called upon the Jewish workers to join the "great world-embracing fighting party of workers" which would achieve "true freedom, brotherhood, and happiness for all mankind without the exclusion of the Jews." This attack on the *Chovevei Zion* movement shows that the workers refused to swallow easily the cosmopolitan theories of their *intelligentsia* leadership. In 1895, A. Martov, later an outstanding Social-Democrat and Menshevik, called in his May First speech for the creation of "a special Jewish workers organization which would be the leader and educator of the Jewish proletariat in its struggle for economic, civil, and political liberation." It would, of course, join the other parties in the struggle. His main reason was his fear that the Russian or Polish working classes might in their difficult struggle yield on certain issues "which concern us Jews in particular, such as, for instance, freedom of religion and equality for the Jews." He also thought that "as long as the present order exists every nation ought to strive, if not for political independence, at least for fully equal rights." "National indifference of one nation to another which is robbed of general civil rights is the greatest obstacle to the development of the oppressed nation." It was the duty of the Socialist Party to awaken it in order that it might liberate itself from civil inequality. Since his ideas were frowned upon by the leadership and members of the Jewish groups, he recanted very soon after.

What individual theorists and propagandists failed to achieve was accomplished by a mass movement. The *Bund* (General Jewish Workers' Alliance) was organized in September, 1897 (the same year in which Theodore Herzl convoked the First Zionist

Congress in Basle, Switzerland) as a culmination of tendencies and discussions about the necessity of the establishment of a Jewish workers' movement within the various propaganda circles and elementary trade unions which conducted their activities among the Jewish artisans and proletarians in Russia. The *Bund* began as an economic organization, and its progress in the direction of a consistent ideology was slow and hesitant. It refused to face the Jewish problem as one international in its scope. It maintained that the Jews having lost the characteristics of a nation could never regain them. At best Jewry can be called a composite of different groups without any strong link of unity. The *Bund* considered itself merely a local Russian party for Jewish worker. Its early leaders were completely neutral to assimilation, linguistic or otherwise. In their minds, assimilation was neither desirable nor undesirable. History alone would determine its future. The difference between the *Bund* and the Russian Social-Democratic movement of that period was the fact that the *Bund* conducted its propaganda in Yiddish among Jewish workers. It maintained its cosmopolitan outlook for some time; but very soon, mainly under the pressure of Zionism and of the initial momentum inherent in its Jewish membership, it began to concern itself more and more with Jewish issues. These tendencies culminated with cultural work in Yiddish and a modest demand for national cultural autonomy for the Jews in Russia, after the Austrian theoreticians had made such demands *kosher* from a socialist point of view. The militancy of the *Bund* and its political action in the early stages of its development fill a glorious chapter in the history of the Jewish labor movement. But it certainly failed to furnish a solution for those desiring a socialist road to Jewish survival.

The attempts to arrive at a synthesis of Zionism and socialism began contemporaneously with political Zionism. Some intellectuals discussed this problem at the First Zionist Congress at Basle in 1897. Individual socialists of prominence (as for instance, Bernard Lazare, Farbstein) were active Zionists since the beginning of the movement. The first man to make a serious attempt at this

task was Nachman Syrkin. His propaganda began with the publication of a series of essays (1898), and culminated in 1904 with
his organization of the first Socialist Zionist group, *Heirut*, in
Berlin. Syrkin's ideology was non-Marxian. He believed that the
abnormal economic situation of the Jewish masses in the Galut,
which is expressed in their frequent migrations, leads them directly
to Zionism. The solution of their problem can take place only
in a free Jewish land of labor and socialism. Attempts at productivization in the Galut can be successful only temporarily, because
as soon as conditions improve a return to middle class occupations
takes place. Because of the interests of the upper and middle
classes in maintaining their economic positions in the Galut, assimilation is their expression. But the Zionism of the proletariat, in
which he also included the petty employers as well as all the working people, has little in common with the various bourgeois varieties, such as the modest colonization plans of the *Chibat Zion*, the
Maskilim's longings for a cultural center, or the West European
Jews' philanthropic approach of saving their poorer brethren. Yet,
he believed in working in common with the bourgeois Zionists.
The task of the proletarian Zionists was to organize the Jewish
masses, to fight against the Jewish moneyed and assimilated bourgeoisie in order to force it to aid the upbuilding of the national
home. The achievement of Zionism was one area in the activities
of the movement, and must proceed independently of the work in
the second area, namely, that of political socialism in the Galut.
Syrkin's "double area" theory of socialist activities did not become
very popular because of the lack of coordination between the work
for socialism in the Galut and the Zionist work for Palestine.
Yet, his ideology has been a factor in the later development of the
non-Marxian groups in the Labor Zionist movement.

At the time when Syrkin was conducting his propaganda in Berlin, there arose (since 1900) different Socialist Zionist groups in
Russia under the name "Poale Zion" ("Workers of Zion"). They
were scattered in different cities without any organizational unity.
At first, their only distinction from the General Zionists was their
working class membership. They denied the connection between

the Jewish proletariat and the socialist and revolutionary movement. Their denial was based on the interpretation that the revolution could not solve the problem of Jewish poverty which sprang from the Galut. Later they maintained that a struggle for socialism in the Galut was impossible because there was no Jewish ruling class and no healthy Jewish proletariat. They did, however, concern themselves with economic issues and conducted trade union work. The ideological leaders of this trend were the Minsk groups.

A different development took place in Southern Russia. There, under the leadership of Borochov, the groups which were also organized under the name of "Poale Zion" based their ideology on a unity between Social-Democracy and Zionism. In those days which Syrkin so aptly termed "the period of theoretical chaos", the different ideologies of the several Socialist Zionist, or rather, Socialist Territorialist groups were slowly and laboriously evolved through a great deal of discussion, pamphleteering, and the appearance of the early press of the movement.

A breaking point in the evolution of the ideologies was caused by the offer on the part of England, presented at the Sixth Zionist Congress at Basle in 1903, to create in Uganda a Jewish national home. This offer was rejected because of the strenuous objections of the Russian Zionists. The Zionist movement split into two warring groups, the pro-Palestinians and the anti-Palestinians. This dispute finally led to the establishment of the "Jewish Territorialist Organization" (ITO) under the leadership of Israel Zangwill.

The same issue came to a head among the various labor groups in Zionism. The enticing offer of Uganda appealed to those who looked for an immediate realistic solution in terms of mass emigration. The possibilities of Palestine as a land capable of absorbing the Jewish masses within a reasonable time seemed to be remote and visionary. Thus the movement was immediately divided into two trends, namely of Palestinism and territorialism. The Minsk groups were territorialist. The Southern Russian group retained their Palestinian sympathies. Out of this chaos of discussions and orientations there arose several distinct movements, all of them orientated on some combination of socialism and Zionism and on the impossibility of solving the Jewish problem without a territory. They were divided on the questions of Palestine, Galut activities, and the theory of non-proletarianization.

The theories of non-proletarianization or limited proletarianization were accepted by all the early Socialist-Zionist and Socialist-Territorialist groups. The proponents of the first theory believed together with all the Russian Social-Democrats of this period that the development of capitalism was constantly increasing the ranks of the proletariat at the expense of the petty bourgeoisie. This in turn would bring about the realization of socialism in the classical revolutionary manner. It was impossible, however, for the Jewish declassed bourgeoisie to become proletarians, because of the competition of their non-Jewish fellow workers and national oppression. Declassment or emigration must be the lot of the Jewish masses. Emigration could be but a temporary relief, for the same process of declassment was bound to be repeated eventually in the new lands. The only way out was the territorial solution. The theory of abnormal proletarianization is different only in degree from the non-proletarianization. It grants that the Jewish petty bourgeoisie is becoming proletarianized, but not to the same degree as the non-Jewish bourgeoisie, because the major basic industries are closed to Jewish workers with the usual resulting evils. Territorialism was to prevent this and allow the Jewish proletariat to develop in a normal manner.

The S. S. (Russian initials for Zionist Socialist) Party, organized after the rejection of the Uganda offer, soon became the strongest group within proletarian territorialism. They, too, arrived at their ideology from a Marxian approach. They maintained that the realization of socialism can be accomplished only through the existence of a highly advanced stage of production and a culturally developed rising proletariat, fully confident of its role in the conduct of the class struggle. The historical mission of overthrowing the capitalistic system would be achieved only by the industrial proletariat. They believed in the theory of non-proletarianization in its pristine purity. The Jewish masses, they taught, cannot be proletarianized or industrialized. Their class struggle is a helpless, negative one. It results are nil. The revolutionary tendencies of the Jewish proletariat are not due to its place in the scheme of production but to ideological motives and particular tendencies to abstraction. The results of the steadily and irrevocably increasing impoverishment of the Jewish masses are seen in emigration, which is a historical necessity and as inevitable a tendency and a positive factor as the role of the basic industries among the non-Jews. Emigration leads to the concentration of the masses in certain territories where the tendency to enter basic industries cannot be satisfied because of the ever repeated conditions of national oppression. Therefore, the emigration movement has to be converted into one of colonization. The basic tendencies in emigration must eventually lead both to class consciousness and to the attempt to settle the Jewish masses in a free territory, where the class struggle will be given a normal expression. Thus territorialism is complementary to the class struggle. The actual realization of territorialism is a long process which will enable the Jewish proletariat to improve its class position through organization and will power. Territorialism cannot be achieved by the proletariat alone. It will be aided in its tasks by the masses and some layers of the middle classes in different countries. The task of the proletariat is to strengthen the territorialist ideology, to struggle for democracy within the Jewish community, to introduce proletarian elements into the process of colonization and socialist ideology into all cultural and educational institutions. The S. S. adopted the name Zionist Socialists and not Social-Democratic Territorialists and continued to participate in the Zionist Congress for a short period because of two very practical reasons. By retaining the name "Zionists" and being counted as such they hoped to gain more adherents. By calling themselves Socialists and not Social-Democrats they hoped to gain the adherence to their movement of an outstanding group of intellectuals which was then in the process of formulating the ideology of a new movement, the *Vozrozhdenye.*

The ideology of the *Vozrozhdenye* (Renaissance) group resembled greatly that of Chaim Zhitlovsky. Its leaders criticized both the indifferent attitude of the Jewish socialists to the fate of the Jewish nation and the one-sidedness of the Zionists who in their hope for the future ignored the needs of the present and the possibilities of the Galut. The *Vozrozhdenye* group believed in the need of the Jewish people for its own national home as a main condition "for the full development of the national potentialities and the completely normal existence of a nation". It had no objection to Palestine as a national home. It would, however—confident in the inevitability of the realization of this idea—"affix our national thought, our national aims, our national forces on one central idea, the idea of the national renaissance", thus leaving the realization of their territorial aspirations in the realm of theorizing. It also denied the theory of non-proletarianization.

Its concern with the Galut later led this group far astray from its original position. Its offspring, the *Seimist* Party (Jewish Socialist Workers Party, *Serp*), abandoned the Marxian interpretation for one similar to that of the Socialist Revolutionaries. The ultimate reason for all historical development was according to its theoreticians the perpetual striving for limitless self-development. They placed the main emphasis on the national aspect of life through which all other aspects find their expression and are reflected. National consciousness thus is the reason for the historical progress and development of both the individual and the national group. The national consciousness of a ruling nation shows very often tendencies of chauvinism and exploitation of other peoples. That of a subject nation is a progressive one. To them, the proletariat was classified according to its nationality. The achievement of socialism in their opinion implied component and separately conducted struggles for economic liberty and for political and cultural salvation.

The *Seimists* also evolved a concept of exclusive Galut work. Territorialism according to them would be a logical result of Galut activities, just as socialism was to develop out of capitalism. It could grow out only of healthy Galut conditions. The salvation for the subdued nationalities would be the change of all multiple nationality states into federations of free nations to be ruled by a parliament composed of the representatives of the different component nationalities. Each nationality would have its own parliament (*Sejm* is the Polish term for Parliament) with the rights of legislation and taxation. The task of the Jewish proletariat would be to force within the Jewish parliament the representatives of the bourgeoisie to follow a policy suitable to the interests of the masses. It would be aided in this struggle by the intelligentsia and by the progressive elements of the bourgeoisie. Thus it would achieve the twofold aim of normalizing Jewish life in the Galut and of obtaining eventually a territorial center. Very soon the *Seimists* followed the logical conclusion of their policy that "the better conditions are in the Galut, the easier it will be to build the national home". They devoted their activities completely to the class struggle, Yiddish, cultural work, and to the strengthening of the *Kehillah,* which they would rebuild into a secular institution, a preliminary step in the attainment of the parliament.

Competition between these different schools of territorialist thought was quite sharp. In the beginning the S. S. was the most energetic in its activities and successful in gaining the most adherents. Very soon it became the strongest competitor to the *Bund.* It was strengthened in 1907 by the adherents of the Minsk Poale Zion, which for a while was organized under the name, Jewish Territorialists Workers Party. The S. S., called Socialist Territorialists in the United States, outnumbered the other two territorialist groups in this country, the Anarchist Territorialists and the *Seimist* Social Revolutionary Territorialists. They were also quite strong in Austria and in other centers of Jewish life in Europe. The *Seimists,* on the other hand, remained a small but vocal and influential party of intellectuals. Very soon they all lost their positions to the Poale Zion, after the unity of this party was achieved as a result of the indomitable efforts of Ber Borochov and his youthful associates.

Borochov set out to solve all the doubts raised by the general socialist movement and by all these different groupings within the Jewish labor movement. In logic Borochov was a thorough-going materialist and Marxist; emotionally he was a Zionist. His theory is a result of both these aspects. He had first to contend with the assimilationist Marxists, hence his general theory of nationalism. He had to justify his belief in Jewish survival, hence his theory of the role of landless nations and territorial concentration. He had to prove that Palestine could be the only territory because he was a lover of this land, hence his theory of the *stychic* process. At the same time he had to reconcile work in the Galut with the task of building the territorial center, hence his theory of the role of the Jewish proletariat and the changes which would take place while the process of immigration to Palestine would go on. His theory had to be materialistic to the core; otherwise he could not gain the following of the Jewish youthful intelligentsia, which at that time, together with the Russian intellectuals, was turning away from the socialist *Narodnik* teachings to dialectical materialism as a result of the propaganda of Plekhanov and his associates.

Borochov saw clearly the errors of his contemporaries in following blindly the utopian notions of cosmopolitanism. Marx failed to formulate clearly a "Marxian" approach to social problems which spring from national differences. Thus socialism in its early stages was cosmopolitan in its outlook, and continually negated or minimized the importance of nationalism in the class struggle. This point of view was largely due to the fact that most of the socialist theoreticians were or considered themselves to be members of majority national groups within a state. Minorities are naturally more concerned with the problem of national survival than majorities because they suffer from national oppression in addition to the usual economic oppression.

Borochov's doctrine of nationalism can be called the earliest successful effort in the direction of evolving a theory of nationalism on the basis of dialectical materialism. The basis for the materialistic analysis of Borochov is a new term which he introduced, namely, "conditions of production" which is an extension of Marx's and Engels' concept of "relations of production". "Conditions of production" include the sum total of conditions under which production takes place: the geographical, anthropological, and the historical, which function both within the respective group and in connection with its relation to other groups.

This concept furnishes the basis for Borochov's approach to the problem of nationalism. According to Marx, social conflicts result from the development of the forces of production and their clash with the existing relations of production. Borochov interprets, in an analogous manner, national conflicts as a result of the clash between the developing forces of production of a nation and the conditions of production under which it lives. To Borochov, a people is "a society which grew out of the very same conditions of production". A nation to him is a people in a higher stage of development which, in addition to springing from the same conditions of production, is also "united by the consciousness of its individual members and a kinship arising out of a common historical past". Nationalism to him is "the feeling of kinship created as a result of a common historic past, the roots of which arise from the common conditions of production". It is a product of bourgeois society. The period of feudalism knew only peoples, but not nationalities, which began to develop with the rise of capitalism. The bourgeoisie with the aid of other classes was able to liberate the entire population from its former masters. The abolition of feudalism was thus a progressive revolutionary step.

The nationalism of the ruling classes is diversified. For the class of the great landowners, the territory is valuable as their chief source of income, which they derive from rent. Their nationalism is a land nationalism. They are not concerned with who controls the market for the products as long as they continue to derive their income from it. In backward states their class is mostly identified with the regime. In more developed states where the bourgeoisie has defeated them, they try to make peace with their former foes through the protective coloring of nationalism and reaction.

The great bourgeoisie knows no traditions. It is not concerned with language and customs which are merely within the needs of the domestic market. The territory presents to this class an operating basis for the purpose of seizing the world market.

For the middle class and petty bourgeoisie the territory possesses significance as a market for consumers' goods. Selling and purchasing of these goods require the use of the same language, hence the concern of this class for the extent of the area of its language and culture. It is the weakest class and is subject to many internal conflicts. In search of support for its continuously tottering position, this group comes to the aid of the reactionary domestic and foreign policies of the landlords and great bourgeoisie.

For the proletariat, the territory has a twofold significance. It is important both as a work-place and as a strategic place for the conduct of the class struggle. The proletariat, too, is not a unified, solid bloc. It is split because of the varying conditions of production. Competition exists between the skilled and unskilled workers. The territory becomes a base for the struggle only after its occupation by the worker as a work-place has become secure. This is the reason for the lack of class consciousness and the presence of nationalistic sentiments among the "proletarianizing" masses in search of work as well as among the natives who are in the defense of their jobs against the influx of foreign workers. The development of the territory as a base for struggle lessens both the individualistic and the nationalistic trends within the proletariat and increases class solidarity.

Among nations which live a normal economic life, nationalism is reactionary and dangerous because it obscures the class relationship. The situation is different among nations which live under abnormal economic conditions because of either national subjugation or the lack of own territories. This uncertain strategic base of the proletariat of such a nation causes its class consciousness to be closely identified with its national consciousness. Its class struggle assumes both objectively and subjectively national characteristics and trends. Its national consciousness is derived only from the desire of the proletariat to overcome the abnormalities of its strategic base. The nationalism of the organized revolutionary proletariat of a subject or landless nation has as its purpose the struggle for a normal work-place and a strategic base. It cannot achieve its aims without striving for the normalization of the conditions of production for the *entire* nation. Its nationalism is thus the only real nationalism since it does not strive to obscure the class relationship nor does it call for class collaboration.

The application of Borochov's theory of landless nations to the Jews follows the same line of reasoning. The Jewish nation has no territory of its own. It falls thus within the category of a landless nation which has entered a foreign system of economy. It has to adjust itself economically to the demands of the majority nations among which it lives. The first factor in this process of adjustment is the inevitable assimilation. Assimilation is counter-balanced by and is in constant clash with the second factor, a negative one—namely, that of isolation. As long as the landless nation is merely exploited by its host nations, its economic position is fairly definite and strong. But as soon as exploitation is re-placed by the inevitable appearance of competition, the minority is bound to lose steadily its economic positions to the majority. National competition forces it to engage in the branches of economy which are the least important and the weakest.

To the Jewish capitalists, Jewish national life does not permit any imperialistic aspirations. This class has managed to adjust itself remarkably well to its environment. If not for the pressure of the hordes of "poor East European Jewry" which constantly bring pogroms and migrations to the attention of their wealthy relatives, this class would not have felt any sense of isolation. Only the fear of the spread of anti-Semitism ties it to the other classes of the Jewish people. Its only expression of this bond takes a philanthropic form.

The middle bourgeoisie has a much closer connection with the masses. First, there are its national interests in the internal market. It has to compete with the non-Jewish bourgeoisie. This introduces assimilation and at the same time sharpens its national consciousness. Since its problem is that of finding a territory upon which to base the struggle for its market, it shows tendencies of dreaming of Jewish independence and a Jewish state. Its members feel most keenly the legal restrictions and the misery of the masses; hence they are more nationally minded. Nevertheless their main tie to the Galut is their immediate economic interests. Their national energy can be partly utilized but cannot form the basis of any serious endeavor for the radical reconstruction of Jewish life.

The Jewish proletariat, too, suffers from the abnormality of the economic development of the Jewish people and its resulting occupational distribution. It is concentrated in intellectual professions and in secondary industries, remote from nature and natural resources. Thus, the Jewish fields of work are of little value both in the economic structure of the country and as a basis for the class struggle of the Jewish workers. The processes of capitalism tend to throw a steadily increasing number of the declassed Jewish petty bourgeoisie into the ranks of the unemployed reserves at a greater proportion than that of the non-Jewish petty bourgeoisie. This influx makes it harder for the Jewish worker to find employment and to conduct a normal class struggle. The Jewish worker is confined largely to small shops and plants and thus is unable to organize properly to fight against his exploiters. He cannot participate properly in the process of bringing about the social revolution. Since the basic industries are closed to him, "he is incapable of paralyzing the economic organism in a single strike ... His exploiter is the small capitalist whose role in production is negligible. When the Jewish worker does go on strike against the industry which exploits him, he does not appreciably disturb the equilibrium of the country. He is not even strong enough to obtain his just demands without the support of the other more fortunate workers of the surrounding nationalities. He cannot obtain even the most minor concession when his national needs do not coincide with those of workers of another nationality." This peculiar, weak position strengthens in turn his sense of proletarian solidarity. Since these difficulties of the Jewish proletariat are based on national factors, he must be, unlike the proletariat of other nations, interested in nationalism.

These shortcomings of the Jewish people and of the Jewish proletariat will be eliminated by the settlement of the Jews in their own land. There the worker will develop under normal conditions and find his strategic base from which to conduct the class struggle and achieve the social revolution.

As opposed to the free choice of territory by the other Socialist Territorialist theoreticians, Borochov propounded his own interpretation of Palestine as the land of future Jewish mass immigration and settlement. Just as the realization of socialism will take place through a *stychic* process of the concentration of capital without dependence on any conscious factors whatsoever, so too will the future concentration of the Jewish emigrants into a definite territory begin *stychically* and independently of anyone's will. This does not mean an immediate return of the Jews to Palestine. The Jewish masses, driven out because of their abnormal situation from the lands in which they reside, must emigrate to any country which will accept them. But even in the more thinly settled lands, they are forced to engage in their former occupations because of the national oppression. The basic industries continue to be closed to them. At the same time the need for new lands of immigration increases because of progressively sharper competition resulting from the steady expulsion of the Jews from their occupations. The absorptive capacity of the new lands of immigration will decrease gradually, so that eventually all of them will bar their gates to the Jewish wanderer. Ultimately, there will remain but one avenue for the masses in their search for a haven. They will have to direct their wanderings to a land where they will be able to enter all branches of production without any great difficulties. This land will have to be able to give the petty Jewish capitalist an opportunity to invest his capital in industry and agriculture; it will have to be able to give the Jewish worker the opportunity to engage in basic industries or to transfer from industry to agriculture without undue difficulty. This land must be semi-agricultural, thinly populated, fitted for the immigration of the petty bourgeois Jew and his small investment, where neither the Jewish capitalist nor the worker will meet with national competition in their efforts to enter the basic industries. This land is, of course, Palestine. Economic necessity will drive the Jews there.

Borochov, like most of his contemporaries in Europe, was not well acquainted with the Arab problem. He considered Palestine as an "international hotel" the same as "Switzerland, Yemen, and Tibet." Countries of this type have their peculiar economic structure, which is characterized by small native or petty bourgeoisie production and by the fact that a large proportion of the population derives its livelihood from the pilgrim and tourist trade. A land of this type has also a peculiar cultural structure. The population is highly cultured but has no culture or its own. The natives depend on the "foreign guests" economically, and they adjust themselves to the incomers culturally. Therefore, they are acquainted with a number of languages, and they lack the feeling of national isolation and are more free from chauvinism. On the basis of this interpretation the Arabs in Palestine are not of an economically or culturally independent type. They are not a nation and will not become one for a long time. They are open to cultural assimilation because they cannot offer economic competition on a national basis. They will thus adopt the economic and cultural characteristics of the incoming Jews. "The development of the forces of production will be taken over by the Jewish immigrants and the present population will eventually become economically and culturally assimilated with the Jews."

The part which the Jewish proletariat is to play in the achievement of the normalization of Jewish life through the immigration of the masses into Palestine is a very important one. It is parallel to the function of the proletariat in hastening the decline of capitalism through the class struggle and the sharpening of class relations. The Jewish proletariat is bound to participate in this process of the settlement of Palestine. The means for its participation is the class struggle, the only weapon of the proletariat. Mass migrations require order and management. The Jewish masses which are so anxious to migrate can certainly not be entrusted with this task. The sorely beset petty bourgeoisie is too individualistic and too disorganized to do it. The upper and middle bourgeoisie cannot do it because they are not sufficiently interested in a basic and thorough solution of the Jewish problem. Furthermore their interests are of a reactionary class position. The revolutionary proletariat is thus bound to undertake the task of introducing order into the process of Jewish migration into Palestine as well as in the process of converting this semi-agricultural country into a place fit for increasing immigration of the masses. This process is a double one. The Jewish proletariat, through its participation in the general class struggle in the Galut, will force the individual governments of the countries in which the Jewish masses reside to adopt a more democratic policy and will strengthen the tendencies in support of the Jewish plans for Palestine (as for instance, by insisting on unlimited immigration). The interest is bound to grow in time. The gradual impoverishment of the Jewish petty bourgeoisie, the poverty and the increasing radicalization of the masses will see to that. Immigration to Palestine will begin with the petty bourgeoisie. Later, international capital too will begin to invade the country, a desirable thing from Borochov's point of view. While the bourgeoisie will assume the task of upbuilding, the proletariat will undertake the task of its liberation from capitalism. During the first few years of colonization, there will be temporarily some collaboration between the proletariat and the bourgeoisie in order to achieve the most elementary aims of the establishment of normal economic relations within a capitalistic society. The partnership will be of the type of the joint action between the enlightened bourgeoisie and the revolutionary proletariat in their effort to overthrow the Czarist despotism in Russia. The class struggle can be mitigated or postponed but cannot be finally averted.

The grave problem of the final achievement of territorial autonomy or perhaps independence of Palestine from the Turkish regime will be solved as a result of this organic process. The Turkish government will most decidedly interfere on behalf of the bourgeoisie in its struggle against the demands of the proletariat. This in turn will bring about the intervention of the powers of Europe which will demand the liberation of Palestine from the despotism of Turkey. As the territorial autonomy will be established, the proletariat will have achieved its only aim, since it has no other national aims. The class struggle will continue until the liberation of the proletariat will be completely achieved.

What of the Jews outside Palestine? Borochov never admitted the possibility of the settlement in Palestine of the majority of the Jewish people. According to him, the majority of Jews will continue to reside throughout the world. The establishment of the territorial autonomy of the Jewish center of Palestine will place the Jews in the Galut in a position of a national minority of the same nature as all other national minorities. This of course will gradually remedy the evils of their exceptional economic distribution due to their present condition as a national minority *without* a center. Eventually all national minorities in general, and the Jewish one in particular, will disappear completely. National autonomy will make this process easier, since it will lessen the clashes between the majority and minority. With the elimination of national oppression under socialism, minorities and nations which are backward economically or culturally are bound to assimilate completely and painlessly among their more developed neighbors. In the same way Borochov foretold the solution of the Arab problem in Palestine—through assimilation with the higher culture of the Jews. His ideas concerning the eventual assimilation were never adopted by the movement. Borochov himself revised them later.

It is easy to criticize the early system of Borochov in the light of more recent changes in Marxian thought and in Jewish life. His mechanistic approach to social problems as characterized by his emphasis on purely *stychic* trends certainly cannot be accepted. The tendency now among the orthodox Borochovists and the less articulate neo-Borochovists is to attempt to prove that Borochov included the element of *will* in his *stychic* process. His own statement as to his materialistic approach would seem to belie it. At best this attempt is similar to present efforts to read new contents into the teachings of Marx on the basis of stray quotations instead of admitting that perhaps even a genius cannot foresee all.

A corollary to this *stychic* process is the disregard for all efforts and factors which are not purely materialistic. Early Borochovism does not concern itself with any moral or spiritual values; it has no concern whatsoever with the individual. It disregards the efforts of collectives and cooperatives which are based on social-spiritual drives rather than on purely economic factors. It tends to look on the proletariat as the exclusive possessor of the mission of bringing about socialism. For this reason its present adherents fail to appreciate, for instance, the return to the Hebrew language in Palestine. They try to interpret it as a deliberate conspiracy against the Yiddish speaking masses, rather than to see it as a spiritual revolt against Galut life and as a return to historical, traditional values.

This particular attention paid to the proletariat is especially unrealistic when applied to Jewish life. Furthermore, Borochovism implies a sacred worship of Borochov's early writings with its concomitant dogmatism, narrow-minded sectarianism, continual hair-splitting, and "holier than thou" attitude of a small group of chosen people who claim to maintain the gospel in its pristine purity. To American Jewry it offers nothing. A theory evolved under conditions of a multi-nationality state, a theory which does not take cognizance of religious and traditional elements in Jewish life and would substitute for it a mere Yiddish speaking community, does not hold water even from its own materialistic approach. The upbuilding of Palestine, too, failed to follow the exact lines of the *stychic* process as indicated by Borochov in his early teachings. The collective will of the Jewish people in its historical settings and the individual determination of a small group of pioneers also played a great part in the task. The twofold task of the "creating" bourgeoisie and "liberating" proletariat failed to function at least in the first stages of the construction of the Jewish homeland in Palestine.

In spite of these shortcomings, Borochov managed to construct a system of ideas which appealed strongly to his own contemporaries and many of which remain unchallenged today. The same standards of criticism that can be applied to Marxism apply to the basis of his economic interpretation. Its acceptance depends on the acceptance of dialectical materialism. Its further development also depends on the liberation of socialist thought from dogmatism and the disease of blind hero and quotation worship. Borochov's greatest contribution to socialist thought, namely his theory of the organic unity between socialism and proletarian nationalism, remains unacknowledged, although it is being carried out to some extent in practice by the same cosmopolitan socialists and communists who fought him so bitterly on this score. In his insistence on united action among the different schools in socialism, Borochov, too, was ahead of his times. His predictions of the role of the declassed bourgeoisie as an aid to declining capitalism, is almost a prophecy of fascism. His synthesis of Zionism and socialism suffers, as he admitted later, from dogmatism. Socialist Zionism of today is too much of a movement of idealists to permit itself to be cramped by rigid materialistic formulas. His analysis of the problem of emigration of the Jewish masses cannot be called completely original. It is a logical development of contemporaneous theories. Yet, he predicted, in 1905, the stoppage of world immigration. The concentration of Jewish immigration towards Palestine has come true in our own day.

Many other accomplishments of Borochov remain unknown in the hustle and bustle of partisan life and arguments. In his studies in the field of the Jewish labor movement, he easily shared the honors with another brilliant young theoretician, Jacob Lestshinsky, then a leader in the S. S. movement. His economic interpretation of Jewish history has contributed a great deal to the direction of scholarly research in this field. It is a fact worth mentioning that most of the younger scholars in the field of Jewish history in Poland and Palestine who adhere to this economic approach are Borochovists. His contributions to clarity in the field of the economic development of the Jews are permanent. His analysis of the class relationship and assimilation within the Jewish community, too, is a synthesis rather than an original contribution. Yet, it still stands the test of time. The outstanding merit of Borochov as a thinker was his ability to analyze things as a man of action, too. His own dogmatic convictions never prevented him from seeing reality. For the sake of practical achievement he, unlike many of the socialist thinkers of his day, was willing to put aside many theoretical reservations. Otherwise, how could one explain his joining together with the Austrian non-Marxist Poale Zion and his efforts to present a united front of Jewish labor before the Socialist International. He never pretended infallibility, though his teachings were the gospel of a movement in his early youth. His gentle cynicism in the latter period of his life, which was aimed at his assertive dogmatic and ideologically self-righteous youth, is a proof of toleration and self-criticism, hardly ever found and thus even more to be desired among theoreticians and founders of social movements.

The early Poale Zion groups, it has been noted, had no common ideology. Their varied beliefs were conflicting, the only point of unity being Palestine. Borochov was successful in neutralizing the *Vozrozhdenye* and Territorialist influences within these groups. Finally his efforts culminated in the Organization Convention of the Jewish Social-Democratic Workers Party Poale Zion in Russia, which took place in Poltava in February, 1906. The police arrested many of its participants, including Borochov. Yet the convention managed to draft a platform, which was later extended and adopted in final form at the second convention which met in Crakow in August, 1907. The platform followed closely the theories of Borochov. It included both *maximum* demands for complete socialization of the means of production and *minimum* aims for the establishment of territorial autonomy for the Jewish nation in Palestine along democratic principles and through the class struggle. The gulf between the Poale Zion and the bourgeois Zionists was stressed. It allowed for cooperation with them only in practical Palestine activities. Participation in Zionist congresses was advocated, but solely for the purposes of criticism, the support of democracy, and educating the proletariat.

At the same time a different development in Labor Zionism took place in Austria, centering in Galicia. The early Labor Zionist movement found its expression in the organization of trade unions, mutual aid societies, and Zionist groups of workers, clerks and salesmen. These groups emphasized the need for democracy within the Jewish community. They did not hesitate to place the *Lumpenproletariat*—the petty merchants and hucksters— on the same level as the factory workers, and they continually asserted their primary allegiance to Zionism. In 1904 a convention of these groups at Crakow resulted in the organization of the Jewish Socialist Party Poale Zion of Austria. From the point of view of theory, this party differed widely from the Russian one. Its ideologists maintained that the Zionist movement was an expression of the entire Jewish people and transcended class interests. Therefore the Party considered itself an integral part of the Zionist organization and fully adhered to the Basle program. It maintained that the position of the Jewish worker and commercial employee was different from that of the non-Jew, since the Jew had to face both exploitation and discrimination. It warned the Jewish workers against following the teachings of the Social-Democrats in Austria who denied this fact. It negated the importance of the socialist solution unless it were combined with a Jewish autonomous territory. It denied the truth of the materialistic view of history, and as a result it also negated the *stychic* process. Instead it stressed the need for the conscious direction of the migration of the Jewish masses to Palestine. It considered their sentimental ties with this country an important factor in the speedy establishment of the Jewish national home.

The Poale Zion groups in other countries followed in their ideology either the Russian or the Austrian schools. The American movement, which was officially organized as a party at the 1905 convention in Baltimore, followed the Austrian school. Very soon, however, there arose within it a strong Borochovist opposition, which later came to dominate the movement. The parties in Argentina, Roumania, and Bulgaria also adhered to the Austrian school. The movement in Great Britain followed Borochov with some divergences. The Palestinian Party, which was organized as a result of the *Second Aliya* in 1905, began on a strict Borochovist basis. The peculiar conditions of Palestine pioneer life, however, modified its orthodoxy to a great degree within a few years.

Reality encroached upon theories. The two divergent schools of Poale Zionism met at Zionist congresses. Both were active in Galut work; both were seeking new channels for practical activity in Palestine. A world convention of representatives from the different countries met in the Hague in 1907 in connection with the Eighth Zionist Congress. Thus, the Jewish Socialist Workers World Confederation Poale Zion was established. Its program, adopted in 1909, attempted to gloss over ideological differences. It called for the abolition of capitalism and complete socialization of the means of production through the economic and political class struggle of the proletariat, as well as for the territorial solution of the Jewish problem through Jewish mass settlement in Palestine and its neighboring countries. But the differences within the two wings could not be eradicated by formulas of compromise. They continued, latent, until moments of crisis when they flared up openly. They revolved mainly about the problem of participation in the Zionist congresses. The Poale Zion became in 1907 an autonomous federation within Zionism. Yet, this was considered as class collaboration on the part of the Russian membership who under the influence of Borochov decided to leave the Congress in 1909. This decision was disputed by most of the other parties. The question was not settled definitely until it became a major factor in the split of 1920. The Russians, too, objected to working for the Jewish National Fund, which they considered an institution created by the bourgeoisie for its own needs. The party substituted for it the Palestine Workers Fund (1909), which failed to gain any appreciable monetary results. Scepticism was also expressed by the Borochovists to Professor Oppenheimer's plans for cooperative settlements in Palestine, which later turned out to be a success.

In spite of these differences the World Party functioned as a united body in other respects. It is impossible to give here a detailed presentation of its activities and achievements. In Russia it was the pioneer in the armed self-defense movement against the pogroms. It conducted trade union activities vigorously. It participated actively in the political life of the country, in the revolution of 1905, in the elections to the Duma and local bodies. It conducted an open fight among the workers against anti-Semitism, which was particularly prevalent in the Polish provinces of the country. It was an active factor in the cultural revival of the Yiddish language. It led a successful fight together with other parties against the self-proclaimed monopoly of the *Bund*. Together with the entire socialist movement it suffered a decline during the reaction which followed the 1905 revolution. In America, it devoted itself largely to Zionist and cultural affairs. It was the first to found Yiddish secular schools where Hebrew, too, was taught, and later was instrumental in the creation of the first American Jewish Congress. In Galicia, it was a potent factor in breaking down the joint monopoly in political and community life of the *Chassidim* and the Polonized wealthy oligarchy, and fought for the recognition of the Jews as a national group even at the cost of antagonizing the local socialist movement. In Palestine, its members were instrumental in the organization of the trade unions and cooperatives. Its efforts to unite all the Jewish labor parties in order to effect a joint representation of the Jewish proletariat as a national unit within the Second International met with failure because of the opposition of the *Bund*. It was equally unsuccessful in gaining admittance to this body as a world movement because of the opposition of the cosmopolitan socialist leadership. Unlike the other parties, it refused to enter it under the guise of branches of the socialist parties in the different countries.

The World War brought new problems to the movement. It was then impossible to conduct the usual socialist activities in most European countries. Unemployment and mass exile caused all the Jewish labor parties to turn their attention to relief activities and the establishment of consumers' cooperatives. The Poale Zion maintained its central offices in a neutral country and continued to exercise its efforts to obtain the sympathy of the socialist world for the Jewish people through a series of memoranda and publications. In addition to the usual socialist demands, the Party put forth a program for Jewish rights which included equality, national autonomy in some countries, freedom of emigration, and mass settlement in Palestine under international auspices. In 1916, it was admitted to the Second International as a representative of the Turkish Socialists bcause of its Palestinian connections. Its demands were included in the 1917 peace manifesto of the International.

At the same time, the World War tended to accentuate the differences within the movement both through the cessation of normal relations between the different countries and through the changes in the economical and political life. The movement in the democratic Allied countries, especially in the United States, abandoned its uncompromising Borochovist ideology and devoted its attention and activities to the fields of relief, community organization and Palestine work of the types frowned upon by the more orthodox Russian brethren. This "ideological retreat" was aided by the presence of Borochov, who came to the United States in 1914 as a refugee from Austria and naturally assumed a position of respect and leadership in the movement.

The later writings of Borochov reveal almost a complete *volte-face* from his early theories. Unfortunately he died before he had the opportunity to revise his system or to construct it anew. During his stay in America Borochov was occupied more with practical problems. We suspect that he too succumbed to the more pragmatic atmosphere of American thought. But there are indications aplenty that Borochov strayed far away from Borochovism. His Russian comrades, whom he met again in 1917 after a separation of almost ten years and who followed his orthodox path, could not recognize him. The man who had analyzed microscopically every iota in the programs of all the Jewish labor parties looked in 1915 upon the differences between the anarchists and socialists as *Zukunfstmusik*. He called himself "a Marxist without 'matter' and a critical empiricist opposed both to materialism and idealism". On the question of the post-revolutionary type of collectivism, he declared himself to be an anarchistic socialist. He declared his willingness to let all "these philosophic questions dream peacefully till after the social revolution". He was for the unity of all those who believe in the necessity of vigorous activity towards the abolition of capitalism, "be they socialists, anarchists, syndicalists, I. W. W.'s, materialists, Kantians, empirical realists, or revolutionaries from the school of Marx, Kropotkin, or the prophet Isaiah". He called for the same type of freedom and unity in Zionism, as long as its purpose was the creation of a national home for the Jewish people in Palestine. This home was to be built by the partnership of the working class and the entire Jewish people. He abandoned his strict interpretation of the *stychic* processes and emphasized the role of will in social movements. "Years ago," he admitted, "we said: Zionism is a *stychic* process. Our only task is to remove all the obstacles which interfere with this process. And we left the creative work to the bourgeois Zionists . . . We erred formerly when we contended that natural emigration waves are already under way. General Zionists were closer to the truth when they said that for the present only the organic process has begun." He approved of the efforts made along the lines of cooperative colonization and called it "the way to a socialist society in Palestine. While this colonization is not in itself socialism, it does teach the Jewish proletariat the elementary lessons of self-help." Borochov also widened his concept of the tasks of the Jewish proletariat. Palestine was to be more than a strategic base for its struggle. The task of the proletariat was to build Palestine as a home for the "entire Jewish people". The proletariat desired to build a new life and Palestine was to be the base for its creativity. Thus he saw clearly the ideological motivation in Socialist Zionism. He saw in the struggle against assimilation something much more than a struggle for a strategic base. Then it was to him the fight of all the Jewish masses against the attempt of national suicide on a part of the Jewish intelligentsia and upper bourgeoisie. The masses, he declared, "will not yield to the notion that the Jew disappear among foreign nations and alien cultures."

Borochov also changed his terminology. The terms, "the entire Jewish people", "the Jewish masses", were used by him in his later stage in addition to the term "proletariat" which he previously employed almost exclusively when discussing any constructive tasks. He advocated making the terminology of the movement more elastic. He looked upon the stern and mechanistic expressions of his younger days as a product of a period during which "no one believed in romance, ornaments, or adornment." He called for an abandonment of the "naively realistic" view on life. Most characteristic is his return to the ancient name, *Eretz Yisrael* (Land of Israel), for *Palestina*. To Zionists the land of Israel *had* to be *Eretz Yisrael*. For young Borochov and his followers, a sentimental name of this type would not befit the territorial center which was to be a result of the *stychic* process. They always referred to it as "Palestina" and abandoned the historical name which was accepted among the Yiddish speaking masses. The later Borochov openly returned to the "emotional terminology"; and to the dismay of his Borochovist comrades, he exclaimed, "Now we can and must proclaim: Eretz Yisrael—a Jewish home!"

It was natural that the new Borochov could not be accepted by the old Borochovists, especially those of Eastern Europe. The Poale Zion movement was never completely Borochovist; it was composed of the two conflicting trends in Labor Zionism, the Marxian and the non-Marxian. As long as both the upbuilding of Palestine and the social revolution were subjects mainly for discussion and petty activities, they could work together. After the Balfour Declaration and the March Revolution in Russia, this unity had to be abandoned. Cooperation with the bourgeois Zionists in their congresses and funds, the establishment of the *Hechalutz* movement and the Jewish legion, the direction of colonization into cooperative channels, the task of obtaining the recognition of minority rights through the Jewish congresses in several countries —all these problems had to be decided upon not as theoretical matters but as the actual needs of the day. On the other side, the Poale Zion had to make up their mind about the future of democracy in Russia and the future of world socialism.

The November Revolution decided all these problems for the movement by causing its split. It is doubtful whether even the commanding personality of Borochov could have stopped it had he continued to live. Most of the Russian Poale Zion who were brought up on Borochovism, which is as revolutionary as the extremist form of Leninism, joined the Bolsheviks. Some began to cooperate with them in city councils and other political activities immediately after the March Revolution. The November Revolution found their leftist elements ready for full cooperation with the Bolsheviks. Many joined the Red Army as special Borochov brigades and units. The organization of the Third International brought them nearer to the communists. In justice to them it must be stated here that they certainly did not anticipate the turn of events which was to take place both in the Soviet Union and in world socialism. Those were the days when the world revolution was almost a certainty to them. The communist Poale Zion hoped for a defeat of world imperialism and for the immigration of the Jewish masses into Palestine with the aid of the World Soviet Republic. Some even planned the organization of a Jewish Red Army which was to drive the British imperialist troops out of Palestine. The majority of the movement went with the communistic wing (which later became known as and still is called the Left Poale Zion) which became weakened because of the steady loss of its membership to the Russian and other communist parties. They looked upon themselves as the future Jewish section of the Comintern. Their negotiations with this body came to naught because of the objections of the ex-*Bundists* and other "Jewish" Jewish communists who still had old accounts to settle with the Poale Zion. Because of their unblemished revolutionary record, a small number of the intransigents who refused to join the general rush into the Communist Party was tolerated in the Soviet Union till 1928. Till that year the Left Poale Zion was an officially recognized communistic party with its own press and youth movement. Almost all of its members joined the Communist Party. Some have figured prominently in the recent Trotskyite trials and expulsions.

The Left Poale Zion have been more successful for some years in Poland and Palestine than in Russia. They have undergone several splits. They are the only orthodox Borochovists left, and their number and influence are constantly decreasing. Borochovism also left some marks on the ideology of *Hashomer Hatzair,* but not enough to call this extremist Marxian wing in Zionism a Borochovist one.

Not all the Labor Zionists in Russia joined the Poale Zion. At about 1906 there arose new youth groups in Eastern Europe under the names *Zeire Zion* and *Hatechiyah.* Their main aim, settlement in Palestine, brought them into close ideological contact with the growing labor movement of this country. It was natural for their settlers to join the non-Marxian *Hapoel Hatzair* rather than the Poale Zion, whom they knew so well from Russia. Meetings of these groups at the various Zionist congresses culminated in the unification of the *Hapoel Hatzair* and *Zeire Zion* groups at the Eleventh Zionist Congress in Vienna (1913) on a platform which called for complete democratization of the Zionist Organization and for support of the Palestine labor movement. Slowly the *Zeire Zion* drifted to the left. Under the influence of the Russian Revolution they adopted a socialist ideology which in its Zionist side was similar to that of the Austrian Poale Zion and which in its views on socialist and national problems resembled that of the Russian Social Revolutionaries. They denied the importance of the class struggle between the Jewish workers and their petty employers; they would substitute for it the productivization of both of these poverty stricken elements to normalize Jewish economic life. The class struggle to them implied all efforts at the improvement of the situation of the workers, including the establishment of cooperatives. They differed radically from the Yiddishist Poale Zion in their demands for the sole use of the Hebrew language in Palestine and for the equality of both Yiddish and Hebrew in the Galut. They paid most attention to Palestine work. This accounts for their organic connection with the *Hechalutz* pioneer movement, the organization and early guidance of which can be attributed to them.

At the Fifth World Convention (Vienna, 1920), the Poale Zion decided to join the Comintern. The adherents of the Right

Wing, who were willing to join this body under the condition that it should include all the revolutionary socialist parties with the right of independent action, organized a new world union. It joined the Vienna International and later was absorbed together with it in the new reorganized Second International. Despite the internal differences concerning the language problem and the participation in Zionist congresses it managed to maintain its unity. The most characteristic aspect of the Right Poale Zion was its desire for unification of the Labor Zionist movement. In 1925 it united with the World Union of the Left Wing *Zeire Zion* (in 1919 this organization was split as a result of its adoption of a definite socialist program) under the name World Jewish Socialist Workers' Party Poale Zion (united with the Zionist Socialist Alliance). The new organization adopted practically a Poale Zion platform, with the only exceptions of the recognition of choice between Yiddish and Hebrew, of the special position of Yiddish in Galut and of the right for minorities to foster Hebrew cultural activities. By this time, no more doubts existed concerning participation in Zionist congresses.

The Right Wing of the Zeire Zion joined the Palestinian non-Marxian *Hapoel Hatzair* in the *Zionist Labor Party Hitachdut.* In 1929 the Palestine Poale Zion known as *Achdut Haavoda* united with the *Hapoel Hatzair* to form the *Mapai* (*Mifleget Poale Eretz Yisrael*—Palestine Labor Party), which was recognized by the Second International as the Jewish Section in Palestine. This action led to the further unity of the movement. The *Hitachdut Party* united with Poale Zion Party in 1931. The two organizations were merged in the U. S. A. in 1931 to form the present United Jewish Socialist Labor Party Poale Zion-Zeire Zion of America. In 1936 a section of the Left Poale Zion in Palestine joined the *Mapai.* Thus the overwhelming majority of the Socialist Zionist movement is now united in one party, except for the communist Left Poale Zion, the youth movement *Hashomer Hatzair* (an extremely left wing revolutionary socialist group and its adult movement the Socialist League in Palestine), as well as some smaller youth organizations. Yet, even these extremist movements are at present cooperating in the *Histadrut,* the General Federation of Jewish Labor in Palestine, and the World League for Labor Palestine. The Labor Zionists have since the World War become the most powerful factor and strongest wing within the Zionist movement.

The united party of today resembles in its composition the pre-War World Party. Though it is well knit and united in action and policies, yet its different component wings are still clearly differentiated. The *Mapai* is the ideological leader of the movement both by the virtue of its numerical strength and the tremendous influence of Palestine today. The adherents of the former Poale Zion of the Marxist variety form its revolutionary Left wing. They still follow to some extent the early teachings of Borochov, though they would modify and reinterpret them. The left wing also includes former Left Poale Zionists, who differ with the communists only on the Jewish problem, and others who joined it because of its concrete Palestinian activities. A very influential group is the former Right Poale Zion of Russia, Poland, and Palestine, who follow the Reformist school of Marxism. They could be classified as adherents of the later Borochov. The former *Hitachdut* or *Zeire Zion* adherents, as well as the Austrian Poale Zion, have retained their non-materialistic approach to social problems. The influence of the former *Hapoel Hatzair*—who seek in their activities a solution to their personal problems as men, look upon the party as a comradely collective, and adhere to the "religion of labor" ideas of A. D. Gordon—is still felt strongly. Naturally, the only reason for the effective unity and joint action among so many different groups is their common desire to reconstruct Jewish life on the basis of socialism and Zionism, and their practical work in Palestine.

The various parties in the Galut are led mainly by the former Poale Zion. They reflect the peculiar conditions of the different countries, both in their ideologies and methods. In Poland and France, for instance, they are largely revolutionary. In the United States and England, they are mainly Reformist. The Polish party has retained more of Borochovism than any other branch of the movement. They, too, are united in their common aims, in spite of so many differences. The most characteristic aspect of the present movement, in contrast to the pre-War period, is the scant attention which is given by it to abstract theorizing in most countries, especially in Palestine. The cause for this change is the preoccupation with the concrete tasks of the construction of the Jewish National Home. This lack of concern with theories makes it impossible to give at the present time an answer to the baffling question: "What remains of Borochov?"

SECTION ONE

IN THE PERIOD OF WAR AND REVOLUTION

THE ECONOMIC DEVELOPMENT OF THE
JEWISH PEOPLE[1]

I.

THE SOCIO-ECONOMIC structure of the Jewish people differs radically from that of other nations. Ours is an anomalous, abnormal structure. Stubborn Galut[2] champions have been wont to reject or ignore this truth. Recently, however, their eyes, too, have been opened; and although very few have been able to offer a satisfactory analysis of our economic abnormalities, no serious student of Jewish life can ignore them.

The case of the Jewish people is analogous to that of the patient who has complained of sundry aches and pains for a number of years, but whose physician has not been able to arrive at any satisfactory diagnosis. There was no doubt about the patient's illness, but in the course of the illness the body developed some measure of resistance to it. As the years progressed and new resistances were built up, the character of the disease changed, new symptoms appeared, and the physician found himself in a continuous state of bewilderment. Likewise, the Jewish nation has not been a passive patient awaiting his inevitable demise. Resistance to the disease has appeared at various times. There has always been the normal effort to regain organic equilibrium. It was not unnatural therefore that the diagnoses of our social "doctors" varied with the morphology of the disease.

---

1 Published in 1916 as a series of articles in the Poale Zion Yiddish weekly, *Der Yiddisher Kaempfer*, New York.

2 *Galut*—exile, diaspora. In the geographic sense, it refers to all territories inhabited by Jews outside of Palestine. *Galut life* refers to the experiences, persecutions, mental reactions, mannerisms, customs, etc., of the Jews living outside of Palestine. *Galut champions* or adherents of *Galutism* refers to the philosophy and view of those who see the solution of the Jewish problem within the territories where Jews reside—excluding, minimizing, or opposing the idea of a Jewish homeland. There are various types of Galutists: the assimilationists, certain Yiddishists, cosmopolitans, extreme radicals, etc.

Some thirteen or fourteen years ago, one such diagnosis, devised by a group of Jewish Socialists, appeared under the name of *non-proletarization.*† Its major thesis was that the Jewish proletariat cannot be proletarized. The obvious contradiction contained in the proposition "that the Jewish proletariat cannot be proletarized" led the Poale Zion, who were the first to develop this theory, to be also the first to renounce it. The Zionist-Socialists (the S. S.)³ retained this illogical theory longest. However, they too attempted to remove some of its crudities by converting it into the "non-industrialization" theory.

Jacob Lestshinsky, the leading economist of the S. S., dedicated his book, *The Jewish Worker in Russia,* to the exposition of this theory. Its major thesis that "the Jewish worker cannot be industrialized" differed only slightly from its prototype. The book, like the principle around which it was built, was an indiscriminate mixture of sound ideas with grave errors.

It is absurd to assert that the Jewish worker cannot be "proletarized". His being a worker is evidence of the fact that he has ceased to be an "owner", that he has placed his labor-power on the market, and has *ipso facto* become a member of the proletariat. The proposition, therefore, that Jewish workers cannot achieve their own proletarization becomes an even greater absurdity when it comes from a *Jewish Socialist Labor* Party.

Nor is it less absurd to contend that Jewish labor cannot be industrialized. Jacob Lestshinsky complained (in the book mentioned above) that around 1897 there did not exist a single factory which employed a thousand Jewish workers. However, the very handbook of statistics (published by ICA⁴) on which he based his work told us (Vol. II, p. 77) of a tobacco factory in

---

† Commonly spelled "proletarianization".

3 An influential faction in the Socialist-Zionist movement which split from the Russian Poale Zion. The S. S. were Socialist-Territorialists who opposed or were indifferent to Palestine as *the* territory for the Jewish Homeland. Their chief activity consisted in aiding Jewish immigration, believing as they did that the course of Jewish immigration would automatically determine the "territory" of the Jewish mass concentration. In America, this group was known as Socialist-Territorialists (S. T.) and among its leaders were Nachman Syrkin and Baruch Zuckerman. In 1909 the American S. T. merged with the Poale Zion.

4 The abbreviated form of the "Jewish Colonization Association", founded by Baron De Hirsch in 1891 for the purpose of aiding Jewish immigration and colonization. It concentrates chiefly on the colonizing of Jews in Argentina.

Grodno, in the years 1898-99, in which 1,594 Jewish workers were employed. The same factory boasted a steam engine of 36 horse-power. Moreover, the literature of the general and Jewish labor movement in Russia contains detailed accounts of numerous strikes conducted by Jewish workers in the Russian Pale of Settlement.[5] The illegal literature of that period (1900-1905) records no less than fifty factories, each employing more than a hundred Jewish workers. The following outstanding examples are also worthy of notice: a millinery factory in Warsaw with 1,000 Jewish employees, a tobacco factory employing 500 Jews, and a glassware factory in Polonoye with 400 Jewish workers.

II.

America opened to the Jewish immigrant even greater opportunities for work than the most highly developed industries in Eastern Europe. No statistics are available concerning Jewish factories in the United States, but of this we are certain: that Jewish labor in America,[6] which is concentrated almost exclusively in the needle industry (in contradistinction to greater diversification of employment in Russia), has definitely assumed the proportions of mass-production that characterize big business. In Paterson, N. J., for example, there are large textile factories with an enormous number of Jewish workers. In Chicago, Rosenwald's clothing shops employ several thousand Jewish laborers.

It remains true, however, that Jewish industries never attain the large-scale development achieved by non-Jewish industries. No Jewish factory, not even the largest, can compare with such gigantic enterprises as Krupp's iron works, or Ford's automobile factories. The Jewish entrepreneur never dreams of industries on this scale, nor does the Jewish laborer have any access to them.

To be sure, the Jewish masses do become *proletarized;* Jewish labor does become industrialized. The process, however, is slow, and its development is limited and unilinear. Moreover, Jewish entrepreneurs seem to have a natural tendency to small scale

---

5 Certain areas largely in Southwestern Russia and in Poland designated in Czarist edicts of 1791 and 1882 as the sole areas where Jews could reside.

6 Cf. Elsie Gluck's "Jewish Workers in the Trade Unions", *Jewish Frontier,* December, 1935.

production. S. O. Margolin, the economist, calls this tendency the *individualization of industry.* A Jew, possessing meager means, often decides to become a boss "on his own" under circumstances in which a Gentile will never dare undertake such a venture. The Jew will often establish a business or factory with negligible "capital" and thus become a "capitalist". The Gentile will more often choose to remain a "wage-slave" for his entire life, even when his savings are larger than those of his Jewish fellow worker. The enterprising spirit of the Jew is irrepressible. He refuses to remain a proletarian. He will grab at the first opportunity to advance to a higher rung on the social ladder.

This desire to achieve "success" is a deeply ingrained characteristic of the Jewish laboring masses. Tailors, shoemakers, and cigarmakers eagerly await the opportunity to rid themselves of their tools, and to climb into the higher strata of insurance, dentistry, medicine, law, or into an independent business. This continuous exodus of thousands from the ranks of Jewish labor, and the necessary influx of thousands to replace them, furnishes the explanation for the instability of the Jewish laboring masses.

These peculiar phenomena of Jewish labor have their roots in the general nature of our economic history.

It would be possible to formulate and explain clearly this uniqueness of the Jewish economic past and present, through recourse to the literature of the Poale Zion in Russia before and during the last decade, but we will base our analysis on literature much older than this. Let us begin with a distinction made by Aristotle, whom Marx frequently quotes with much respect (a distinction which Marxists unfortunately have forgotten or neglected). Aristotle distinguishes between two modes of gaining a livelihood: first, the livelihood gained from nature; and second, the livelihood gained from man. The farmer, mountaineer, or fisherman gains his livelihood from nature; the business man, the banker, or physician gains his from man.

In terms of this distinction, it is obvious that Jews, in contradistinction to all other nations, *derive their livelihood exclusively from man.*

We carry our analysis a bit further by availing ourselves of the economic theory of Otto Effertz.[7] He classifies human production on the basis of the share of labor and land (or elements derived directly from land) in it. If we use the farmer as an illustration, there can be no doubt that his work in producing a crop is both difficult and important; nevertheless, the part played by the soil in the production of the crop is greater than that of the human labor involved. The farmer tills, fertilizes, plows, sows, and in the end harvests; but ultimately it is nature that provides the most important factors in the production of the crop. On the other hand, the human labor involved in the production of a garment far exceeds the contributions of nature. The sheep and wool are the products of nature; but from the moment the shears sever the wool from the sheep's back, and on through the long process of cleaning, spinning, dyeing, and weaving, it is human labor exclusively that brings a piece of cloth to its completion. Nor has labor finished its task before the tailor cuts the cloth and tailors it into a suit of clothes. In this long succession, the contribution of nature is negligible in proportion to the overwhelming demands put on human labor.

In terms of this second distinction we discover that in Jewish production, again in contradistinction to that of all other nations, the proportion of human labor far exceeds the natural elements involved.

This analysis explains why Jewish economics is a "luft" economics and why Jewish life is a "luft" life. The term, *luftmensch,* was Max Nordau's[8] contribution to our literature, and it expresses all too well the severance of Jewish labor from the soil. To be sure, no nation's economic life is founded on land alone. All economic life consists of both elements, land and labor.

---

7 Otto Effertz's works may be classified as being between bourgeois and Marxian. His contributions were not essentially original, but his surplus value theory is considered as an improvement over Marx's.

8 Max Nordau (1849-1923), the philosopher, was among the first to join Herzl in the founding of the Zionist Congress. An able orator, journalist, and leader, Nordau is particularly known in Jewish communal life for his addresses at the Zionist Congresses, depicting the tragic conditions of the Jews in the various countries.

Indeed, the development of industry is invariably accompanied by an increase in the element of human labor, and a proportional decrease in the elements of nature in production. Although the elements of soil and nature are decreasing in the economic life of other peoples, they are almost absent from Jewish production, which is built exclusively on human labor.

Further, within the labor element in production we should distinguish between physical labor and mental labor. It is a commonplace that in Jewish economic life occupations that require mental labor far outnumber those requiring physical labor. Of course, we must not overlook the fact that among other nations, too, the proportion of mental workers increases with the cultural development of the people. In the case of no other nation is the proportion as high as among the Jews.

The capitalist, or entrepreneur contributes *mental labor* to his enterprise. His work is that of organizing and managing the business. The wage-earner's contribution consists chiefly of *physical labor*. The natural gravitation of the Jew toward the occupations that require mental labor exemplifies the entrepreneuring spirit which drives the Jewish laborer to become a small, but independent, business man. This so-called economic individualism is deeply rooted in the landless history of the Jewish people.

To recapitulate: two important phenomena may be observed in Jewish economic production:

(1) The preponderance of the element of *human labor* over the elements of nature.

(2) The preponderance of *mental labor* over *physical labor*.

III.

The products of human enterprise are generally divided into three classifications:

(1) Production goods, e. g., machines, raw materials, tools, etc.

(2) Means of communication and transportation, e.g., railways, coaches, wagons, ships, telephone, telegraph, etc.

(3) Consumers goods, e. g., food, clothing, houses, furniture, dishes, books, pictures, musical instruments, etc.

Within these classifications of human production, still further divisions may be made, using as a criterion the proximity of a product to, or its remoteness from, nature. The story of the pair of shoes begins with the farmer's raising and feeding the animal. Then come the slaughterer, the tanner, and the various other craftsmen of the leather industry whose task it is to refine the leather to a specific degree. Finally, out of the hands of the shoemaker emerges the finished product.

Accordingly, we must distinguish in production the following levels:

(1) The *primary level* of production, in which we include the branches of production nearest nature, e. g., agriculture, gardening, ranching, etc. Here the element of soil, or nature, is preponderant over that of the human labor.

(2) The level of *basic industry,* in which we include mining, quarrying, forestry, etc. On this level there is an increase in the proportion of human labor.

(3) The *secondary-middle level* of production. This level is even further removed from nature. It includes the metal, building, and textile industries.

(4) The *tertiary-middle level* of production. In this category we include the chemical industry, the lumber industry, the production of leather, paper, etc. Here we approach the level of the consumer and are still further removed from nature. The occupations of many Jews fall within this category.

(5) The *final level* of production, which includes the needle trades, baking, printing, etc., and serves the consumer directly. On this level we find the greatest concentration of traditional occupations of the Jew. Here the elements of soil and nature have vanished completely, and human labor is the only constituent.

In the light of this classification, let us see what information is obtainable from our statistical tables. In Table I, which is based on the Russian Census of 1897 and the Austrian Census of 1900, Jewish occupations are arranged in the order of their remoteness from nature. The table also furnishes us with the percentages that the Jews constitute in relation to the total num-

TABLE I.

Occupational Distribution of the Jews and Their Percentage in the Total Population of Those Occupations

(Based on the Russian Census of 1897)

Level of Production	In The Russian Pale		In Galicia	
	Jews	Per Cent	Jews	Per Cent
1. PRIMARY LEVEL OF PRODUCTION				
Agriculture, gardening, cattle raising, etc.	35,822	0.6	47,996	1.5
2. THE LEVEL OF BASIC INDUSTRY				
Mountaineering, Mining	1,006	1.8	1,053	8.3
Quarrying and Digging	5,187	12.5	696	10.6
Forestry	3,200	12.4	928	10.6
Total	9,393	7.7	2,677	9.5
3. THE SECONDARY MIDDLE LEVEL				
Metal Industry	40,082	21.2	4,410	15.9
Textile Industry	33,200	19.0	1,421	14.7
Building Industary	37,136	18.9	3,110	13.0
Total	110,418	19.7	8,941	14.5
4. THE TERTIARY MIDDLE LEVEL				
Lumber Industry	41,359	27.2	4,229	18.1
Chemical Industry	6,514	34.1	1,430	37.9
Leather and Paper	20,446	43.9	1,938	39.2
Total	68,319	31.3	7,597	23.7
5. FINAL LEVEL OF PRODUCTION				
Foods	44,797	34.8	11,036	48.9
Liquors and Tobacco	23,548	38.3	22,981	70.8
Clothing and Hygienics	244,534	48.1	20,298	35.2
Printing, Etc.	18,996	53.9	450	21.4
Jewelry	5,240	66.5	....	......
Total	337,115	45.5	54,765	47.7

TABLE II.

Comparison of Occupational Distribution of One Hundred Jews and One Hundred Non-Jews

Branches of Occupations	Italy 1901		Germany 1907		Austria 1900		Russian-Pale 1897		United Stat 1900	
	Jews	Non-Jews	Jews	Non-Jews	Jews	Non-Jews	Jews	Non-Jews	Jews	No Jeu
1. Agriculture	0.3	53.3	1.3	33.1	12.8	58.1	2.5	53.0	10.0	3:
2. Industry	8.7	22.4	21.9	37.4	27.5	22.3	36.2	14.6	48.4	24
3. Commerce and Transport	50.3	8.3	50.5	11.1	34.4	5.1	34.6	7.4	28.2	16
4. Servants	0.3	1.4	0.5	1.6	5.2	2.2	11.9	11.8	11.2	1!
5. Professions, Social and Government	18.7	6.4	6.5	5.1	8.3	4.5	7.2	8.2	2.2	4
6. Unclassified	21.7	8.2	19.3	11.1	11.8	7.8	7.6	5.0	......	
Total	100.0	100.0	100.0	100.0	100.0	100.0	100.0	100.0	100.0	10

Editor's Note—J. Lestshinsky has published the following comparable data in *Ekonomische Schriften*, Vol. I, 1930, Yiddish Scientific Institute, Vilna.

Occupational Distribution of World and European Jewry in Percentages

	A	B	C	D	E	F
	Agriculture	*Industry*	*Commerce and Transportation*	*Professions and Government Service*	*Domestic Service and Unskilled Labor*	*Unclassified*
World Jewry (15,800,000)	4.2	36.4	38.6	6.1	2.0	12.7
European Jewry (7,306,541)	5.5	32.8	41.9	6.1	1.6	12.1

It is also interesting to use Professor Salomon Goldelman's classification of the data ("Juedische Galuthwirstchaft", Prague) for the same occupational categories to compare the distributions of gainfully employed Jews and non-Jews in the European agricultural countries.

		A		B		C		D		E		F	
Year	Country	Jews	Non-Jews	Jews	Non-Jews	Jews	Non-Jews	Jews	Non-Jews	Jews	Non-Jews	Jews	Non-Jews
1927	Soviet Russia	9.8	81.4	35.1	7.6	27.3	1.2	2.2	2.2	8.6	2.6	17.0	5.0
1921	Poland	9.8	80.7	32.2	7.7	35.1	1.5	2.7	1.7	4.4	2.3	15.8	6.1
1921	Carpathian Russia	27.7	74.9	25.7	8.5	24.5	0.7	3.4	2.0	5.0	3.3	13.7	10.6
1913	Roumania	2.5	82.3	42.5	7.0	37.9	1.9	3.5	1.8	3.2	2.0	10.4	5.0

Comparing the average occupational distribution of 100 Jews and non-Jews of the above countries we find the respective number of Jews and non-Jews to be: A—10.2 and 84.5; B—34.1 nd 5.8; C—28.4 and 1.0, and D—2.8 and 1.4.

In the semi-agrarian territories (Hungary, 1920; Slovakia, 1921) the average occupational distribution of 100 Jews and non-Jews respectively was: A—5.6 and 61.6; B—29.9 and 18.0; C—43.7 and 3.3; D—2.8 and 32. In the industrial countries (Bohemia, 1921; Silesia, 1921; nd Germany, 1907) the average occupational distribution of 100 Jews and non-Jews respectively was: A—1.6 and 33.4; B—23.4 and 38.4; C—52.6 and 7.6; D—0.9 and 3.7.

It should be remembered, of course, that the occupational distribution of the Jews in ussia has been changed considerably as a result of the two Five-Year plans. In Poland and oumania a change occurred as a result of the boycott policies of those governments. The tuation in Germany, too, has changed with the rise of Hitler and the corresponding mass nigration of German Jews.

The economic structure of American Jewry has as yet not been thoroughly investigated. rom the materials that are available we know that its structure does not differ *basically* from at of European Jewry.

(The reader is referred to footnote 10, p. 73 for a study of the economic structure of the ws in Palestine.)

bers employed in the various branches of production. The table reveals the following information:

(a) *Jewish occupations are remote from nature.* In Russia only 0.6% of those engaged in agriculture are Jews, and in Galicia only 1.5%.

(b) *The percentage of Jews in any level of production varies directly with its remoteness from nature.* On the level of basic industry, 8 to 9% of the laborers are Jews. On the secondary-middle level the percentage of Jews rises to between 15 and 20. In the tertiary-middle level it reaches 25 to 33%.

(c) On the final level of production Jewish labor represents 50% of the total; i. e., the Jews have their highest representation in occupations that are at the greatest distance from nature.

(d) The vast majority of non-Jews gain their livelihood from nature (in levels 1 and 2, i. e., agriculture and basic industry), whereas the majority of Jews earn their living directly from other men. In Russia and Galicia 70-80% of non-Jews earn their livelihood directly from nature; a similar percentage of the Jews earn theirs from men.

These figures are based on official government statistics. They incorporate no Zionist theories and are not motivated by the remotest concern with Jewish problems. The above are the writer's own classifications. He was compelled to make them for two reasons. Firstly, because occupations are classified differently in Russia and in Austria. Secondly, because the classifications of the government statisticians are too general; we find, for example, in these government statistics that large scale metallurgy, which rightfully belongs in class 3, and small metal work like that of the blacksmith, locksmith, or tinsmith, which rightfully belongs in class 5, are all in one category. Were official statistics anything better than the indiscriminate jumble that they actually are, they would display the economic condition of the Jewish people much more clearly. Even the veil of official figures, however, cannot obscure the prevailing law of Jewish economics, namely, *that the concentration of Jewish labor in any occupation varies directly with the remoteness of that occupation from nature.*

It is as if an inexorable whip of history were driving the Jews further and further away from soil and nature, and higher and higher into the insubstantial ether of social stratification; it is as if history had conspired never to liberate the Jews from the shackles of economic landlessness.

The story told by the figures of Table I (see page 66) is that of a people far removed from the most important, most influential, and most stable branches of production—far removed from the occupations which are at the hub of history. Instead of concentrating about the vital center of economic life, the Jews are scattered on its periphery. Obviously, the fate of society does not to any extent rest on the needle or tobacco industries. This superficies of social life, which is made up of the give-and-take of finished goods, must draw its sustenance from labor in such central branches of production as agriculture, sheep raising, mining, railways, shipping, etc.

The moral of this story told by dry statistics is, that as long as the Jewish people remains remote from nature and basic industry, Jewish economic life will remain stagnant, Jewish culture will be at a low ebb, and the political welfare of the Jews will remain the plaything of chance. These figures force upon us the inevitable conclusion that in *international* Socialism, the class struggle, and the revolution, the part played by *Jewish* Socialism will be as insignificant as the Jewish needle and flatiron are when compared to the non-Jewish tractor, locomotive, or steamship.

Such is the chronic malady of Jewish history. Those who seek to strengthen the attachment of the Jews to the rarefied economic stratosphere of the Galut, those who seek comfort for the Jewish people in Exile songs and Exile hopes, merely help to perpetuate our chronic malady.

IV.

From this analysis of the chronic economic ailment of the Jewish people in terms of current concepts of economic theory, let us now pass to an analysis of the same group of phenomena in Marxian terms.

Marx divides modern capital into two categories: (1) *constant capital,* which consists of the means of production such as land, factory buildings, raw materials, coal, machines, implements, etc.; (2) *variable capital,* which consists of human labor-power. In the capital invested in any enterprise we must, therefore, according to Marx, distinguish between these two categories. The investment in rent, coal, machinery, freight, etc. is the constant part of the capital; the investment in salaries and wages is its variable portion.

All capital, both constant and variable, is, of course, created by human labor. Let us not fail to observe immediately that, since the number of Jews in the production of buildings, machines, means of communication, and raw materials is negligible, the Jews as a whole participate but little in the production and in the distribution of *constant capital.* Jewish labor is invested in the production of variable capital, and here, too, Jews are subject to competition on the part of non-Jewish labor.

The next step in our analysis is the observation that both kinds of capital are in a process of continual expansion. The rate of growth of constant capital, however, is greater than that of variable capital. In a developing technological economy the amount of work done by machinery constantly increases, at the expense of human labor. Workers are dropped as new machines are introduced into the process of production. This law, that *constant capital grows at the expense of variable capital,* is one of the most important generalizations in Marxian economic theory.

Marx establishes the fact that the machine displaces the worker, and that constant capital displaces variable capital. Since Jewish labor is concentrated exclusively in the production of variable capital, we must conclude that *Jewish labor is being increasingly displaced by non-Jewish labor.*

This is the obviously logical conclusion to which we are driven by Marx's economic theories. The failure of Marx's followers to observe this can be attributed only to their complete failure to examine Jewish economic conditions in the light of scientific principles. The development of technology will inevitably throw Jewish workers out of employment. Jewish labor will inevitably remain technologically backward, because the machine is its most formidable enemy. And all this, in turn, can be explained only by the fact that the Jew is divorced from nature.

Fortunately, the displacement of Jewish labor is a slow process rather than a sudden catastrophe. In Europe, Jewish weavers, shoemakers, cabinet makers, and cigar makers are being gradually displaced by non-Jewish labor. With the introduction of the power-loom, Jewish weavers in Lodz and Bialystok have become almost entirely a thing of the past and non-Jewish labor operates the machines. The shoe industry in Warsaw and Odessa has passed through the same evolutionary process. The large tobacco factories in Russia are now almost entirely in the hands of Gentile labor.

The Jews are compelled to seek new work; and under this compulsion they migrate to the four corners of the earth, in search of opportunities to develop new industries. Even in the countries where Jews have most recently found a haven, however, they are relentlessly pursued by the spectre of displacement. In England, where Jews founded a large, modern needle industry, Jewish labor is being displaced by Gentile girls. In America, too, Jews are losing control of the needle trade of which they were the founders. Gradually, step by step, they are being eased out of their jobs in the American needle industry by the influx of Italians, Poles, Lithuanians, and Syrians.

As we proceed, it becomes more obvious that the Jewish economic structure is malformed because of its remoteness from nature. The so-called Jewish malady is a result of historic conditions, and is therefore chronic. It is well known that an organism afflicted by a chronic malady may survive for a long time. This is just what has happened to the Jewish national organism: it has adapted itself to this chronic ailment that has tortured it for almost two thousand years. But the Marxian analysis has brought to light another, and more disquieting, complication. It warns us that, under modern capitalism, the process of displacement will continue to aggravate our condition. After two thousand years, our malady has ceased to be quiescent. It has become acute.

The landlessness of the Jewish people is the source of its malady and tragedy. We have no territory of our own, hence we are by necessity divorced from nature. Therefore, given the recently developed environment of capitalistic production and competition, this abnormal circumstance quite naturally assumes proportions of an acute and dangerous nature.

Table II will furnish us with the data on the efforts the Jewish nation has made to combat this disease.

In Italy, where the number of Jews is very small, their economic, political, and cultural conditions compare favorably with those of their brethren in any part of the world. Jews frequently occupy positions of importance in the political and intellectual life of the land. Our statistics, however, tell us a different story. The economic structure of Italian Jewry is one of the most abnormal and unproductive.[9] Agriculture is something almost totally foreign to the Italian Jew. Less than 9% of the Jews are engaged in industry; moreover, not as workers, but as entrepreneurs. Half of the Italian Jews are merchants. *Almost all Italian Jews obtain their income from the exploitation of foreign labor, chiefly in the non-basic industries.*

The situation in Germany is not much different. The number of Jews in Germany is twelve times the number in Italy. Their part in the political life of the country is less conspicuous. The economic picture of German Jewry, however, shows a larger proportion of productivity. As many as 22% are engaged in industry. Nevertheless, the major contribution of the Jews to the economic life of Germany is still that of capital used for exploitation.

Austria has twice as many Jews as Germany. Galicia, Bukovina, and Vienna are densely populated by Jews. Among these masses one observes an urge to return to productive, "natural" occupations. More than one-fourth of the Jews are engaged in industry, and in the majority of cases not as capitalists, but rather

---

9 In Zionist literature, the terms *productive* and *unproductive* are used in a very special sense. They refer to presence in or absence from the basic industries rather than to an evaluation of economic or social usefulness.

as wage-earners and small-scale owners. Almost 13% of the Jews of Austria are engaged in agriculture. In general, then, we have a picture of a substantial number of Jews who have penetrated into the primary and basic levels of production.

In Russia, too, we can discern a similar return to productive occupations. Whereas in all other countries of Europe the Jew lives chiefly by commerce rather than industry, in Russia there is a greater tendency to industrialization. This development has been taking place despite the enormous obstacles imposed by the government. Despite the government restrictions that forbid the Jew to live in rural areas outside of the Pale of Settlement, we find many Jews forcing their way back to the soil, to nature.

A slow, but fundamental, revolution has been taking place in Jewish life. We have been witnessing the slow transition of the Jewish masses from unproductive to productive occupations. Emigration is the culminating point of this process. American statistics tell us that productive work has become the basis of Jewish economic life; and the Jewish proletarian, the true representative of Jewry.

No statistics are available concerning Palestine and the Argentine, but there is all reason to believe that in these two countries Jewish work has become even more productive, closer to nature and more deeply rooted in the soil than in the United States. And there is further reason to believe that in Palestine, with its Jewish colonies and Jewish agriculture, the economic position of the Jews is still more secure and less subject to the whims of chance.[10]

10 That Borochov's predictions of a relatively more normal Jewish economic structure in Palestine was not a chance prophecy may be seen from the statistics listed below, published by H. Frumkin (*Jewish Frontier*, March, 1936).

	Providers Beginning 1936	%	Providers and Their Dependents	%
Agriculture	23,000	16.1	50,500	13.5
Building	19,000	13.3	49,600	13.2
Industry	35,000	24.5	89,500	23.9
Transport and Transit	8,500	5.9	25,000	6.6
Liberal Professions	13,500	9.4	31,800	8.5
Administration and Police	2,000	1.4	5,200	1.4
	101,000	70.6		67.1
Commerce, Housework, Misc.	42,000	29.4	123,400	32.0
	143,00	100.0	375,000	100.0

The diversity of Jewish labor may be seen from the following table showing the

For hundreds of years the Jewish masses have blindly searched for a way that will return them to nature, to the soil. At last we have found it. *Zionism is the way. Zionism is the logical, the natural consequence of the economic revolution* that has been going on within Jewish life for the past few hundred years. Even in the Galut, our people have been striving to turn to more "natural" and more productive occupations, but this radical change cannot come to its full fruition in the hostile atmosphere of the Galut.

Zionism is the only movement capable of introducing reason, order, and discipline into Jewish life. Zionism is the only answer to the economic and historic need of the Jewish people.

distribution of 98,636 members of the Histadrut (General Federation of Jewish Labor in Palestine) which embraces 80-85% of all Jewish workers in Palestine, as of January 1, 1937.

Jews in agricultural settlements (private colonies):

Male workers over 18 years of age	11,136	
Female workers over 18 years of age	3,426	
Housewives	4,646	
Working youth	899	
		20,107

Jews in agricultural settlement (communal and cooperative colonies):

Male workers over 18 years of age	6,044	
Female workers over 18 years of age	5,520	
Working youth	889	
		12,453

Total of Jews in agricultural settlements		32,560

Jewish workers in cities:

Construction	8,829	
Building materials	750	
Painters	1,149	
Quarrymen	457	
Stone dressers	179	
Metal and electricity	4,678	
Woodworkers	2,334	
Stevedores and other port workers	2,146	
Railway, postal and telegraph	489	
Leather workers	655	
Weavers	795	
Needle workers	1,266	
Baking, meat, and food	1,677	
Printing and paper boxes	1,030	
Various factories	2,222	
Restaurant and hotel	1,802	
Domestic services	1,633	
Clerks, etc.	4,985	
Art workers	290	
Janitors, guards, policemen	420	
Engineers and technicians	557	
Teachers and kindergartens	562	
Medical workers	1,877	
Agriculturalists and gardeners	492	
Housewives	15,704	
Working youth	889	
Unclassified	7,751	
		66,076
		98,636

"JEWISH ANTI-SEMITISM"[1]

IT IS a well-known and tragic fact that many a Jewish worker who has slaved away for years in a growing Jewish industry awakes one fine morning to find himself ruthlessly displaced by a non-Jew from the very factory to which he has given so much of his sweat and blood. This problem becomes particularly acute when the industrialist introduces modern methods of production, that is, when he substitutes machine labor for hand labor. It has become almost axiomatic that Jewish workers are not privileged to work at the machines but are doomed to hand-labor.

Our movement (the Poale Zion), as early as ten years ago, called attention to this phenomenon in Jewish life. Another faction which to this very day considers itself the "sole representative" of the Jewish labor movement (the *Bund*[2]) mocked the Poale Zion and heaped ridicule upon our thoughts and actions. But contemporary life has demonstrated the correctness of our

---

1 An uncompleted manuscript written sometime before the World War under the title, "What Can Be Done to Check Discrimination."

2 The General Jewish Workers' Alliance, the *Bund*, was organized in 1897. At first it was affiliated with the Russian Social-Democratic Party but soon withdrew, because of the latter's attitude toward nationality sections. The *Bund* embraced workers' groups in Russia, Poland, and Lithuania. When first organized, its chief Jewish characteristic was that it employed Yiddish—the most convenient language in which to carry on propaganda among Jewish labor. The basic tenet from which it has not deviated to this date is that the Jewish problem must necessarily await the advent of Socialism, which will automatically solve it. Hence it considers the Jewish problem of sectional rather than international importance. From this arises its bitter opposition to territorialism, and particularly to Zionism.

In the course of the development of the *Bund* it has greatly modified its attitude toward nationalism. It no longer considers itself to be merely a Yiddish-speaking Socialist group; it has embodied in its program Jewish culture and Jewish national minority rights, though it is still opposed to Hebrew.

The accomplishments of the *Bund* are not to be minimized. It was the first Jewish labor party to organize the Jewish worker for his political and economic struggle. "The Jewish labor movement will erect in honor of the great accomplishments of the *Bund* a great memorial—in Jerusalem," said Borochov.

However, its failure to discover the root of the Jewish problem and its fomenting of antagonism to Palestine are undermining its position. Outside of Poland, the *Bund* now plays an insignificant role.

view and has forced our opponents to take cognizance of the real conditions. And now, when the elimination of Jewish workers has reached the stage of a veritable epidemic, when the tragic news of the dismissal of Jewish weavers, spatsmakers, and tobacco workers has become an open secret, they awake from their slumber and evince an interest in this tragedy of Jewish labor. It is natural that those who only now have recognized this malignant condition are puzzled and bewildered. They neither analyze the symptoms of the disease, nor propose a cure.

I.

What accounts for this state of affairs? To date, numerous theories have been advanced. Our optimists,[3] who seek to minimize Jewish tragedies, have attributed this plight to insignificant and incidental causes. The optimists maintain that this abnormality has its origin in the fact that Jews lack craftsmanship, that they are unaccustomed to physical labor. They conclude that were the Jewish workers to receive a good vocational training, there would remain no obstacle in the effort to penetrate the primary levels of production. Those publicists and "community leaders" who uphold this view have not the least understanding of the history of the Jewish working class, nor of the laws of capitalistic development. In the first place, it is erroneous to assume that it is because of lack of proper training that Jews are excluded from factories. Are the peasant boys and girls who make up the bulk of the workers in the large factories better trained or more skilled? On the contrary, modern industry demands unskilled labor power; only the foremen and the technical experts need have special training. Secondly, the Jewish workers did not become workers over-night. For hundreds of years a working class existed in the Jewish Ghetto. Moreover, Jewish craftsmen had their own guilds with their trade rules just like the workers of other peoples. The Jewish shoemaker, tailor, bookbinder, or upholsterer received the same training as did his German contemporary. In the course of centuries, Jewish workers

---

3 Borochov refers to the so-called Jewish communal leaders who have a tendency to minimize the economic problem of Jews in Galut.

developed their own labor traditions and techniques. That these traditions and techniques were more adapted to Ghetto life than to the outside world: that the Jewish weaver has for centuries specialized in making a *tallit*[4] and not a shawl, the Jewish cap-maker, a *yarmulke*[5] and not an officer's cap—all this does not prove that the Jewish laborer has no tradition or historical past. For if our "community leaders" would speak less and investigate more, they would discover that even in Western Europe today, it is claimed that the modern hand-worker does not easily adapt himself to factory work and that no amount of vocational training in the most advanced country can fully prepare the worker for modern industry.

A second reason frequently given is that the Sabbath[6] hinders the Jews from penetrating into the large industries. Our optimists who cling to the Sabbath theory fail to understand that, for the Jews, the Sabbath is not only a religious tradition, but a deeply-rooted social-economic institution. The Sabbath should be an advantage rather than a disadvantage to the Jewish worker; for the Jewish employer is also accustomed to rest on Sabbath, and were he not to entertain any particular hatred for the Jewish worker, he would certainly employ him. The fact that the foreman and the expert are in most cases imported non-Jews for whose sake the employer is "forced" to keep his factory open on the Sabbath, provides no valid excuse. In the first place, the foreman is not the owner, and secondly, there are many Jewish workers who *would* work on Saturday. In many instances, Jewish workers have agreed to work on Saturday, but were refused employment.

A third reason commonly advanced is that the Jewish worker is culturally on a higher level than his non-Jewish competitor. The Jewish worker demands better pay and better working condi-

---

4 A shawl with fringes on the four corners worn by Jews when praying.

5 A skull-cap worn by orthodox Jews.

6 One of the reasons advanced by Gentile employers for not employing Jewish labor in America is "that work is disturbed by absence on Jewish festivals and holy days". See J. X. Cohen's pamphlet *Jews, Jobs and Discrimination*—A Report on Jewish Non-Employment (in America) published by the American Jewish Congress, New York, 1937.

tions, and most important, the Jewish worker is a frequent striker.[7] The Jewish industrialist who fears the strike of the Jewish worker refuses to employ him. This assertion is true. The Jewish worker and his non-Jewish comrade, as well as the employer, are equally aware of it.

In the five-year period, 1900-1904, the numbers of striking workers per thousand were: Germany 55, Belgium 70, England 75, France 150, and Russia 130. Among Jewish workers in Russia, 240 of every 1,000 struck. Are we, then, to conclude that the big Jewish industrialist is justified in his fears? No. For the majority of the Jewish strikes occur in small shops and not in large factories. The following figures clearly illustrate this: in the small work-shops, 17.5% were lockouts; in small and middle sized factories, 50% of the strikes were provoked by the employers; and in the large factories (employing 200 workers or more), 67.5% of all strikes were forced by the employers, and only 25% were called by the workers.

The Jewish striker meets with a smaller measure of success in the large factories than in the small work-shops. The handworkers had a complete victory in 72.7% of all strikes, and suffered a complete loss in 7.9%. The Jewish workers in the small factories (employing from 20 to 50 workers) scored a victory in 68.7% of the strikes and suffered a loss in 14.9%; in the middle-sized factories (employing from 51 to 200 workers), they scored a complete victory in 56.9% and suffered a complete loss in 20.7%; and *in the large factories (employing 200 workers and over), they scored a complete victory in 27.6% and suffered a complete loss in 41.7% of all the strikes.*

---

[7] The same reasons are advanced by Jewish plantation owners of Palestine against employing Jewish workers. Moshe Smilansky, leader of the plantation owners and an enemy of Jewish labor, wrote in 1932 ". . . In the orange grove where the work is done wholly by Jewish workers, there are always negotiations about one thing or another." This is why some Jewish plantation owners in Palestine prefer to hire the unorganized, underpaid Arab workers—very often under the guise of "internationalism" and "friendly relations with our Arab neighbors". See D. Ben Gurion's pamphlet, *Jewish Labor*, published by the Hechalutz Organization of England, 1935.

* During the same period government statistics show that there were only 481 strikes in European Russia, affecting 1,030 factories. Belgium in the same period registered 487 strikes; and Switzerland, in the course of 40 years (1861-1900), had 1,001 strikes.
In general, the Jewish striker was not less successful than the non-Jewish. Whereas only 7.5% of the strikes in Belgium were won completely, 9% in Austria, 3% in France,

These figures prove that the complaints of the big industrialists against the audacity of the Jewish worker are groundless, for in most cases the employers were the aggressors. If anyone has a right to complain, it is the small owner, for in his workshop the Jewish worker is truly a frequent striker. In this respect, the big Jewish capitalist might consider himself fortunate. Nevertheless, *the small owner continues to employ the Jew, even though the latter is a striker.* The small owner may make frequent use of the police; he may suffer financial losses; however, he does not replace the Jewish worker with a non-Jew. Who, then, is responsible for the expulsion of the Jewish worker from Jewish industry? It is the big capitalist, the "Lord Manufacturer". In order to pacify the Jewish community, the big capitalist rationalizes his refusal to employ Jewish workers by claiming that the Jewish worker is a chronic striker.

II.

If we wish to investigate the real causes of the displacement of Jewish workers, we must consider the problem in its two parts: *isolation and discrimination.* We must give due consideration to the fact that historically the Jewish worker has been torn away from nature (agriculture), from the natural resources (mines, quarries, and forests), and from those industries which produce the means of production and the transportation facilities (metallurgy, manufacture of machinery, steamships and railroads). The Jews have been removed for centuries from the basic branches of production upon which the economic structure depends. The Jews are concentrated in the final levels of production—those

30% in Great Britain, 49.5% in Germany, and 26% in European Russia, the Jewish workers in the Pale won 63.5% of their strikes completely, achieved partial victory in 22.5%, and suffered complete defeat in only 14% of the strikes.

The intensity of the economic conflict between the Jewish employer and the Jewish worker, too, is greater than among the non-Jews, as is evident from a comparison of the "resistance coefficients" of the strikers. Thus, for example, in the aforementioned five year period the number of strike days per striking worker in European Russia was 4.7 as compared with 9.5 days for the Jews in the Pale. The power of resistance of the Jews was twice as great as that of the non-Jews. [The preceding data, both of the text and the footnote, are also found in *The Jewish Labor Movement in Statistics* (Berlin, 1923), which was the result of seven years of research by Borochov into the status of the Jewish workers in the Russian Pale. The study covers the period 1895-1904 and was intended merely as an introduction to a larger, more comprehensive work concerning the class struggle as it affected the Jews.—Editor.]

branches which are far from the core of our economic structure (the production of consumers' goods). This phenomenon cannot be attributed to anti-Jewish discrimination. Jews were not forced out of metallurgy into locksmithing. They were not transformed from railroad men to teamsters; from farmers to tailors, cobblers, and cigar makers. They were not forced out of forestry and thrust into the match industry. True, the Jews have not engaged in basic industries since their dispersion, but neither the Sabbath nor the economic struggle of the Jewish worker are responsible for this state of affairs. Its root lies in the unique history of Galut Jewry.

Our severance from nature and the basic industries is the chief characteristic of the Jewish economic life in Galut. Under the capitalist economy, however, we note the additional anomaly that even in those branches of production in which the Jews have long been engaged, they are restricted from entering the more developed forms of industry. This second phenomenon is not an historical one, and the two-thousand-year-old wandering of the Jew which is responsible for the first anomaly is not at all responsible for the second. These phenomena are often confused. We shall differentiate between them by calling the first, *isolation,* and the second, *discrimination.*

We already know the cause of our isolation.[8] What, however, is the cause of the discrimination? Its cause may be attributed to the assimilationist tendency of the Jewish bourgeoisie. The Jewish manufacturer who is about to become a big capitalist wants to sever, as soon as possible, his relations with the Jewish community from which he emerged. He does it for two reasons. He wants to conquer the Gentile market and be on the same footing with the Gentile manufacturer. His Jewishness is in this respect a disadvantage, since his competitors refuse to recognize him as an equal. He is, therefore, eager to display his *goyish* (non-Jewish) patriotism. Secondly, to the extent that he is traditionally bound up with his people, he seeks to govern them. He

---

8 See the essay, "The Economic Development of the Jewish People."

utilizes his influence in the *kehilla*[9] and in the charitable institutions as a means of crushing the Jewish masses and public opinion. The fewer ties he has with the Jewish community, the less he fears its control. He is anxious to employ Gentile workers and managers and, to as great an extent as possible, restrict his commercial intercourse to Gentiles because he wants to identify himself with his Gentile competitor and rid himself of Jewish public control. To the Jews, he offers charity and faith; in his business, however, he prefers to associate with Gentiles or with Jewish assimilationists of his own kind.

The Jewish employer, upon introducing steampower into his factory (the symbol of large-scale production), substitutes the Gentile for the Jewish worker. Being an enemy of *Jewish* labor, he is particularly angry when the latter protests or strikes. Hence, he justifies his acts with the Sabbath excuse, or the pretext of the inexperience or physical weakness of the Jewish worker. But these are not his real motives. The truth of the matter is that he wants to rid himself of the Jews and of the Jewish environment. And when our "sole representative" (the *Bund*) and its bourgeois allies take the contentions of the Jewish capitalists seriously, it only proves how short-sighted they are and how superficially they interpret Jewish reality.

III.

We have noted two diseases: isolation and discrimination. Two types of treatment are possible: one is in the form of a palliative; the other is a radical and lasting cure. Marx often quoted William Petty: "the land is the mother, and labor is the father of wealth". As long as the Jewish people lives in the Galut, it will never have a "mother". The remedy will come only with an economic revolution in Jewish life, only when the Jewish people will have its own land, its own territory. Palliatives are of little help in the Galut. *The only cure for isolation is Zionism.*

Such is not the case, however, as regards discrimination. Here

---

9 *Kehilla* refers to the Jewish community (chiefly Eastern Europe) of a given town or city which was empowered by the Government to assess or collect taxes and regulate all Jewish religious and communal affairs.

our enemies want to rob us of positions which we have won with our sweat and blood. They want to expel us from those fields into which we have penetrated. This we must firmly oppose. If we possessed the power to win our economic positions, then regardless of our present weakness we must be strong enough to retain them. *We must strike at the anti-Semitism of the Jewish capitalists.*

Let us pause awhile and ask ourselves: What is our aim? Do we wish to render only temporary relief to the Jewish workers, or do we wish to make impossible their continued displacement? Do we want first aid for the unfortunate, or are we interested in finding a radical solution?

At the present time, the masses are so depressed that they long for even a modicum of relief. Therefore, the agitation for first aid, for weak and even demoralizing palliatives—and we certainly have an over-abundance of palliatives—finds fertile soil among the masses. The bourgeois nationalists prescribe philanthropic remedies and the *Bundist* guardians deliver social sermons. The Galut nationalists reproach the Jewish industrialists for being "bad Jews", having no pity on the poor Jewish workers. They appeal to the national conscience of the capitalist. The Jewish "communal leader" often succeeds in arousing the capitalist's pity to the extent of bringing about re-employment of a few Jewish workers. The *Bundists* don a *kosher* proletarian mask and reproach the Gentile Polish workers for being "bad Marxists". They appeal to their sense of solidarity; they write humble letters to their Polish comrades, appealing to the latter's sense of class justice. The results are nil. The tactics, both of the Galut nationalists and of the *Bundists,* are as ridiculous as they are harmful.

Of course, an appeal to national pity and class philanthropy sometimes helps. Reproaches are temporarily effective. When the manufacturer succumbs to the newspaper sermons and the spark of Jewishness flares up within him, he sometimes consents to take back a few Jewish workers. In such instances, how does the worker feel towards his boss who has become a man of "good" deeds? The boss is a "great and pious Jew" and the worker will have to pay bitterly and dearly for his boss' justice. The worker is no longer a proud, dignified man, but an uninvited beggar. The boss' pity is a strong weapon with which to break the spirit and resistance of the Jewish worker.

Socialist pity, likewise, may occasionally be of help. Through such pity, the Jewish weavers in Bialystok persuaded their Gentile comrades to permit them to work. But do not for a moment imagine that all Jewish workers were accorded this right. No. The class compassion of the Polish workers led them to introduce a system of *numerus clausus*[10] for the Jews. Previously, we were blessed with a *numerus clausus* in schools, and now, class solidarity as conceived by the *Bundists* has blessed us with a *numerus clausus* in the factories. What a remarkable victory!

One who is overjoyed at the great victory which we scored in Bialystok, one who can humble himself by appealing to the class consciousness of his comrades (as did the shoemakers in Warsaw), is not fit to defend his honor and has lost all courage to struggle for his interests. Such demoralization has been introduced into the ranks of the working masses by our "sole representative", the *Bund*. *We must understand once and for all that one who has no national dignity can have no class dignity.*

---

10 The laws of the various anti-Semitic Governments which limited the number of Jewish students who may attend schools or colleges usually to the proportion of the Jews in the country. Such laws are in force now in Germany, Poland, Hungary, etc.

NATIONAL HELPLESSNESS VERSUS NATIONAL SELF-HELP[1]

I.

THE MOST important question facing the Jewish worker at the present phase of history is: How can our nation be insured against the recurrence of the horrible persecutions and tragic events which so often befall it in the various countries?

Each nation has its troubles. The Italians are not assured against earthquakes; the Chinese, against floods; the Indians, against failure of crops, cholera and pests. Nature is responsible for these catastrophes. Human knowledge, however, can combat these blind elements of nature.

Other nations suffer from continual oppression: Ireland and India are under the yoke of Great Britain, and Russia is under the yoke of the Czar. These peoples suffer because they are not sufficiently conscious of their nationality nor are they internally united. They cannot, therefore, successfully revolt against their oppressors.

Some nations are being ruined by the World War, in spite of the fact that they do not want war and are not to be blamed for it. Among these nations are the Serbians, Belgians, Poles, Latvians and Armenians. Nevertheless, they find a double consolation in their sufferings. They are not alone, not deserted, nor persecuted; they have someone to come to their aid. A great many nations came to the support of the Serbians and Belgians, and Russia pretended to come to the aid of the Armenians. Of greater importance is the fact that these nations may sooner or later expect

---

[1] Published in the *Yiddisher Congress*, New York, August 6, 1915.

to receive recompense for their sacrifices. *They struggle for their own national cause.* Should they lose in the struggle, the loss is not permanent; for they remain on their own soil and can always wait for the opportunity to arise and regain their rights.

The Galut condition of the Jewish nation is not only tragic, but also hopeless. Our Galut tragedy is not temporary, but permanent. We do not fight for a Jewish cause; we suffer for foreign interests. We do not possess our own land, and are neglected by this colossal world which has its own troubles. We have no side to join in a war; the world is hostile towards us and wishes to wipe us out. Under the best conditions, the world is indifferent to us. Our fate is always determined by the fate of other nations.

How can we escape from this extraordinary condition? Are we absolutely helpless, or can we extricate ourselves?

The Jewish workers receive various answers to this question. Some Jewish Socialists place their entire faith in *assimilation;* others, in the *progress of humanity.* We Socialist-Zionists are convinced that our freedom depends primarily upon the *national self-help of the Jewish masses.* And the latest, most dreadful of all catastrophes befalling the Jews, the World War, substantiated our viewpoint.

II.

Death and suicide are the most radical reliefs from disease. Similarly, assimilation is the most radical solution to the Jewish problem. If there were no Jews, there would be no suffering from the Jewish tragedy. Nevertheless, no medical expert would advise his patient to take poison for a cure. No honest statesman or idealist ever attempted to solve, for example, the Polish question by suggesting that the Polish people should cease existing. And how would the Belgians, in their present plight, look upon anyone who gave them the excellent advice to assimilate with the Germans, and cease to exist as an independent nation?

Only to us Jews have self-appointed "physicians" had the audacity, the shamelessness, to preach national suicide. It is beneath the honor and dignity of our great heroic and martyred people to take the assimilationist Utopianists seriously. The Jewish nation *lives* and *will* live! Other nations may love us or hate us, but they will never succeed in wiping us out, either by persecution or by assimilation.

Nevertheless, were assimilation possible, we might have considered it. The truth of the matter is, however, that assimilation is nothing more than a harmful illusion. The Jewish masses become assimilated only to some degree. At most, they accept *the external characteristics* of the neighboring nations: the clothes, the language, certain foods and habits. But inwardly, in their spirit, they remain strange to the culture of their neighbors. Even the most assimilated Jews cannot intermingle with their neighbors, and always lead a distinct Jewish life.

As long as other nations exist, the Jewish nation will also exist. A part of the Jewish intelligentzia and upper bourgeoisie strenuously attempts to commit national suicide, but the Jewish masses, the Jewish working class, will not yield to the notion that the Jew disappear among foreign nations and alien cultures.

III.

"Progress of humanity" is a beautiful idea, but we must always be aware of one thing: progress does not create man, but man creates progress. Progress is not self-made, but must be won, step by step, by the masses. True, there is such a thing as technical, scientific, and economic progress. We continually become wiser, keener, and more experienced in the control of nature. That alone, however, cannot make our character more humane, our feelings more refined, our motives, nobler. Political institutions do not of themselves become ennobled, and social justice does not just "happen".

Social and political rights grow only through bitter struggle. Oppression maintains itself as long as the oppressed have not the strength to throw off the yoke and institute a new *equilibrium*. The moral progress of mankind is nothing more than a result of this bitter struggle for this equilibrium. Wherever might and helplessness meet, oppression will be the inevitable result. The only defense the weak have is their own organized effort and their common struggle for their interests. The law, the police, and the courts of justice will at most come to the aid of the innocent, suffering *individual,* but not to the aid of the oppressed *group or nation.* Every law, every statute is passed and controlled by the powerful, who utilize technical progress for their own purposes. The laws and judicial practices can improve in favor of the oppressed classes and nations through no means other than their own efforts.

The World War has clearly demonstrated that even the best of mankind will not cease to oppress the weak if the latter comes into conflict with its own interests. In proof of this truism, we submit the example of the German Social-Democratic Party which consented to the military move of the Imperial Army in occupying neutral Luxemburg and Belgium. No one will deny that the German Social-Democrats are good Socialists. But when it seemed to them that it was essential to violate the neutrality of weak neighbors, they did not hesitate in the least. The Belgian and French Socialists acted similarly.

In short, the weaker element, be it class or nation, should not depend on the humaneness and justice of the stronger. The basic principle of Socialism is that the emancipation of the working class must come through its own efforts and through its own struggle. What a fine thing it would be if the worker depended on the moral progress of the capitalist to cease exploiting him!

IV.

And are we not naive in assuming that the Jews will cease to suffer and will be guarded against all catastrophes when the nations shall have become more humane and shall no longer persecute weaker peoples? We Jews should trust no one but ourselves. *The emancipation of the Jewish people can be gained only by our own efforts.*

The only solution to the Jewish problem is the creation of an equilibrium of power which will not permit other nations to persecute us so freely without being called to account. The uniqueness of the Jewish tragedy resides in the fact that Jews have no land of their own. For that reason Jewish interests and needs do not evoke respect.

Consider a tiny country like Montenegro which has a quarter of a million poor, semi-barbarian inhabitants without any influence whatsoever on world civilization. Then consider the Jewish nation, a cultured people of over thirteen million, with a thousand-year-old culture, a people of great capitalists and great revolutionists, of Rothschilds, Poznanskys, and Schiffs, and of Marxes, Lassalles, and Gershonys; a nation which has everywhere statesmen, journalists, artists, poets, teachers, and social leaders; a people of great capabilities, exerting a powerful influence on human civilization.

Whose interests will be taken into greater account—that of the thirteen million highly cultured Jews, or that of the quarter million Montenegrins? Whose voice will ring clearer in the international chorus of the movements for freedom? The answer is plain. The Montenegrins are in a better position to struggle for freedom than are the Jews. The interests of the Montenegrins will be taken into greater account for they do not depend upon assimilation and human progress, but on their own small forces and planned connections with the great powers of the world. This must also be the national political slogan of the Jewish worker: *organized national self-help. We must unite ourselves in the struggle for our own future.*

FACING REALITY[1]

ZIONISM IS facing reality, while the enemies of Zion are turning their backs on it.

What we predicted about fifteen years ago, and again at the beginning of the World War, has now become a fact. The question of a Jewish national autonomous homeland has been placed on the agenda of world politics. For the present, this is all—no more, but also no less.

This is unquestionably a victory for all Zionists. Were it not for the twenty years of intense Zionist propaganda, and were it not for the ten years of practical revolutionary work in Palestine, this question would never have been seriously considered and world diplomacy would never have been seriously interested in it. Only people with a naive conception of politics could imagine that this question would have been given any consideration if there were no great Zionist movement. As a matter of fact, the Zionist movement has played second fiddle to none in bringing about this result—not even to the British march on Palestine. It will be well for our friends to remember this and surely it will not be harmful for others to take note of it.

No question of rights is ever raised until those directly interested demand them. History proves that the Jews secured their rights only 'after they demanded them and only in that measure in which they fought for them. The English and Dutch Revolutions of the seventeenth century did not bring equal rights to Jews because the Jews did not ask for them. The first French Revolution did not bring full equality because the Jews made their demands too late. Before the Revolution of 1848, the

1 Originally published in the American Poale Zion weekly, *Der Yiddisher Kaempfer*, May 4, 1917.

Jewish emancipation movement[2] was very weak; and, therefore, that revolution brought them but little relief.

For fifty years Jewish emancipation movements were active in Russia. Hence, the Russian Revolution immediately broke the chains of the Jewish people. The Russian Jews, however, were almost as instrumental in bringing about their freedom as was the Revolution. If our hearts are filled with gratitude to the Russian nation and the Russian working class for our emancipation, we must also give the same wholehearted thanks and recognition to the Jewish *Maskilim*[3] of the 60's and 70's, to the Jewish Socialist *Bund,* and to the Socialist-Zionists, through whose struggles the result was made possible.

I go further. Outside agents often have less influence in bringing about the emancipation of an oppressed people than does the conscious effort of the people itself. Emancipation is after all the concern of the enslaved, of the working class, and of all oppressed peoples. Civil rights for the Jews of Central Europe in 1867-1870 were not effected by a revolution, but came as the result of an active struggle for these rights and as a result of the strengthening of constitutional principles in Austria, Hungary, and Germany.

The factors responsible for the recognition of our civil rights, will also bring about the recognition of our national-political rights in Palestine and our autonomous national rights[4] in the Galut. To be sure, external political situations must be favorable;

---

2 The movement in Jewish life which sought to obtain equal civil and political rights for Jews.

3 The bearers of the *Haskala* movement. *Haskala*—literally enlightenment; in Jewish history, *Haskala* refers to the movement aiming at the breakdown of the Jewish Ghetto through the introduction of secular studies (Europeanization).

4 More commonly known as "minority rights"—that is, the rights granted by a government to a minority population (which differs from the majority in race, language, or religion) to regulate its own communal, religious, and educational affairs. In the broadest sense minority rights imply self-government of the minority population, its language being recognized in the government courts and institutions. In the narrower sense, minority rights refer only to the cultural autonomy granted to the minority population. After the World War minority rights were incorporated in the treaties made with most of the East European countries. At present, minority rights remain in force only in Finland and Czechoslovakia. In Palestine the Jewish community enjoys *autonomy* rights. The Jewish Assembly (*Kennesset Yisrael*) has the power to tax its constituents and to administrate all internal affairs (religious, educational, health, etc.) of the Jewish community.

but what we need primarily is a strong movement within Jewry to focus world-wide attention upon our interests—a movement which shall make use of every favorable political situation, and, whenever necessary, take advantage of every suitable alignment with other political forces.

From a political point of view, propaganda is less productive than action. *Create facts and more facts—that is the cornerstone of political strategy.* Facts are more convincing than phrases. Accomplishments are of greater influence than proclamations. Sacrifices are better propaganda than resolutions. The *Bund,* for example, played a more important role in the emancipation of Russian Jewry than all the apologetic literature on the question of Jewish rights produced during a period of fifty years. The *Bund* did not content itself with talk, but fought and made sacrifices. It created political facts, small and insignificant in their isolation, but in combination building up one great fact which has now borne fruit. (I refer, of course, only to the former *positive* achievements of the *Bund.*)

The same is true of Zionism. The practical colonization work in Palestine, with its experiences, its sacrifices, its inevitable mistakes, has created those political *facts* which have paved the way for our present status. No matter how small and weak the Jewish colonies might be, no matter how great the shortcomings in their system of colonization—they did more towards enlightening the Jewish nation than a thousand beautifully-worded programs and diplomatic negotiations. A fallen *Shomer*[5] plays a greater role in the realization of Zionism than all declarations.

The best guarantee of Zionism lies not in a charter but in the Zionist movement. The guarantee lies in the organization of the Zionists and Socialist Zionists. I said this fifteen years ago, and I will not cease reiterating it even now when the world is so carried away by current political and diplomatic events. I am not fearful about the disillusionment which may follow. The sole

---

5 *Hashomer* was the name of a semi-professional organization of armed watchmen in pre-War Palestine which protected the Jewish colonies from thieves, plunderers and attackers. Its members were known as *Shomrim* (the Hebrew for guards; singular— *Shomer*). In modern Palestine the Jewish colonies designate members for guard duty as well. (See *The Terrorist and the Shomer*, p. 120.)

danger lies in confusion. One must not fail to see the trees because of the forest. The beautiful forest of political perspectives for Zionism can exist only because of its trees—the practical accomplishments of the Zionist movement.

Meanwhile, our goal has not been fully achieved. It is still in the process of realization. We must remember that Palestine is not yet ours. We still have no official promise that we are going to get Palestine. It is true, nevertheless, that Zionism has finally become a serious matter in world politics. This great victory for the Zionist movement must ultimately result in substantial dividends—even though we may suffer temporary setbacks. Ostensibly, the first Russian revolution (1905) was a fearful fiasco, but today it has borne fruit with a vengeance. That tragic revolution with its tragic disappointment dealt the true death-blow to Czarism. Likewise, our latest victory has dealt a death-blow to the Galut ideology and to reactionary anti-Zionism.

Anti-Zionism has been mortally wounded. The world may now see that anti-Zionism has no sound psychological or social foundation, that it is thoroughly decadent, that it represents reactionary and obscurantist issues in Jewish life. The enemies of Zion, who brazenly turn their backs on life and freedom, do not realize that life has answered them in kind by turning her back on them.

I repeat, the gain will be permanent even if the existing diplomatic negotiations bring no positive results.

Let us hope that world events will so shape themselves that they will contribute to the highest interests of mankind and the Jewish people. The World War is progressing from its imperialistic phase to its revolutionary phase. Let us hope that it will end with a thorough emancipation of all peoples.

It is almost certain that England will conquer Palestine, Mesopotamia, and Syria. It is almost certain, too, that revolutions will make an end of the Hohenzollerns, the Hapsburgs, and the chauvinism of the Young Turks. If so, a Jewish republic in Palestine is destined to come.

But, who knows? Is it not possible that the wheels of history will take a queer turn and Zionism, like other revolutionary hopes, will be disappointed; that the knights of Jewish assimilation and Galut opportunists, together with other reactionaries, will once again come out the "victors"? Yet, one positive fact will remain. Once placed on the table of world politics, the Palestine question will not be removed from there. The Zionist movement will, through its practical accomplishments, bring the problem to its ultimate solution—an assured and autonomous homeland for the Jewish people in Palestine.

Zionism is the only answer to the economic and historic needs of the Jewish people. It will be realized through the Zionist movement, through the Poale Zion, and through our labors and struggles.

ANTI-ZIONIST FRONT[1]

THE SOCIAL barometer of present Galut life forecasts stormy days. The soaring of commodity prices, the exorbitant military budgets, the feverish and unsuccessful efforts of diplomacy to check the growing war-spirit, the constant rise of tax-levies and interest rates, and the vacillating stock exchange—all these indicate that we are approaching the end of the industrial prosperity which prevailed during the last few years. No capitalistic maneuvers can check the impending crisis. A new act in the drama of history is about to be staged. It seems as if the greatest upheaval confronts those regions densely populated by Jews, i. e., Eastern Europe and North America.

No sober person regards the coming events as the "final conflicts" or believes that this new chapter of history will usher in the millenium. The final victory of *Ahura-Mazda* over *Angra Mainyu*[2] is still a long way off. The will to freedom of the various peoples is not yet sufficiently powerful for them to gain mastery over their oppressors.

On the contrary, the impending period of enthusiasm and Messianic hope will end in disillusionment and despair. That will be a welcome yet tragic phase in the development and decay of the capitalistic order. Like one of those stormy waves which precedes the final overpowering ninth wave, this period will leave deep scars on the old world. Herein lies the historical value of the impending events.

The tension which embraces the social strata of all nations leads to the alliance of groups having common interests. The

---

1 Published in 1911 in the Russian periodical, *Razvest,* under the title "The Anti-Zionist Concentration".

2 In Persian mythology, the god of good and the god of evil.

alliances proceed along the horizontal class lines and the vertical lines.

What re-groupings can we expect within Jewish life? What changes in the social psychology of Jewry will these processes call forth? To the thinking person these questions are very pertinent.

I.

In periods of turbulent social change, Jewry, being the landless and the weakest among the conflicting elements, is hardest hit. It brings the greatest sacrifices to the altar of progress. Therefore, the alignment of forces within Jewry assumes a distinct and peculiar form.

Among other nations, the alliances usually proceed along class lines. The ruling classes unite and build one reactionary bloc whereas the suppressed groups form a revolutionary bloc. These blocs are not always internally harmonious, but they exhibit a tendency toward class unity. Even today this trend is manifest in many countries.

Among the Jewish people, however, the grouping does not occur on a class basis, but on the basis of the varying national aspirations. Within Jewry the chief struggle is not between the proletariat and the bourgeoisie, or between the urban and agrarian populations, but between Zionists and Galut champions[3] of all classes. The concentration of anti-Zionist forces usually precedes Zionist consolidation.

This does not mean to imply that there is no class struggle within Jewry. On the contrary, the class struggle within the Jewish people is more intense and involves the masses to a greater extent than it does within other nations. But the class struggle in Jewish life has meager social content. Its historical horizons are limited. The class struggle of the Jews is primarily on the economic front.[4]

We lack, however, the political class struggle; for the Jewish people is now divorced from state functions and political rule as a unit. Under the prevailing conditions in Galut, it is really im-

---

3 See footnote 2, p. 59.

4 See p. 78.

possible to engage in this struggle. Instead, each class, guided by its own interests, participates in the political struggle of the people among whom its members reside. Although in its struggle against the general bourgeoisie, the Jewish proletariat cannot avoid a clash with the Jewish bourgeoisie, that struggle is not for dominance within Jewish life, for there is no one to divest of or invest with power. In Jewish life, only the *economic* class antagonisms find full play; the political conflicts go off on a tangent.

I admit that with the achievement of national autonomy[5] in Galut we shall gain a base for a political class struggle within Jewish life. But even this base will be narrow and limited in its social aspects. Our autonomous Galut life will never be a substitute for a Jewish national home.

Small wonder then, that among Jews there is no conflict between class ideologies. The classes of our people possess different psychologies and opposing ideals, but their class psychologies are derived not from Jewish life, but from the surrounding environment. These ideals (contrary to the views of our *nationalists*) are not abstractions, nor are they a product of rationalization; they are living and creative, for they have their origin in our everyday life. However, it is not from Jewish life that we derive our socialism, radicalism, liberalism, and clericalism. Our differing social ideologies are mere reflections of the life of our neighbors.

Within Jewry there does not exist the class struggle in its usual forms; we have among us a struggle between national factions. Once this struggle took place between the champions of *Haskala*[6] and Orthodoxy,[7] then between Zionism and assimilation, and now between Zionism and *Galutism*. It is unnecessary to point out that assimilation has today lost its ideological grounds. Only tattered remnants remain of its former ideological garb and these are clumsily patched on to other ancient but seemingly progressive ideologies. Fifteen or twenty years ago, the enemies of Zion (irrespective of class) negated the principle of Jewish nationality. Today, however, Zionism faces an enemy under whose banner are

---

5 See footnote 4, p. 90.
6 See footnote 3, p. 90; also the following chapter.
7 See the following chapter.

united various ideologies, the majority of which contain national aspirations. The hodge-podge of Yiddish culturists, the autonomists, the Social-Democrats, and the various shades of bourgeois radicals, the staunch nationalist *Seimists,*[8] as well as the hazy territorialists who suffer from an anachronistic hatred for Palestine —all join hands to form the anti-Zionist front.

Contemporary events have produced a mass of facts which point to the unquestionable consolidation of these forces. I believe that the coming era of social unrest will tend to strengthen this anti-Zionist front.

II.

When Zionism appeared as a modern, positive force (*Chibat Zion*[9] and *Herzlism*[10]) two ideologies were current in Jewish life. One was the Orthodox ideology which accepted Messianism literally and pinned its hopes for national salvation on the miraculous; the other was the *Haskala* ideology which preached the adaptation of the Jew to universal culture. We have long since learned to distinguish between assimilation as an established fact and assimilation as an ideological rationalization. Assimilation as a fact, or as a genuine process, affects all Jewish groups. Assimilation *ad perfectio* as an ideology, however, is a comfortable and profitable "philosophy" for those apostates who have no sincere interest in the Jewish nation. Paradoxical as it may seem, assimilationists often display a profound interest in the Jewish people; in most cases, however, their inquiries seek but a justification for their

---

8 *The Seimist* movement was organized in 1906 as an outgrowth of the intellectual *Vozrozhdenye* group and later became the Jewish Socialist Labor Party *(Seimists* or *Serp).* It was non-Marxian, in close contact with the Socialist Revolutionary Party. It believed that the future of the Jewish masses lay in national political autonomy with a separate Jewish Parliament *(Seim* is the Polish word for parliament). It did not negate territorial concentration, was not opposed to Palestine, but believed the realization of a territory for the Jews should come after the establishment of the *Seim.* After the Russian Revolution it joined the S. S. to form the United Jewish Socialist Party in Russia. Later they united with the *Bund* and the Communist Party. Its present adherents are active mainly in the territorialist *Freiland* movement.

9 *Chibat Zion*—literally, love of Zion. Before the formation of the World Zionist Organization in 1897 by Theodore Herzl, there existed *Chovevei Zion* ("Lovers of Zion") societies in a number of countries, with the Russian groups as the driving force. These societies supported colonization in Palestine without waiting for a formal charter from the Turkish regime. They were therefore known as practical Zionists as distinguished from the later Herzlian political Zionists. The *Chovevei Zion* played a leading role in the establishment of the World Zionist Organization.

10 *Herzlism* refers to political Zionism.

rationalization. We are not speaking of individuals, for it is possible for an assimilated Jew to be a bitter enemy of assimilationist ideology, and for a Jew who has preserved all the customs and characteristics of his people, to be the most fervid devotee of assimilationist ideology. Assimilation is here considered purely from the viewpoint of a possible solution to the Jewish problem.

Prior to Zionism, assimilation, as advanced by the *Haskala* champions in their fierce struggle with orthodoxy, was the only ideology of the upper classes of the Jews who came in constant contact with the analogous groups of other nations. This was in direct conformity with the time-honored tactics of the Jewish *shtadlan*.[11] The first assimilationists really believed themselves to be the representatives of the Jewish people, its champions before the rulers and aristocracy of our neighboring nations. The Jewish masses kept aloof from this ideology and would have none of its politics.

The *Haskala* movement rendered valuable service to the Jewish people. It prepared the ground for the later modern movements in Jewish life. But Zionism, having awakened the dormant hopes of the Jewish masses, made surprising and violent inroads into the idyllic *Haskala* philosophy. Simultaneously, the rise of a Jewish migration movement and the later development of organized Jewish labor began to undermine the already weakened foundations of assimilation. Assimilation, which until now had monopolized "modernism", "Europeanism", and "progress", suddenly clashed with mighty cultural forces within Jewish life. The "celestial light of the *Haskala*" began to fade with the dawn of Zionism, the labor movement, and the era of migration.

Zionism translated into terms of everyday creativeness that which the people had until recently conceived of as a transcendent heavenly promise. Zionism illuminated the past and future of the Jewish people. The labor movement drew the Jewish masses close to the cause of human emancipation, binding their hopes

---

11 *Shtadlan*—usually an influential Jew who took upon himself or was delegated by the community to represent it before the authorities. While the office of *shtadlan* was a necessity in certain periods of Jewish history, there would be no need for it in a democratically organized Jewish community. At present a *shtadlan* implies a self-appointed, self-seeking politician, running back-door politics.

and struggles with those of humanity. The dynamic forces of Jewish immigration wrought their effect upon the minds of the most lethargic. How impotent was the artificial culture of the *Haskala* intelligentzia compared to the dynamic and vital culture of the masses!

At the beginning of the Russian Revolution the assimilationist ideology collapsed and its essence—the ties with the Galut—was inherited by other movements. The former indifference to the Jewish people gave way to the unique Galut nationalism, which, as early as 1905, gained a stronghold on Russian and Galician Jewry. Galut nationalism also crossed the Atlantic to America.

It is important that we differentiate between the three types of Galut nationalism. The first type was the inconsistent assimilationism which though employing the term "nation" actually did not aspire to the full content of nationalism. Such was the "autonomism" advanced by the *Bundist* intelligentzia in the first stages of its development (1897-1908), and such is the current lip-service nationalism of the Jewish intelligentzia. The second type was the inconsistent nationalism that fell just short of Zionism. This was the Galut nationalism of the past two or three years which paraded under the slogans "Yiddish culture and autonomy". (Dubnow's "spiritual nationalism" with its profound attempt to establish a base for the national idealization of the Galut was likewise an inconsistent Zionism.) The third type of Galut nationalism was an abstract territorialism which attempted to solve the Jewish problem solely by immigration. Despite the great antipathy of the territorialists towards the Galut, their very soul is bound to it. Only boycotts, pogroms, and persecutions torment them in the Galut. Their analysis of the Jewish problems fails to take into account the national, historic, and even economic factors; it merely considers the geographic. One who would solve the Jewish problem with a "tract of land"—somewhere near the Antipodes— has not yet broken with the Galut.

The identification of the Jewish masses with the cause of universal progress brought about Zionism and *Galutism,* the latter adorned with the gay mantel of nationalism. The united front of the *Galutists* in the revolutionary period was in reality the first concentrated effort to form an anti-Zionist front. But the inherent chaos of the capitalistic system on the one hand, and the Jewish dispersion on the other, hindered the development of an anti-Zionist front. This alignment is not an absolute fusion; it never was and never can be such—though its general tendencies lead in that direction.

We shall first consider the anti-Zionist alliance in the political field. Both before and during the Russian Revolution, proletarian and bourgeois Galut champions formed an alliance. The *Bund* conceived its greatest mission to be the attack on Zionism by any and every method, not excluding libel. The assimilated Jewish bourgeoisie rendered moral and material support to their proletarian allies and recognized the *Bund* as the "sole representative". of the Jewish labor movement. During the elections to the second Duma an unsuccessful attempt was made to form a bloc of these same elements, disregarding all class differences. These mutual sympathies are felt even now. The *Groupists*,[12] "empowered" by the Kovna Conference,[13] pretend to be the "sole representatives". Hence, the "sole representatives" of all classes united . . .

In Galicia, where political life is aflame almost exclusively at elections, we saw (in 1907 and particularly in 1911) the solidarity of assimilationists and *Chassidim* with the Social-Democrats. On both these occasions the Galician *Bundists* enthusiastically joined this smart set in a coalition directed against the Zionists. As a result of pre-election agreements, an even firmer anti-Zionist front was forged in the shape of an alliance between the Galician *Bundists* and the Jewish section of the Polish Socialist Party, the strongest opponents of the Jewish national renaissance movement.

The anti-Zionist front is far less noticeable in Jewish communal activities. And yet, it is an undeniable fact that such institutions as the *ICA,* the *Haskala* societies, and the loan and the immigrant information bureaus are centers around which the most diverse elements make common cause. In this field, we find a silent, bitter struggle for supremacy between the anti-Zionist

---

12 *Groupists* refers to the semi-assimilated bourgeois party in Russia.

13 Kovna Conference—a conference of self-appointed Russian leaders who pretended to speak on behalf of Russian Jewry.

elements, who until now reigned supreme, and the Zionists who are beginning to make their influence felt. The leaders of these institutions, the philanthropists and key-men as well as the officials and employees, are imbued with the Galut ideology. They think of community problems as if the fate of the Jewish masses were eternally and inextricably bound up with the Galut and moreover, as if the organization of Galut Jewry were the sole concern of our best minds. In this field, too, we note a silent "class collaboration."[14]

The forms of the anti-Zionist alliance on the literary front are most amusing. A gentlemen's agreement seems to unite the non-Zionist bourgeoisie with the proletarian elements, and not long ago they conducted with rare avidity a joint struggle against Zionism in all its implications. It is significant to note that to this very day these class enemies have avoided attacking each other. The ideological attack of the *Bund* on the Jewish bourgeoisie was aimed only at Zionism, as if Zionism were synonomous with the bourgeoisie. But the most laughable feature of all was the lusty applause with which the bourgeois assimilationists greeted this identification. Barbs aimed against the bourgeoisie in general, including the assimilationists, crept into the *Bund's* systematic attack upon Zionism. But the bourgeois colleagues of Jewish labor's "sole representative" indulgently accepted the *Bund's* demonstrations, well realizing that these attacks were merely a matter of form and only a sop to world Socialism. At no time did the assimilationists

---

14 The type of class collaboration to which Borochov alludes seems to have crossed the Atlantic together with the Jewish mass immigration from Eastern Europe. Beginning with the first attempts at the democratic organization of American Jewry—and notably with the organization of the American Jewish Congress in 1915—we have been witnessing a silent, united front between the wealthy, assimilationist elements composing the American Jewish Committee and the once large but now diminishing section of anti-Zionist Jewish Socialists. Not only do these two otherwise dissimilar groups have in common an obstinate opposition to Zionism and Jewish nationalism, but they often take the same stand toward Jewish problems in Galut. In recent years the Jewish Labor Committee (headed by B. C. Vladeck) and the American Jewish Committee issued joint statements in connection with the struggle for Jewish rights, wherein they criticized severely the American Jewish Congress both for the exclusively Jewish as well as public character of its protest against the German and Polish treatment of Jews. Their own activities have been characterized by an apologetic tone and a constant attempt to prove that the Jews are not what their enemies portray them to be (as for example, their statements about the role of the Jews in the Bolshevik Revolution and the place of Jews in the German Communist movement). This also holds true with regard to the position of these strange allies on such problems as Jewish relief, philanthropy, immigration, Jewish education, and the organization of American Jewish community life. This is an example from the American scene of the class collaboration pointed out by Borochov.

and Galut-Nationalists of the bourgeois camp attack their proletarian allies. They were content mildly to repulse the attacks
of the *Bund*. Certain publications follow these tactics even now.

It is noteworthy that the anti-Zionist alliance meets its most
formidable obstacle to inner harmony on the literary front. Politics is a matter of action, literature of talk. In practice, the *Bund*
may engage in activities which have no bearing on the class struggle; however, our "sole representative" does talk a good class
struggle. The Galut nationalists are willing to place their press
—with but few restrictions—at the disposal of the "orthodox"
(Marxist) brethren; and the latter, despite their collaboration in
other fields, dare not accept the offer. Freedom of press would
indeed have surpassed itself with such a motley crew gathered
under one literary roof.

The Jewish people is small in numbers and exerts but little
socio-political influence. Therefore, its various social processes
appear trivial. The anti-Zionist manifestations, which we have
pointed out, do not seem sufficiently important to command our
attention. But one must remember that history wends its way
through a road littered with the seemingly insignificant. Neither
can we ignore the influence that the anti-Zionist intelligentzia
exerts on our people and our future. The intelligentzia has ap-
propriated to itself the Jewish labor and immigration movements.
It rules the *Kehillot* and the Jewish communal institutions. It
obtrudes itself at the first sign of the organization of mutual aid,
and is successful because it is united and because its proletarian
allies, who make holy vows of class struggle, practice class collaboration. The anti-Zionist intelligentzia does not fear, and even
welcomes, the various class elements. It tolerates freedom of
speech in order to obtain unity of action. These tactics boldly
reveal that both allies are busy bolstering their positions in Jewish
life.

The fact that our Galut life is not a resplendent one by no
means minimizes the historical significance of these phenomena.

III.

How can we explain the deep hatred between Zionism and the so-called *Galutism* in Russia and Galicia? It is very naive to assume that the ceaseless attacks on Zionism by the *Bundists,* or the brutal attack by the united front of the bourgeoisie, *Chassidim,* and Social-Democrats in Galicia, drew their sustenance from theoretical differences. The bloodshed in the streets of Drohobitch[15] is the strongest refutation of such an innocent interpretation of the struggle in Jewish life.

It is clear that that was a struggle for supremacy, a bitter conflict for material interests. It is equally clear that this was not merely a struggle of class interests. The struggle for and against Zionism may be compared to the struggle between the freethinkers and clericals of Europe; the iconoclasm of the radical bourgeoisie and of the conscious proletariat are no more identical than are the interests of the anti-Zionist allies.

There is no people in the world whose members are so efficient, alert, stubborn, and adaptable in their struggle for personal existence as the Jewish. Likewise, there is no nation in the world so weak and spineless, infirm and supine in its struggle for national development as the Jewish. One of the contradictions in the Jewish Galut life is the extraordinary strength of the individual and the unparalleled weakness of the group. Our people is not capable of harnessing the individual energy of its talented members for collective creation. Assimilation in its various nuances finds support among those individuals who are unconsciously dominated by careerism, and who seek anxiously to assure their own future even at the price of breaking their bond with their unfortunate and landless people. On the other hand, it is clear that the Jewish people as a whole, which is being deserted by irresponsible individuals seeking only personal success, needs strength and unity in order to become independent. Zionism in all its shades is postulated upon the collective fate of the Jews. *The paths to individual*

---

15 The Zionist and national elements of Galicia put out an independent political ticket in elections held at that time. This aroused the anger of Jewish assimilationists and their political allies, and they incited the police to interfere in these elections.

success and national welfare lie in different directions. This situation gives rise to the conflicting, antithetical, "material" interests within Jewish life.

Assimilation was unaffected by the antagonism between the individual and the group interests. But when Zionism called upon the individual to sacrifice personal interests for the sake of the national renaissance, the assimilationists instinctively felt the danger of Zionist agitation. To defend the rights of individual careerism, assimilation armed itself with a well-equipped arsenal of bogeys—depicting Zionism as "reaction", "chauvinism", "narrow-mindedness", etc. Indeed, Zionism was based on and drew its nourishment from the conflicting interests of the individual and the group; Galut nationalism unconsciously attempted to "reconcile" the interests of the individual and the group.

The individual on whom benign fortune smiles warmly does not desire to leave his well established Galut domicile. Galut is his home and the non-Jewish environment, his Fatherland. But the Jewish people, as a historic organism, as a material and spiritual tradition, as a mode of living and as a cultural, psychological type has its effect upon every individual. True, the Jewish people does not have a very strong material tradition. We have few petrified relics of the collective efforts of earlier generations. We do not possess the power of the soil, the magnetic force of the black earth. Instead, we have many cultural traditions—our thought processes, temperament, and intellectual inheritance. These traditions rarely allow an individual to escape from their tenacious grasp. In general, the Jew, with all his careeristic strivings, remains within the fold. This is the source of the inner contradiction of assimilation.

On the other hand, the Jewish community must fortify itself and become rooted in the surrounding environment, tying itself organically to the soil of the neighboring peoples. A whole people cannot live as if in a hostelry. A neglect of this truth caused the inner contradiction of General Zionism.

Formerly, assimilation offered a more subtle way of solving the above contradiction. As soon as the theoreticians of assimilation were convinced of the impossibility of obtaining security for themselves by purely individual endeavor, they instinctively began to seek those paths which the masses were following in their inevitable attempts to become rooted in the Galut. The assimilationists who fell heir to the influence of the old custodians of the Jewish people, of the plutocracy and communal leaders, found open before them (in this period of transition) all doors to the Jewish masses, to their institutions and organizations. The older generation ruled the *Kehillot,* the Jewish Charities, and educational institutions. Their descendants gained control of the modern societies, mutual aid organizations, and workers' associations. These new rulers have demonstrated their ability to exploit the hereditary habits of the Jews in order to strengthen their own positions. As the "sole representatives" of Jewry, or of their own class, they received the recognition of the corresponding groups of the neighboring peoples.

Without any original desire to serve the Jewish people, these leaders returned to the fold thanks to the failure of their personal, careerist assimilationism. These talented and active intellectuals were to a certain extent valuable. They organized charity, cheap credit, education, statistical surveys and emigration bureaus, and also led strikes and political labor demonstrations. They almost completely monopolized Jewish communal affairs, in keeping with the historical principle of "priority rights". And all of these activities had one aim—*to obtain the recognition of the neighboring peoples, and to achieve personal integration in the Galut through the medium of the Jewish people.* Thus, our *Galutistic* intelligentzia, which in spirit remained indifferent to the fate of the people whom it served, brought no sacrifices for the sake of the group. Personal ambitions were thus happily harmonized with service to the community.

The services which this intelligentzia rendered the Jewish people were not fundamental but superficial, for they were confined to the limits of the Galut. These services satisfied only the most temporary needs. Hence certain groups and individuals profited thereby, while the basic problems of the people remained unsolved. All this activity on the part of both the bourgeoisie and the proletarian intelligentzia was and remains opportunist, because it arose out of personal and transient rather than national and fundamental needs.

Since these activities brought some amelioration, the *Galutistic* intelligentzia boasted to the outside world of the partial confidence in them displayed by the Jewish masses. They were responsible for the unpleasant atmosphere of loud self-advertising and partisan mud-slinging. That was the cause for their ideological shallowness, their avoidance of all organic unity with Jewish life, their fanatical falsification of all positive values of the Jewish people, their fear of facing the naked truth. Their chief concern was to be the "only representative" of Jewry to the mighty, enticing, outside world. Therefore, they maintained that "within the Jewish people, under our care, peace must reign".

This extremely vapid and negative ideology enabled the intelligentzia to abandon their former assimilationism. The demise of assimilation did not drive them to tears, called forth no memories, since it did not shatter their personal careers. [The tears shed at the Sixth Zionist Congress over the question of Uganda vs. Zion (as the territory for the Jewish people) is a superb example of the collective feelings of Zionists.]

With characteristic shrewdness, the intelligentzia, even before the 1905 Revolution, turned from assimilationism and cosmopolitanism to a distorted Galut nationalism.

Zionism. on the other hand, underwent quite a different evolution. Zionism was created by that section of the Jewish intelligentzia which was most sensitive to the terrible blows of social and state anti-Semitism. They were unable to link the happiness of their people with personal careerism. These Zionists renounced the Galut, seeing in it the chief source of Jewish suffering and sterility. The Zionist intelligentzia, however, swung to the other extreme and turned a deaf ear to the positive everyday realities of Jewish life.

Highly inspired by the ideals of our national rehabilitation in Palestine, Zionism's vision was far too lofty to see the needs of the passing moment. During the first twenty years, Zionists did not think of capturing and fortifying our positions in the Galut and did not deem it necessary to combine their personal interests with general interests. The Zionists viewed the economic struggle of the workers, the fight for civil rights, and the development of the Yiddish language, and intra-diasporic migrations as futile. Since the basic work was to be done there, in the historic home of the Jewish people, of what avail were temporary efforts in the Galut?

Meanwhile, the anti-Zionist elements gained control of the communal institutions. Their extreme intellectual poverty was offset by their great sense of practicality and organizational prowess; Zionism, despite its courageous and penetrating thought, proved itself organizationally impotent.

Every social upheaval had its repercussions among the Jewish people, bringing new hopes, grave dangers, and alluring prospects. Zionism banked on the dangers and worries of the Galut, while Galutism fortified itself with bright prospects and hopes. At first Zionism tried to ignore these hopes and prospects and with a sickly joy grasped at everything that was tragic and horrible in Jewish life in order to obscure the bright spots. Anti-Zionists on the other hand underestimated the gravity of the situation, and met the upheaval smilingly, with a soothing self-deception; it was not courage but vacuity that closed their eyes to the depths of the cavern. None in the Jewish community called out: "With head held high are we going to meet our fate!"

Zionism grumbled and waged an ideological battle, while its enemies built strongholds in Jewish life. In those dark, yet important years, one after another of the most active and most mature elements deserted Zionism. A new form of Galut nationalism arose from the bosom of Zionism, more profound and genuine than the wordy nationalism of the semi-assimilator. Even workers who theoretically remained loyal to Zionism deserted it in spirit to unite their immediate tasks with the ideal of vitalizing the nation in its land of residence. Finally, after this fermentation had carried off the most radical and sober, the headquarters of the

Zionist army began to fight for positions in the Galut. The *Helsingfors* program [16] in Russia and the formation of the Jewish National Party[17] in Austria initiated a new trend in Zionist politics. Thus Zionism at last began to resolve the contradictions of its role. Instead of merely dreaming of saving Jewry at one stroke, Zionism began to strengthen Jewish Galut positions.

Zionism became synthesized and integrated. It encompassed every need of Jewry in the Galut and in Palestine: in the present, and in the future. But most Zionists were so psychologically unprepared for these tasks that only lately have they undertaken them in practice. Unfavorable circumstances undoubtedly contributed to this backwardness, particularly in Russia. Besides, the most important communal positions were already in the hands of the enemies of the *real* renaissance of the Jewish people. It was difficult for Zionists (if we exclude the Poale Zion who have long since understood the question and developed their tactics accordingly) to become accustomed to the thought that Zionism is facing a *struggle for power* within Jewish life.

In short, Zionism must take over all that has been usurped by its enemies to the detriment of the people. The positions that the anti-Zionist intelligentzia had held were not taken away from Zionism; they simply never were under Zionist control. It is noteworthy that where Zionism strives to penetrate into Jewish life, it is received warmly by the masses. It was so in the elections to the first and second Duma, and in Galicia a year or two earlier. To date Zionism has failed to utilize the potent sympathies for it that lie dormant in the Jewish masses.

On the threshold of a new era in universal and Jewish history, when the Jewish people faces new dangers and contemplates glorious visions, we pose these questions: How can we overcome the organizational weakness of Zionism? How can we develop the maximum of activity among the masses so sympathetic to the ideal of rebirth in our national home?

The answer is: *A national front against the anti-Zionist front.*

---

[16] Helsingfors program—the national Galut program adopted by Russian Zionists in Helsingfors, which was then under Russian rule.

[17] Jewish National Party refers to the Zionist elements in Galicia who appeared in the local political 'elections not as a Zionist, but as a national grouping, with a program of national rights.

NATIONALISM AND THE WORLD WAR[1]

I.

IT IS absurd to contend that nationalism alone is responsible for the present World War. It is a grave injustice to burden the national impulse with sole responsibility for this bloodshed, for this holocaust of wild passions and sufferings, for this destruction of cultural treasures. Yet it is equally absurd to ignore the harmfulness of present-day reactionary chauvinism.

Only those whose minds are still dominated by the cliches of the old radical canonical code will seriously believe that it is nationalism that is guilty of bringing on the current catastrophe. It is argued that were there no nations and no nationalism, there would be no quarrels among the peoples and all would live in unity and peace. Therefore it is the sacred task of all radicals to vilify all nationalism and to strive for the abolition of all nations.

We might, if we wished, develop prettier notions. By following this logic of an intoned A. B. C. of Marx, we can reason that inasmuch as the instinct of self-preservation drives human beings to compete with one another, and in this process the weaker are exploited by the stronger, it is the sacred duty of every friend of mankind to fight this instinct of self-preservation.

The same profound scholastics have discovered an additional series of syllogisms against nationalism, syllogisms whose validity is on a par with the one cited above. It is argued that since national sentiments are easily exploited for militaristic purposes, therefore all national sentiments should be rooted out from the human heart. To be consistent, all sentiments of heroism, courage and

---

1 Published in the *Yiddisher Kaempfer*, New York, 1916, under the title "Healthy and Diseased Socialism".

ambition—which are frequently exploited for militaristic purposes and may consequently be harmful—should also be done away with. Similarly, since militarism makes use of iron, steel and copper, bread and boots, these too should be branded as reactionary tools.

Some of the more profound philosophers of this type contend that territorial boundaries are responsible for all human conflicts. Nations may continue to exist as long as they do not possess definite, demarcated territories; boundaries should cease marring the face of the earth. When the boundaries of the various fatherlands disappear, there will be no more wars. A nation that possesses boundaries automatically desires to expand its frontiers and does not permit another nation to encroach upon its own. Proletarians have no fatherlands, but if they have one, their attachment to it must be uprooted.

To this day the Jews have been an exceptional case among all the nations of the world. All nations have boundaries, and fight and suffer for their fatherlands; only the Jews, faring better, have no land for which to suffer. The Jewish people can proudly claim, with Sholom Aleichem's *Motel Paisie,* the cantor's son, "How lucky I am to be an orphan". There you have an easy solution to the woes of the world: let all the nations become orphans; let there be indiscriminate assimilation; let all the nations of the world become landless like the Jews instead of letting the Jews become a normal people on its own land.

II.

Such was the philosophy which dominated pre-war Socialist thought, with the force of a holy creed given to Moses direct from Mount Sinai. The World War smashed those ideas, and turned those social cosmopolitans into social patriots.

They leaped from one absurdity to another, substituting one A. B. C. for another. They scrapped the A. B. C. of the class will snatch the heavenly fires for himself and for the Jewish people. patriotism. Karl Marx was replaced by the old Imperial Majesty and the verses of the Communist Manifesto were discarded for the tune of "How Fine It Is To Be a Soldier".[2] Instead of "Proletarians of all lands, unite" the new slogan became "Citizens of all lands, to arms against one another!"

The case of Gustave Herve is a typical illustration of this change. He who had always been on the extreme opposition at all the congresses of the Socialist International, he who continually demanded that energetic steps be taken against militarism, that the general strike be used against war, that war declaration be met with barricades on the streets—he was the one to change the name of his militant organ *The Social War* to that of *The Victory*. At these International Socialist congresses, little heed was paid to him; his fiery speeches were received with condescending smiles. He was too logical and too consistently unilinear. But, theoretically it was impossible to dissent openly from his views. No one dared and no one could, for Herve was simply pushing the Socialists' absurdities to their logical conclusion.

Unlike his comrades Herve had the courage to be absurd. He maintained that "the proletarians have no fatherland"; for it is not our fatherland, but that of the rich and mighty, that of the capitalists. This was Herve's dictum, one befitting a courageous man who speaks out honestly. It was the Socialists who said, "True, we have no fatherland, yet we must defend the fatherland" who were illogical.

---

2 Borochov opposed America's entry to the World War. Of those Socialists who preached "the call to arms" in the name of "historic necessity", Borochov wrote:

We know that when Marx said that Socialism will come with mathematical certainty and because of the "historic necessity", it was only a great wish of a great spirit; and his pupils who studied and popularized his wish were simply hypnotized by Marx's superb dialectics . . . But since we have no historic or supernatural guarantees that "historic necessity" must come, it pains us all the more to see how the official priests and custodians of these ideals endeavor to belittle their own teachings. No matter what syllogisms we shall make use of, Socialism and militarism do not go hand and hand; for militarism is the opposite of Socialism. Militarism aims at letting loose man's instincts and enslaving humanity; Socialism aims at creating a humanity which will control its instincts. Militarism aims to convert nations into armies, men into soldiers; Socialism aims to free men and nations.

"Historic necessity" is but a wish. Socialism is abused when it is coupled with the spirit of war.

We must guard ourselves lest Socialism meet a similar fate as Christianity. Christianity, too, believed in the historical, supernatural guarantees and has patiently awaited the coming of the savior. In the meantime, Christianity gradually compromised until little remained of all of its precepts and ideals. *We must beware lest Socialism become a new labor edition of Capitalism.* (From the article, "New Socialism and Old Christianity", *Die Warheit*, Dec. 24, 1915.)

Herve lambasted this inconsistency, mocked this line of thought, and spent his days in jail for his anti-war propaganda, in a French jail on which was inscribed "Liberty, Equality, and Fraternity."

Today Herve is still the same open, brave, and courageous fighter. He does not conduct diplomatic negotiations with his own conscience. What his comrades murmur he promptly proclaims to the world.

On changing the name of his organ, he announced, "I can no more call my organ *The Social War*. For sixteen months this organ has openly and consistently advocated the sacredness of national unity, and is determined to continue this policy even after the war.

"I find it necessary to proclaim that we feel ourselves bound more closely to the clerical and reactionary French patriot who is willing to continue the war until Prussian militarism is destroyed, than to the so-called Socialists of Zimmerwald who are too willing to accept a 'German Peace'.

"We want no more social war, no more civil war. Today it is just war; tomorrow it must be unity among the French, so that justice and brotherhood may prevail at home and abroad."

Thus wrote Herve because he wished to be consistent, because his conduct was motivated by principles of sobriety, clarity, and intellectual honesty.

It was the same in Germany. If Socialists may become loyal to the Kaiser, His Majesty can also become a Marxist! We actually heard how "Comrade" Wilhelm II declared himself in love with Socialism . . .

III.

We have described the two maladies and have observed the symptoms. We have noted the heat generated by the chauvinists and the chauvinistic reaction among Socialists, which resulted from their earlier over-simplified anti-nationalist stand. One who today demands that all national boundaries be abolished, may tomorrow shout hurrah to the Kaiser and find joy in the Imperial cannons. Such men cannot adhere to a healthy Socialism.

Marx was quite correct in saying that proletarians have no fatherland. In his day (70 years ago), healthy, progressive nationalism had hardly yet pecked its way out from its bourgeois liberal shell. But since then, progressive nationalism has become a unique historical phenomenon. Nationalism is not the reactionary product manufactured by petty bourgeois agitators; it is the instinct of self-preservation in nations, their healthy urge for self-determination.

It is thus understood by international Socialism. Mankind is divided into nations and classes. Nations existed before they were split into classes. Nations remain, while classes change. In the middle ages classes were different from what they are today. Then, the division was feudal—burghers and serfs; today the division is capitalist and proletarian. The nations underwent cultural modifications, but in essence they remained the same, like water changing into ice or steam, though retaining the same chemical elements.

This instinct of self-preservation in nations cannot be destroyed. It is rank dilettantism and sheer nonsense to demand that nations lose their identity and shake off their loyalty to themselves.

The national instinct of self-preservation latent in the Socialist working class is a healthy nationalism. Only international Socialism based upon a realistic approach to nationalism can liberate sick humanity 'in this capitalistic era, and cure this society of the social and national conflicts.

DIFFICULTIES OF POALE ZIONISM[1]

I.

"HOW DIFFICULT it is to be a Poale Zionist!" exclaimed an old Party comrade at a jubilee celebration of the Warsaw organization. "How much easier to be a *Bundist*,[2] or a member of the Polish Socialist Party! In those organizations one is little perturbed by questions that provoke thought or study. How difficult and responsible, however, are the burdens of a Poale Zionist!"

We can fully appreciate the complaints of our devoted comrade, who, though paying for his Party convictions with a life-sentence to Siberia, still remains a devoted Poale Zionist. In spite of all difficulties, we firmly adhere to our principles. Wherein lies the power of this mission, which, while so complicated and so difficult, is yet so dear to us all?

There is a law of nature known as the law of the economy of energy. Each creature strives to achieve the maximum results with the minimum of effort. This law operates in both the organic and inorganic worlds. The growth of plants, the expansion of roots, the movements of microscopic creatures, the instincts of the animal world, the conscious as well as the unconscious life of man—all are influenced by this law of nature. This law is felt in human culture, in industry, science, morals, and art, in the ever-changing conflicts of social thought and in national and class struggles. In brief, *humanity strives to achieve in all its endeavors the greatest results with the least exertion.*

This tendency to economize energy is in itself not a simple, but rather a complicated affair. There is no absolute measure

---

1 Written in 1913 and published in the organ of the Poale Zion *Yiddisher Arbeiter* (Lemberg, now Poland) on the occasion of the tenth anniversary of that publication.

2 See footnote 2, p. 75.

of economy, for its degree always depends upon given circumstances. Thus, theoretically speaking, the shortest distance between any two points is a straight line. This, however, does not take into account the practical complications of a given situation. Imagine for a moment that between two given distances there is a mountain or a lake; it soon becomes evident that the straight line is by no means the shortest or the easiest way. To avoid unnecessary difficulties one would have to go in a roundabout route or construct a tunnel or a bridge. In other words, the simplest is not always the true or correct path. Human life, both individual and group, is so complex that a simple solution is often an impossibility.

Nevertheless, under this law of economy, man strives first of all to achieve his goal in as simple a manner as possible. He first attempts to follow the short way, the straight way. But the realities of life often force him to adapt himself to complicated conditions by employing new and rational means. Such is the case in the history of the individual and the group. In the past, for example, men sought to conquer distance by the simplest means of transportation—horse, camel, or sail. Now, however, it is very difficult for a man during a short lifetime to master the techniques of transportation which have become complicated as a result of the introduction of railways, steamships, automobiles, and aeroplanes. *The development of human culture finds expression not through simplification but through differentiation and refinement of the mental and physical faculties. Simplicity of thought and social tactics are often a sign of primitiveness.*

There is another aspect to this problem. The law of the economy of energy refers not only to the exertion of the least amount of energy, but also to the achievement of the maximum results. In its most elementary and abstract expression, the simplest form of action is inaction; the simplest form of thinking is no thinking. Thus we would conserve all energy. But, man's ideal is the attainment of the maximum amount of productivity with the minimum of effort. Marx clearly points out both aspects of this law in his thesis that the history of humanity depends upon the development of the forces of production.

It is really difficult to be a Poale Zionist, for Poale Zion thought and practice are more complicated and possess finer and more varied nuances than the thoughts and practices of other Jewish parties. Nevertheless, within Jewish life today, with its intricate Galut problems and its striving for renaissance, the Poale Zion program offers the maximum results with the minimum of effort. The *Bund* demands less spiritual and physical effort on the part of the Jewish proletariat, but it is also satisfied with more limited objectives.

We desire to revitalize Jewish life, Jewish labor, and Jewish energy in all fields of endeavor. We cannot be content merely with the results obtainable in the Galut. But even in our Galut work, our program for the Jewish proletariat opens a much vaster vista than the programs of the other Jewish parties. According to the Socialist-Territorialist,[3] the Jewish problem can be solved solely by a program based on emigration. To the *Bundist,* the Galut problem is somewhat broader, but its program and activities are limited only to the most direct forms of struggle with the bourgeoisie and the State. Hence, while the Socialist-Territorialists perform constructive work only in the fields of emigration, and the *Bund* among Jewish workers on strike, the Poale Zion endeavors to do constructive work along all economic, cultural, and political fronts.

It becomes obvious that the complexity of our program does not in any way hinder its practicability. Though the Socialist-Territorialists speak of the need for regulation of Jewish emigration, they let the practical work be conducted by the bourgeois territorialists and assimilationists. The Poale Zionists, however, do not limit themselves to propaganda and have already, in the course of their short existence, achieved something through their own institutions (e. g., the Palestine Workers' Fund[4] and the

3 See footnote 3, p. 60.

4 Established by the World Confederation of Poale Zion to extend aid to all organized workers in Palestine irrespective of party affiliation. It was particularly useful as a financial agency during the World War. In America, this fund is popu-

Information Bureau in Jaffa[5]). Though the *Bundists* constantly propagandize on behalf of the Yiddish language, literature, and schools, they have done very little for Jewish culture, science, and education in comparison with the youthful Poale Zion Party.

The above clearly demonstrates that of all programs of the Jewish parties—both bourgeois and proletarian—the Poale Zion program presents the most inclusive solution to the Jewish problem. Therefore, it is really difficult to be a Poale Zionist—for Poale Zion thought and practice demand of the Jewish worker the greatest exertion of his spiritual and physical faculties. And yet this exertion is a bare minimum in comparison with the all-embracing program of Jewish life to whose attainment the Poale Zionists strive.

II.

Primitive mind presupposes that truth is simple. Complicated and well-founded thoughts puzzle the uneducated man.

The question of the so-called "consistency" of program and tactics of social movements is complicated. The undeveloped and insufficiently conscious Jewish worker assumes that "consistency" means one of two things: here or there, Galut or Zion. He cannot comprehend the integration of the two.

In Socialist thought, too, the question of consistency arises. Thus, for example, the Anarchists, who desire to simplify the tactics of the labor movement, accuse scientific Socialism of inconsistency. The Anarchists would indeed be right in their criticism were Socialism to preach *social revolution* on one day and *social reformism* the next. But actually, Socialism integrates in its program both the struggle for social revolution and for immediate reform. Thus, scientific Socialism is more complex than Anarchism, and though the common mind may not fully comprehend it, it is, nevertheless, consistent. Socialism then has to bridge the gap between reform and revolution, just as Poale Zionism has to integrate the Galut and Zion.

---

larly known as the *Geverkshaften Campaign.* It raised more than a million dollars during the past decade, thus aiding the various institutions of the *Histadrut* (General Federation of Jewish Labor in Palestine).

5 Established by the Palestine Workers' Fund to aid new immigrants.

The whole is greater than any of its parts. Since Socialism is a basic element of Poale Zionism the difficulties of Socialism are also the difficulties of Poale Zionism.

Scientific Socialism demands that our ideals be based on the objective forces operating in society. It is not sufficient that individuals or even the masses feel a need for something; it is essential that these needs and desires, expressed as vital elements of a Party program, be in harmony with historic trends. The objective forces which form the basis for an ideal also create the "historic necessity"[6] for this ideal.

The prime difficulty of the Poale Zion program is that it demands of the Jewish worker who supports it to be thoroughly convinced that the social program of the Galut and the national program of Palestine are not only beautiful ideals, but also objective possibilities.

We can now fully comprehend the demands that scientific Socialism makes of each Poale Zionist. First, he must become acquainted with the conditions of our present day social life and he must study the essence of the historic necessity of Socialism. Second, he must fully comprehend the nature and solution of the economic and cultural problems of the Jewish working class. Third, he must orientate himself in the problem of nationalism in our own times and particularly in the Jewish national problem.

One should not err, however, in concluding that every Poale Zionist must necessarily be a great theoretician. Not every Poale Zionist need thoroughly master the Socialist, the Poale Zion, or anti-Poale Zion literature; nor need he necessarily be an expert in all questions pertaining to the Socialist movement of each nation and the Poale Zion movement of each country.

Through active participation in the Socialist Party, the worker acquires what is commonly termed a Socialist consciousness which is of greater value than his mastery of books. This is, in reality the essence of Socialist education. The very fact that the masses participate in Socialist work in increasing numbers is sufficient proof of its historic necessity. The course of historic necessity of

---

6 See footnote 2, p. 111.

Socialism cannot be charted with mathematical accuracy. Human knowledge is as yet not sufficiently developed to be able to foresee historic developments with mathematical precision. It is not correct to assume that Marx, or for that matter any other thinker, has succeeded in proving beyond any doubts the historic necessity of Socialism. Theories can illustrate and interpret—not prove historic necessity. But that which theory cannot do, life can. His daily experiences rather than books will convince the worker that the struggle between himself and the capitalist becomes ever fiercer.

In a similar manner, our education aims to develop a Poale Zion consciousness. That consciousness even more than our literature will solve the theoretical difficulties of our program. Poale Zion literature can illustrate and interpret our program; it cannot prove its merits. The fact, however, that our movement grows and develops is in itself sufficient proof of its historic necessity. The steady growth of national consciousness among the Jewish masses, the gradual rise of respect for the Jewish personality, the growth of the movement for Jewish national rights, the growing Jewish labor movement in Palestine—all these are the objective facts, the *real* factors which find their theoretical expression in the Poale Zion program.

Our program is more difficult than that of other parties which content themselves with a narrower perspective. Our task, however, is not impossible of achievement; for our theory is based on the needs of Jewish life, and on the living experiences of the organized Jewish proletariat. Like Socialism, Poale Zionism will solve its *theoretical* difficulties only in its *practice*.

THE TERRORIST AND THE *SHOMER*

EDITOR'S NOTE: In 1916 the American Poale Zion published a Yiddish volume, *Yizkor* ("In Memoriam"), dedicated to the *Shomrim*—the fallen Jewish guards of Palestine. Borochov's essay, "The Terrorist and the *Shomer"*, was published in the same year in the New York Yiddish daily, *Die Warheit*, on that occasion.

Yizkor is a record of the men and women who came to Palestine with the second *Aliya* (the immigration stream of 1905-1914) and fell in its defense. Palestine, until the World War, was under the Turkish regime. The isolated colonists were not given any protection by the government, and hence the Jewish colonists were harassed by Arab thieves and murderers. The Jewish pioneers. therefore decided to form a semi-professional organization, *Hashomer,* to guard the life and property of the Jewish colonists. (Some of these *Shomrim* came from the Russian Poale Zion of Homel who organized one of the first self-defense groups, which may be considered a forerunner of the *Hashomer*.)

The Jewish pioneers and guards of Palestine felt that that which was produced by the sweat of their hands must be guarded with their own blood. Self-defense was organically integrated into the Jewish labor movement as being as fundamental and noble a task as draining swamps.

In the course of that period, hundreds of men and women fell. *Yizkor* symbolizes their ideals, which are also the ideals of the Jewish labor movement in Palestine: labor, peace, and self-defense.

A SLIGHTLY built peasant, with an unkempt beard and humble gray eyes bespeaking ceaseless toil, was crouching on his prison bed. Hopeless, embittered, he was perhaps dreaming of the broad earth and of freedom. I shared his prison cell in Southern Russia, together with several Gentiles who had been arrested for political activities. Once he turned to me of a sudden and asked:

"Pray, esteemed one, will the two new prisoners be hanged?"

"I don't know. Probably." The answer tore itself out of my burdened heart.

"Why? They were fighting our cause. Is there not enough land for all . . . The governor thrashed all of us . . . we blessed them when they shot the governor. Why will they hang them and not us? Is that justice, esteemed one?"

Again he became motionless, and I continued to knead the black prison bread into checkers.

"They are our *heroes!*" His frightened thoughts stopped there, his eyes opened wider, and the unimpressive figure of the village rebel seemed to shrink.

"They are our *heroes!*" For the first time, the peasant understood that strange word. Now he began to grasp the meaning of the word "hero", which he had heard somewhere but which had meant nothing to him.

"They are our heroes"—that naive and pious exclamation rings in my memory when I pore over the *Yizkor* book. Every line, every picture pulsates with this thought: "They are our heroes." One of those two heroes who was about to be hanged for defending the tortured peasants was a Jewish lad. He gave the ardour of his youth and his life for a strange people, an alien nation. He gave his life for freedom in a strange land. He was neither a deep thinker nor a theorist; he did not participate in any discussions at secret gatherings. A fugitive conspirator, he dropped his own name and gave himself Christian names—a different one in every town. To this day, I have not learned his Jewish name; I only knew him from occasional meetings at which I discussed the Jewish problem with him.

"Oh you chauvinist, you bourgeois—you do not realize that everything depends on the agrarian problem. Give the Russian his land and his freedom and you dispose of the Jewish problem."

This reply used to ring with pleasant firmness. He looked at me as a wealthy philanthropist looks upon an arrogant beggar who spurns his charity. His eyes gleamed with the silent reproach: 'I want to offer my life for the cause of freedom, for the land, for the peasants and for you—and you, foolish chauvinist, don't want to accept my sacrifice!"

No. I appreciated his sacrifice, and the sacrifice of hundreds of other Jewish youths like him, who gave up their dreaming heads for others. But I was not satisfied. They were not *our* heroes.

And many of that wonderful generation of enthusiasts died, surrendering their last breath to the Czar's hangmen. The rest became wiser: they gave up their desire for the welfare of the world and turned to material gains. The erstwhile revolutionists became careerists.

But the spirit of our Jewish youth was not entirely crushed in the pursuit of pleasure and of a career. Somewhere that idealism survived. In the depths of the people's hearts there smoldered that urge for great historical deeds. The national spirit glowed with holy ecstasy. And instead of *their* heroes came *our* heroes who gave their lives for the Jewish land and Jewish freedom.

The condemned Jewish terrorist found a worthy heir in the Jewish *Shomer.* The terrorist denied his Jewish name, and went to the gallows with a Christian stamp on his brow. The *Shomer* changed his ghetto-name to a national name—one symbolic of our past history and future hopes.

Their Berl and *Velvel* became *Anthony* and *Konstantin. Our* new heroes, the Palestinians, come with new names, with names of our own land and freedom—*Shmueli, Achduti, Reubeni.* To-day there are hundreds of them; tomorrow there will be thousands. Some of them have already devoted themselves whole-heartedly to fructify the Jewish land, to renew her with young blood and muscle, so that green shoots of Jewish freedom might sprout from her bosom. The *Shomrim* were the first defenders of the Jewish strongholds in Palestine, the guards of the Jewish national treasure. Some of them fell while performing their voluntary duty. The Russian terrorist was ready to kill and be killed because in his zeal he intended to destroy the ancient structure of despotism, to batter down with his own head the towers of false-hood and darkness. The modern Jewish pioneer went to Palestine not to destroy, but to build; not to kill and be killed, but to enrich the soil with his peaceful, fruitful labor. However, under the brutal, stubborn conditions of that desolate land, he was compelled to arm himself against his semi-barbarous neighbors.

Our heroes were the opposite of the terrorists. The *Shomrim* fell with full understanding of the cause they defended.

By the graves of the fallen Jewish workers and guards Jewish youth composed a new and glorious prayer—a prayer of freedom and hope, of pride and dignity, and this prayer was bequeathed to the world in the form of a book. This black-bound book of memories and deeds is known as *Yizkor*. This new *Yizkor* does not bewail the death of these martyrs, it does not wring its hands in the helpless sorrow of *El Malei Rachamin*.[1] *Yizkor* commemorates the souls of the fallen as only a comrade can. The authors of *Yizkor* are not mourners and orphans, but warriors who pronounce a solemn oath at the graves of their fallen comrades.

And on Sunday, the living workers and *Shomrim* will assemble. Then the black-enveloped book will be distributed along with the only bequest of the dead. That bequest is the idealism which the fallen have entrusted to the living.

As we assemble, we shall commemorate the names of those young men who abandoned the crowded cities and narrow towns for the glorious hills and broad deserts of Eretz Israel. And over our heads will hover the silent wings of the immortal spirit of the departed—the spirit of peaceful labor, of an emancipated land.

---

1 "God who is filled with compassion." The beginning words of a prayer for the departed.

ERETZ YISRAEL IN OUR PROGRAM
AND TACTICS

EDITOR'S NOTE—The essay "Eretz Yisrael in our Program and Tactics" is an excerpt from an address delivered in Kiev, September, 1917. This excerpt was taken from the minutes of the conference as recorded by S. Har.

After the Kerensky revolution Borochov left America to attend the Conference of the Holland-Scandinavian Socialist Committee in Stockholm. He was then also invited by the Russian Poale Zion to attend its Third Conference. In accepting the invitation, Borochov wrote to the Central Committee of the Russian Poale Zion that he had heard that the Russian Party had turned Bolshevik, whereas he himself was still a Social-Democrat. The Central Committee informed him that the rumors were exaggerated, and that many things would be clarified upon his return. As S. Har writes: "It seems that his fears were not without cause. There existed a chasm between Borochov and his Russian comrades (Borochov had been away from Russia for ten years), not so much with reference to his general views, as to his Jewish views which he expressed in his literary and Party activities in America."

Borochov came to the convention and delivered this famous address. To the young reader it may seem to contain nothing revolutionary. But a thorough study of Borochov's earlier theories will reveal the profound changes that had occurred within him.

With the exception of his unrealistic stand on the Jewish National Fund and the Zionist Congress, Borochov formulated a new orientation. (The symptoms of this orientation were visible in almost all of Borochov's writings during the World War.) The new terminology which he employed gave expression not only to Borochov the thinker, but also to Borochov the man of sentiment. Therein he proclaimed his faith in the Jewish cooperative colonization movement; he proclaimed anew the belief in Jewish Nationalism. Whereas formerly he had contended that we go to Palestine not only because of our historic and cultural ties with that land but chiefly because of the pressure of the objective forces, he now proclaimed as a justifiable motivating force our desire and longing for a Jewish National Home. *Eretz Yisrael,* unlike Palestine, is not only our "strategic base" but is our National Home. "We must not hesitate to proclaim loudly 'Jewish Nation'," he said. "When we say 'Jewish Nation' we know that it has existed even before the class division in modern society.

124

We also know that the proletariat at one time will constitute the nation and that the working class is the one that creates the nation." How similar this is to Ben Gurion's maxim, *mimaamad l'am* (from class to nation)!

The effects of the speech are revealed in the following description written by S. Har. "The speech made a very strong impression and was received with great enthusiasm by most of the delegates at the convention . . . Among the leaders, however, there reigned confusion. Some of the leaders combated the new revolutionary orientation, quoting ancient statements from Borochov's own teachings. In the midst of these polemics, many phrases were flung: 'Borochov has betrayed his own theory'; 'we do not accept the new Borochov'; 'we believe in the theory of the old one'!"

Though Borochov was successful in persuading the convention to adopt his point of view, the further developments of the Russian Poale Zion widened the schism that existed between the followers of the old Borochov and the adherents of the author of "Eretz Yisrael in Our Program and Tactics."

TIME IN its flight has not passed us by; it has brought to the fore new slogans and deeds. Some twelve years ago, our Party, the Poale Zion, made its first appearance as an organized body. Since then, the proletariat in general and the Jewish proletariat in particular have advanced.

Hitherto the proletariat sought to remove only its immediate obstacles; now, it strives to create a new society. Our program, too, must keep pace with our growing aspirations.

Our terminology must be made richer and more elastic. Formerly, we approached life in general from a naive, abstract point of view, and only our immediate demands were prompted by purely realistic conditions. Now, however, there have arisen in Jewish life cultural and aesthetic needs which demand immediate self-expression.

Socialism has several aspects. Economically, it means the socialization of the means of production; politically, the establishment of the dictatorship of the toiling masses; emotionally, the abolition of the reign of egotism and anarchy which characterizes the capitalistic system.

And so it is with Zionism. Economically, it means the concentration of the Jewish masses in Palestine; politically, the gaining of territorial autonomy; emotionally, the striving for a home.

Recent times have witnessed a desire on our part to give expression to these emotions. And we need not fear what our neighbors will say . . .

Twelve years ago, we clung to the epigram "Better a Jew without a beard than a beard without a Jew." Then we did not attach any significance to form and to the aesthetic aspects of life. It had to be that way, for then our battle was fought on two fronts: the *Bundist*[1] and the General Zionist.[2] Lest we be confused with the latter we had to be cautious in our terminology. But even then, we did not fear non-*Kosher* terms. Our program of that time always employed the term "Jewish Nation".[3]

But times have changed. The difference between our Party and the others is sufficiently clear. No one will mistake our identity. It is therefore an opportune time to introduce a newer and richer terminology. Now we can and must employ an emotional terminology. Now we can and must proclaim: "Eretz Yisrael[4]— a Jewish home!"

Our chief concern, however, is our program. The class interests of the Jewish proletariat remain unchanged. Our ultimate aim is Socialism; our immediate need is Zionism. The class struggle is the means to achieve both.

Our class struggle, however, is an abnormal one. It is largely thwarted by the prevailing conditions under which our people live and by the national struggle—the conflict between the forces of production and the conditions of production, as I have outlined elsewhere.[5]

---

1 See footnote 2, p. 175.

2 In the beginning of the Zionist movement, General Zionism was the main force embracing bourgeois as well as liberal elements. Nowadays, General Zionism is divided into two main groups: Group A includes the progressive and pro-labor Zionists; Group B, the reactionary and anti-labor elements.

3 In the earlier periods of the Jewish Socialist and Labor movements which were affected by cosmopolitan thought and phraseology, the term "Jewish Nation" was avoided. Kautsky's volume, *Are Jews a Race?*, is also characteristic of this cosmopolitan outlook on the Jewish people. Assimilationism and Reform-Judaism agreed upon and created an ideological philosophy that Jews are a religious *group* and *not* a nation.

4 Literally, Land of Israel. For the same reason as in (3), the term "Eretz Yisrael" was taboo; also because of the religious, historic and sentimental connotations. Even today the Yiddish daily, *The Forward*, which has of late accepted a positive attitude toward Zionism and Eretz Yisrael, still avoids the use of "Eretz Yisrael". Instead it always refers to it as "Palestina".

5 In his essays "Our Platform" and "The National Question and the Class Struggle".

In the past, the international Socialist proletariat was weak. It was not interested in foreign policy nor in the national problem. But times have changed. The Socialist conferences in Zimmerwald and Stockholm indicate a new epoch in the struggle of the world proletariat. But does the Jewish worker keep pace with these new trends? In spite of his enthusiasm and tremendous revolutionary energy, the Jewish worker exerts but little influence. He is as impotent as the rock-bound Prometheus. This tragic plight compels him to demand a home for the Jewish people. This home will serve as a strategic base for the creative efforts of the Jewish worker in all fields of human endeavor.

Years ago we said: Zionism is a *stychic* [natural, objective, or dynamic] process.[6] Our only task is to remove all the obstacles which interfere with this process. And we left the creative work to the bourgeois Zionists.

---

6 The concept *"stychic process"* is found in all his major writings. In fact this concept constitutes a basic element of Borochov's theory. The word *styhic* is derived from the Greek meaning "order". In religious literature this concept is frequently used to denote the elements of nature operating in the cosmos. In Russian Marxian and in sociological literature, the concept denotes processes which are not within the sphere of man's consciousness and will.

In his earlier writings, Borochov contended that the immigration of Jews into Palestine and their concentration in it will come about not solely because of our Zionist aspirations or because of Jewry's sentimental attachments to its old home, but primarily because of the natural, objective, or dynamic tendencies of life which force the Jew to immigrate into Palestine.

A. Revusky, in his article, "Ber Borochov and Present Jewish Realities" (*The Pioneer Woman Magazine*, February, 1936), explains this concept as follows:

There is no better example of a *stychic* process than the present Jewish immigration into Palestine, where individuals from different countries, each driven by his own misery, form a great mass force, molding a new commonwealth out of chaos. Germany with its barbaric Hitlerism; Poland with its economic crusade against Jewish existence; Yemen with its medieval persecutions—all are aspects of the same acute Jewish problem. They are creating a desperate demand for a new haven of refuge. In other countries where the attacks on Jewish positions are proceeding at a slower pace, large sections of the Jewish population are being up-rooted every year; and many others, threatened with extinction, are in dire need of a secure haven. All this helps to broaden the *stychic* process of Jewish immigration to Palestine and to lend it tremendous momentum.

The phenomenon of the present Palestine immigration, over-flooding the facilities of organized Zionism and always meeting greater restrictions imposed on it by the present mandatory rulers of the country, is exactly the kind of a *stychic* process anticipated by Borochov thirty years ago. Can it be denied that it is the *stychic* process which is responsible for the scope of present-day Palestine, and that our organized activities play merely an auxiliary role in this great historic drama which unfolds itself before the astonishing eyes of the world?

Borochov's strong belief in *stychic* process does not imply inactivity. It is not to be confused with fatalism. Any interpretation which is guilty of such confusion is based on malice or lack of understanding. As Borochov himself repeatedly stated, processes that are taking place in a human environment are of the organic kind. They do not exclude organized activity of

There are two types of natural processes: the mechanical and the organic.[7] We erred formerly when we contended that natural emigration waves are already under way. General Zionists were closer to the truth when they said that for the present only the organic process has begun. It is clear now that what motivated our previous mechanical conception was our reaction to the Zionists' assertion that the will[8] of our nation is the *sole* determining factor in Zionism.

Our experiments in Palestine have taught us a new lesson. Colonization in Palestine is an especially difficult task. But in spite of the difficulties and temporary failures, colonization in Palestine is developing and is gradually approaching the Socialist ideal. I refer, of course, to the co-operatives[9] and particularly to

---

individuals. Quite the contrary, this organized pioneering activity is strongly spurred by the conviction that it is much more than a product of multiple individual whims, that it is basically rooted in a strong historical necessity.

This thesis was accepted by certain factions in the Socialist-Zionist movement, and rejected or minimized by others. It is not the task of the editor to solve this age-long philosophic battle, which of the two—man's *will* or *circumstances*—operates as the determining factor in our social life. The history of the immigration movement into Palestine contains in its records both the human material whose driving force to Palestine was Hitler, and the heroic movement of the *Second Aliya* ("immigration stream" during the period 1905-1914) which had the choice of emigrating to America or Palestine but voluntarily chose the latter.

[7] By "organic process" is meant that process which is directed by man's consciousness and free will. By "mechanical process" is meant those forces which operate apart from man's efforts.

[8] The assertion made by some that Borochov was a *thorough* materialist is questionable in the light of his later writings of which the following citation is characteristic:

Men, at different times, have in their own way envisioned "the days to come". Some envisioned it through the power of prophecy; others, at a later period, envisioned it through mystical ecstacy; and still later, others have envisioned it by cabbalistic calculations. The great revolutionists of England and France have by means of their "common sense" and "mathematical proof" predetermined that "day to come". Marx did it on the basis of his "historic necessity", concentration of capital, and the laws of proletarization. In my opinion, all were correct; for after all, these predeterminations, whether made by mystics, logicians, or scientists, were guided by the powerful voice of man's *will*. They dreamed because they wished, and all of them wished freedom, fraternity, and equality. Each conceived it differently, in accordance with the spirit of his time; each interpreted it differently in accordance with his particular terminology; yet, each desired the same. And today we witness the fact that the will for independence rules the world—that is the *will* of which it was said "where there is a will there is a way". ("The *Hagada* of a Freethinker", *Die Warheit*, April 8, 1917.)

[9] It will not be an historical error to state that the co-operative movement developed in spite of the ill-natured opposition or indifference of orthodox-Socialists, who regarded the co-operative movement as Utopian or even harmful to the cause of the "class struggle". Borochov, in his early years, did not look with great favor upon the co-operative movement, but in his later years he modified his views as this article indicates.

those pursuing the Oppenheimer[10] plan. Co-operative colonization in which the Jewish worker plays a very great role is also the way to a Socialist society in Palestine. While this colonization is not in itself Socialism, it does teach the Jewish proletariat the elementary lessons of self-help.

Small as the *Yishub*[11] is, the Jews enjoy an autonomous life and have their own courts, post-offices, and banking system.[12] Jewish labor has gradually become enrooted even in such a small *Yishub*. The Jewish working class is not as yet large; it nevertheless plays a prominent role. Its organizations and institutions, such as the *Hashomer*[13] and the "Palestine Workers' Fund",[14] are publicly recognized.

It is important to note that Palestine is a semi-agrarian country, and hence it is adapted to the Jewish city-bred immigrant. Palestine is also the center of Jewish public interest. It may also be said that Palestine is the cynosure of all Jewish eyes—its every activity commands the attention of friend and foe. In the last analysis this is the best guarantee for Palestine's proper development.

Many point out the obstacles which we encounter in our colonization work. Some say that the Turkish law hinders our work, others contend that Palestine is insignificantly small, and still others charge us with the odious crime of wishing to oppress and expel the Arabs from Palestine.[15]

According to the latest investigations (for example, Ben Zvi's), Palestine's boundaries include some eighty or ninety

---

10 Franz Oppenheimer, a German-Jewish economist, devised a plan for co-operative colonization in Palestine, the central idea being that the members of the colony be treated as ordinary workers under the guidance of experts. When the members of the colony will have undergone the necessary training, they are to manage and administrate the work themselves. This experiment was first tried in Merchavia in 1909, having received the approval of the Ninth Zionist Congress of the same year.

11 *Yishub*—literally, settlement; in Zionist literature it refers to the Jewish community in Palestine.

12 During the World War, the Jewish Community in Palestine had a monetary system of its own.

13 See footnote 5, p. 91.

14 See footnote 4, p. 116.

15 This is a charge often made by Communists and Arab reactionaries. Even the official government report of Palestine refuted the charges that Jews are responsible for allegedly landless Arabs. See A. Revusky's *Jews in Palestine*, pp. 332-3.

thousand square kilometers, a land capacity sufficient to hold tens of millions of inhabitants. But even in its present limited boundaries, Palestine's twenty-seven thousand square kilometers can accommodate up to nine million people, whereas now it is even short of a half-million. It is understood, of course, that the Turkish rule and the prevailing system will cease. The War will create a change.

When the waste lands are prepared for colonization, when modern technique is introduced, and when the other obstacles are removed, there will be sufficient land to accommodate both the Jews and the Arabs. Normal relations between the Jews and Arabs will and must prevail.

I repeat that we must originate independent activities in Palestine. We cannot merely content ourselves, as we have done until now, with the work of bourgeois Zionists and with our critical attitude towards it.

We must define anew our stand towards the various Zionist institutions. We cannot participate in the Zionist Congress[16] as long as it is a Party tribune. We will, however, participate in a World Jewish Congress because it will be a national tribune, having a semi-parliamentary status.

---

16 Among the numerous schisms in the Poale Zion movement (1905-1920) one occurred on the question of participation in the Zionist Congress. The "later" Borochov was an anti-Congressist. Some self-styled Borochovists (e. g. the left Poale Zion) maintain to this very day the attitude that Socialists *cannot* and *must not* practice class collaboration. Since the Zionist Congress includes non-Socialist elements they contend that the proletariat cannot participate in it. With reference to the principle of class-collaboration, Borochov the anti-Congressist said:

The traditional attitude of the American Poale Zion is that even though Socialist-Zionists constitute a separate Party, they must nevertheless participate in the World Zionist Congress and in all its institutions. The Russian Poale Zion consider themselves as a separate proletarian organization and regard the Zionist Congress and its institutions as purely bourgeois instruments . . .

But this has nothing to do with the question whether or not we participate in the Congress. *Even if the Congress is a bourgeois institution, the Poale Zion may deem it expedient to participate in it for tactical reasons,* i. e., to influence bourgeois Zionism along our lines. The dispute regarding the Zionist Congress is but one small aspect of the entire question: How should the Poale Zion regard the Zionist organization—as a bourgeois organization or as an all-inclusive movement which embraces all classes of Jewry? Workers may participate even in certain bourgeois organizations, if participation benefits the working class. But the chief difference is as to whether we regard the Zionist Congress as a strange and bourgeois organization or as our own Poale Zion institution and an all-inclusive organization of the Jewish masses. ("Zionists and Poale Zionists", *Die Warheit,* 1915.)

How different is the above from the early writings of Borochov, the champion of the Zionist Congress! In "Our Platform" (1905) Borochov vigorously attacked those Socialists and Socialist-Zionists who preached against participation in the Congress. To the charges that were advanced that the Zionist Congress had no right to speak in the name of World Jewry, Borochov said:

Because the immigration into Palestine embraces more and more the interest

We are sympathetic to the Jewish National Fund,[17] and as individuals we may even give it our support. But our official fund is the Palestine Workers' Fund, which deserves our full support. Similarly we must support the co-operative colonization movement.

In short, we must initiate a Socialist program of activities in Palestine. Then the Jewish worker, like the rock-bound Prometheus, will free himself from the vultures that torture him and will snatch the heavenly fires for himself and for the Jewish people.

---

of the Jewish masses, the voluntary Zionist institutions have a right to speak in the name of the Jewish nation and thereby influence its course.

To those protagonists who maintained that there was no sense to the participation of the Jewish proletariat in the Zionist Congress because, unlike a parliament, it had no means of compelling, Borochov replied:

. . . Police and prison are not the only means to compel obedience . . . When there exists a relationship between economic interests, courts and police are not essential . . . The voluntary initiative of social forces which find expression in the Zionist organization can achieve all that is necessary in the way of the regulation of immigration.

17 The objects of the Jewish National Fund as redefined by the resolution of the London Zionist Conference in 1920 are:

(1) To acquire the land in Palestine with the voluntary contributions of the Jewish people, such land to be the common property of the Jewish people.

(2) To lease the land exclusively on hereditary leasehold for cultivation or building thereon.

(3) To facilitate the settlement of working farmers.

(4) *To ensure the cultivation of the land by Jews.*

(5) To combat speculation in land values.

Why then does Borochov say that "as individuals we may *even* give it our support"? This may be explained by the fact that Borochov in common with other, so-called orthodox Socialists, believe that institutions not created or solely controlled by the worker could not be considered his *own*. In the early stages of the Jewish National Fund (it was established in 1901), there were some Poale Zionists who opposed it or, at best, were indifferent to it. That the Jewish National Fund would be that agency which would enable the establishment of the more than 100 *moshavim* (co-operative small-holder settlements) and *kvutzot* (collective land settlements, or communes) which primarily benefit the worker (and, employing Borochov's own concept, creating for him "the strategic base") Borochov could not at that time foresee. Later, however, Borochov modified his stand somewhat. Today the Left Poale Zion alone still cling to this anachronistic concept, though they, too, do not hesitate to share in the benefits of the Jewish National Fund. In spite of their theoretical opposition some of their members are settled on Jewish National Fund land.

In saying, "We are sympathetic to the Jewish National Fund", Borochov already displayed an altered viewpoint. Admittedly, the Jewish National Fund, too, had changed. In the pre-war days there were some cases where the Jewish National Fund aided Jewish colonists who boycotted organized Jewish labor. It was only later that the principle of "Jewish labor on Jewish National Fund land" was incorporated. This may partly explain Borochov's previous contention that the Jewish worker can rely only on his own institutions. As said before, with the change in policy of the Jewish National Fund, Borochov, too, modified his views. The following citation clearly indicates it:

The Jewish National Fund strives to redeem the land of Palestine not for the individual Jew, but for the Jewish people; not as the private property of the rich Jew, but as the national property of the entire people. The original purpose of the Jewish National Fund was that the land which it was to acquire and all the buildings, machines, and inventory thereon should belong to the entire people. In the course of time, the Jewish National Fund incorporated another aim in its program, and that is, that all the work performed on its land should be done by Jewish labor. These, then, are the two basic principles of the Jewish National Fund—the nationalization of the land and the nationalization of the labor on it. (From the article, "The Jewish National Fund", *Die Warheit*, December 24, 1916.)

SECTION TWO

CLASS AND NATION

THE NATIONAL QUESTION AND THE CLASS STRUGGLE

I. THE TWOFOLD DIVISION OF HUMAN SOCIETY

IN THE preface to his book, *A Contribution to the Critique of Political Economy*, Marx states: "In the social production which men carry on, they enter into definite relations that are indispensable and independent of their will; these relations of production correspond to a definite stage of development of their material powers of production."[1]

In order to live, men must produce. In order to produce, they must combine their efforts in a certain way. Man does not as an individual struggle with nature for existence. History knows man only as a unit in a social group. Since men do live socially, it follows that between them certain *relations* are developed. These relations arise because of the production. Indeed, Marx terms them: *relations of production*.

"The sum total of these relations of production constitutes the economic structure of society—the real foundation, on which rise legal and political superstructures and to which correspond definite forms of social consciousness."[2] Thus, the relations of production in China, or in France, for example, are the basis for the whole "social order" of Chinese or French society.

But when we refer to societies by different names, we imply that there are *several* societies. These societies are in some manner *differentiated* one from the other. If this were not so, we could not speak of an English bourgeoisie, for example, and a German bourgeoisie, of an American proletariat and a Russian proletariat.

---

[1] *The Essentials of Marx,* edited by Algernon Lee, Vanguard Press, New York, 1931, p. 176.
[2] Ibid.

Then we would speak only of mankind as a whole, or at least of civilized humanity, and no more. But the English and the Germans, the Americans and the Russians, are each a part of mankind, and if you will, of civilized humanity, and yet they are differentiated from one another. We therefore see that humanity is divided into several societies.

The above is common knowledge, and it would never occur to anyone to deny it. The question is, however, how can we explain the causes which make for this division of humanity? To be sure, many explanations have already been offered. One has but to inquire of those who speak in the name of "national ideologies", of a "pure Russian spirit", of a "true German spirit", of "Judaism", and so on. The problem for us, however, is to explain this in terms of the materialistic concept, which teaches us to seek the basic causes of every social phenomenon in economic conditions.

We know why men are divided into classes. We know that all members of a given society are not in the same position in the relations of production. Each group in society takes a different part in the system of production (feudal or capitalistic). Each group bears a specific relation to the means of production. Some are the entrepreneurs, others the workers, a third group are peasants, and so on. The groups which are so differentiated from one another represent the different *classes*. Every society is therefore divided into classes.

But what is responsible for the differences between the various societies which give rise to the whole national question and its concomitant struggles? On what grounds do these differences arise, and what are the conclusions to be drawn from the previously stated Marxian theory?

II.   CONDITIONS OF PRODUCTION

We stated above: in order to live, men must produce. In the process of production various *relations of production* arise. But the production itself is dependent on certain *conditions,* which are *different* in *different* places.

Citing Marx above, we said that the nature of the relations of production are independent of man's intellect and volition. The character of the *relations* of production depends on the state of the forces of production which are in the control of man. But the state of the forces of production and their development are primarily dependent on the natural conditions which man must face in his struggle for existence. The condition of the forces of production is therefore dependent on the geographic environment, and the latter is, of course, *different* in *different* places.

What is true of the forces of production is also true of the development of production. This development is always influenced by certain naturally and historically different conditions, which result in *different* economic structures among different peoples.

The conditions of production vary considerably. They are geographic, anthropological, and historic. The historic conditions include both those generated within a given social entity and those imposed by the neighboring social groups.

These conditions are recognized by Engels in his second letter in the *Socialist Academician*. He states therein that among the many factors which make for different economies are also the geographical environment, the race, and even the human type, which hes developed *differently* in different places.

In the third volume of *Capital* Marx also states that one and the same economic base can develop in different ways because of different conditions, such as natural environment, race, and external historic influences. Therefore we see, according to the teachers of historic materialism, that one and the same process of development of productive forces can assume various forms according to the differences in the conditions of production.

Of the above-mentioned conditions of production, the natural, non-social factors predominated firstly. As society develops, however, the social and historic environment gains in importance over the non-social, natural conditions, just as man in general assumes mastery over nature.

In this conception of the "conditions of production" we have a sound basis for the development of a purely materialistic theory of the *national question.* For in it is contained the theory and the basis of national struggles.

For scientific accuracy, however, we must add the following explanation: the foregoing citation from Marx speaks about historic influences acting *from without.* When we say "from without", it means that the thing which is being influenced is a *distinct entity* from the other. It therefore has an internal and an external life. But is there anything in the world which is an absolute totality in itself? No. And yet we do speak of certain totalities. It is common knowledge that to the present day humanity must still be considered an aggregate of certain entities which are *to an extent* distinct one from the other. Thus, for example, everyone knows that the French masses are distinct from the German masses, and so on. Scientists very often do speak of various things which are in some measure connected one with the other, and yet are considered distinct entities. Why is this so?

As we have already emphasized, there are many things which are *to a certain extent* totalities in themselves. True, they are not absolute, but only to *an extent,* in other words, *relatively* distinct entities. Humanity must to the present day be considered an aggregate of *relatively* distinct entities. It is therefore apparent that when speaking of such *relatively* distinct entities, we can also speak of *internal* and *external* relations. In speaking of "influences acting from without" Marx by that alone recognizes the *relative* totality of modern societies.

What, however, brings about this relative totality of the social life of a certain group, so that we may consider it a closed entity? Why do we consider England as something different from France, although both these societies have an identical capitalistic system of production? We may speak, and do speak of a *relative distinctness* of social groups only because there is a relative distinctness in the *conditions* of production under which each group must develop its life. Sometimes such a group is called a socio-economic organism.

We, therefore, come to the formulation and explanation of the following two sorts of human groupings: (1) the groups into which humanity is divided according to the differences in the conditions of the relatively distinct productions are called *societies,* socio-economic organisms (tribes, families, peoples, nations); (2) the groups into which the society is divided according to their role in the system of production itself, i. e., according to their respective relations to the means of production, are called *classes* (castes, ranks, etc.).

III. THE NATIONAL STRUGGLE

Having ascertained the causes for the division of humanity into societies, we can now proceed to a discussion of the national struggle and the grounds from which it arises.

We know that the class struggle arises because the *conditions* of the various classes in the system of production are different. The position of one class may be better or worse, more advantageous or less so, than the position of a second class. The striving of the various groups within a given society to gain for themselves a more advantageous position, or to retain for themselves an already achieved position, results in the class struggle.

The class struggle assumes the character of a social problem wherever *the development of the forces of production disturbs the constitution of the relations of production,* i. e., when the constitution of the relations of production is archaic, obsolete, and no longer suitable to the further development of production.

The same is true of the *national struggle.* The situation as regards one set of material conditions of production may be more advantageous than the situation in another set of material conditions of production; and there develops a striving of the same character as that previously described in connection with the class struggle. The result of this striving is the struggle between social entities.

Nor is it even necessary that the conditions should differ as to relative advantageousness. For no matter how advantageous the position of a given society may be in the sphere of its usual conditions of production, it may nevertheless strive to expand its production, to increase the sum total of its energies. It therefore becomes necessary in the process of enlarging the scope of its conditions of production to annex those of other social entities. And here we perceive the same phenomenon: one body seeks to annex the field of the other, or to defend itself against that other; in other words, we are witnessing a *national struggle*.

We have thus demonstrated two bases which give rise to the struggle between social entities. We may quite simply state that a national struggle takes place whenever the development of the forces of production demands that the conditions of production belonging to a social group be better, more advantageous, or that in general they be expanded. In other words a national struggle comes about when the existing conditions of production are no longer compatible with the further development of production. *The national problem therefore arises when the development of the forces of production of a nationality conflicts with the state of the conditions of production.*

Every social phenomenon is primarily related to the material elements of society. A struggle is waged not for "spiritual" things, but for certain economic advantages in social life. The class struggle is waged not for "spiritual" values, but for the means of production. So too, with the national struggle.

The class struggle is waged for the material possessions of the classes, i. e., for the means of production. The means of production may be material or intangible. Material wealth is for the most part something that can be expropriated, such as machines. Intangible assets, on the other hand, are those which cannot be expropriated, as for example, technical proficiency, skill, and so on. Despite the fact that the struggle between classes very often asumes the form of a conflict between cultural-spiritual ideologies, such a struggle is not waged for the possession of intangible assets, but for the control of the material means of production.

The national struggle is also waged for the material possessions of social organisms. The assets of a social body lie in its control of the *conditions of production.* These, too, may be material or "spiritual", i. e., such as can and such as cannot be expropriated. The material conditions consist of the territory and all the products of the material culture which have been developed by man, particularly the tangible conditions of production. The "spiritual" conditions consist of languages, customs, mores, *weltanschauungen,* in other words—the "historic" conditions of production.

The national struggle is waged not for the preservation of cultural values but for the control of material possessions, even though it is very often conducted under the banner of spiritual slogans. Nationalism is always related to the material possessions of the nation, despite the various masks which it may assume outwardly.

But first it is necessary to determine what is "nationalism". The terms "nationalism" and "national question", are directly linked with the term "nation", and it therefore becomes imperative to ascertain precisely what we mean by this latter term.

IV. PEOPLES AND NATIONS

The terms "people" and "nation" each denote a different stage or degree of development in the life of a given society. In order that we may better understand the distinction between the two, we may bring as an illustration the single word "class", and the interpretation of which it is capable. It is well known that the meaning of the word "class" as employed by Marx is ambiguous and somewhat complicated. On the one hand, Marx considers as a class every social group which differs from other groups in the same society as regards its participation in production or in its relation to the means of production. It is in this sense that Marx and Engels stated that the history of humanity is a history of class struggles.

But then again we find passages in Marx which indicate that he employed the term "class" in another, much narrower sense. Here it appears that he understands a class to be not merely any economic group occupying a special place in the system of production, but such a group as has already achieved a measure of self-consciousness and has appeared on the political arena with clearly expressed interests and demands.

These two meanings of the word "class" are to be found in Marx's *The Poverty of Philosophy.* In one instance we find,

"The working class will substitute, in the course of its development, for the old order of civil society an association which will exclude classes and their antagonism . . ."[3] In another instance we find, "So long as the proletariat is not sufficiently developed to constitute itself as a class, so long as, in consequence, the struggle between the proletariat and the bourgeoisie has not acquired a political character . . ."[4] And in still another instance we find, "Many researches have been made to trace the different historical phases through which the bourgeoisie has passed from the early commune to its constitution as a class."[5] In these last two examples we have the second meaning of "class". Here Marx distinguishes between the two different conditions of the group; one, when the group is a class only in relation to the other groups; and the second, when it enters the political arena and becomes a class in its own consciousness.

A whole society may also find itself in one of these two conditions: in the first, when it appears as a relatively distinct entity only in relations with other social organisms; and in the second, when it appears as a social organism with a consciousness of its own.

When we wish to denote the respective states of groups which developed under different *conditions of production,* we have two terms. Thus, a social group which developed under the same conditions of production is commonly called a people. And the same social group which is united also through the consciousness of the kinship between its members is commonly called a nation. In fine, a people becomes a nation only on a higher plane of its development.

V. NATIONALISM

The psyche of every personality adapts itself, in a greater or lesser extent, to the conditions under which its group lives. In

---

3 *The Poverty of Philosophy,* translated by H. Quelch, Chas. H. Kerr & Co., Chicago, p. 190.
4 Ibid., p. 136.
5 Ibid., p. 189.

this way there develops a group psychology, and definite earmarks of a group character emerge. The keen observer will always discover in these traits some relationship to the material conditions of a given system of production or to a definite stage in the development of the system. This relationship may, however, often be obscure.

Furthermore, although the members of each group, be it a class or a society, may have certain generally common characteristics, it does not yet follow that this similarity denotes the community and solidarity of their interests. And even where there is such community of interests, there may not always be any consciousness thereof.

There are some groups among whose members there can be no mutuality of interests, because they are in constant conflict with one another as a result of inner group contradictions. And even groups which really have common, harmonious interests do not easily become conscious of them, for this consciousness can develop only in the course of a more or less extended period of time.

But in groups which are organized so harmoniously that their individual members adapt themselves uniformly to their environment, there sooner or later develops also the consciousness of this harmony. Thus we perceive that because the group lives under uniform and also harmonious conditions of production or relations of production there sometimes develops, in addition to the group character, also a group-consciousness. All the emotions which result from this group-consciousness give rise, in the main, to what is commonly called the feeling of kinship or affinity.

Life under *relations* of production which are harmonious for the individuals of the group evokes *class solidarity*.

Life under one and the same *conditions* of production, when the *conditions* are harmonious for the members of a society, evokes the *national consciousness* of that society, and the feeling of *national kinship*.

This kinship is felt by the individual members as something associated with their common past. Naturally, this does not always mean that they really have a long common past. Sometimes the antiquity of the common past is purely fictitious.

This feeling of kinship, created as a result of the visioned common historic past and rooted in the common conditions of production, is called nationalism.

VI. NATIONALISM AND THE TERRITORY

We previously stated that, in the last analysis, nationalism is always related to the material resources of the nation. What are the material resources of a nation?

The resources of a society, in general, we have pointed out, are the conditions of its system of production. These may be material or spiritual. *The most vital of the material conditions of production is the territory. The territory is furthermore the foundation on which rise all other conditions of production,* and it serves as a base for the introduction of all external influences.

In addition, every nationality also has fashioned certain instruments for the preservation of its resources. These are its political unity and the political institutions, its language, its national education, and nationalism itself.

But here it is necessary to remember that the nation is divided into classes (in both senses of the word). They are each in a different position in the system of production of the nation; their places in the *relations* of production are not the same. Therefore, the conditions of production can under no circumstances be of equal value to all. Each class has a different interest in the national wealth and therefore possesses a different type of "nationalism". If we should formally define nationalism as a striving to preserve the national interests, which are always in some manner or other related to the *base* of the conditions of production, the *territory,* and to its instruments of preservation, then we have, because of the diversity of national interests, also *various types of nationalism.*

The national interests may be directed internally or externally; they may be conservative or progressive, aggressive or defensive in character. All this naturally accounts for certain variations in the types of nationalism.

VII. THE ORIGIN OF NATIONALISM

There can be no nationalism where the conditions of production have not yet been nationalized, i. e., where the relatively distinct society has not yet become segregated from without and united from within.

Both conditions mentioned above—the segregation from the outside world, and the internal unity—must be met. The feudal system satisfied only the first condition—it only served to segregate one society from another, but it did not unite the members of each society with a strong internal bond. The feudal era was not possessed of a harmonious wholeness in the conditions of production. Consequently it had no conception of the existence of nations, but only of "peoples". And therefore, too, it had no conception of nationalism and the national question.

The nationalism of ancient times was purely political in character. It often flared up spontaneously at times when the external relations between peoples became sharply strained. This sort of nationalism came to life and subsided together with the great wars, which, however, were not waged because of national interests, and were not, therefore, national in character.

When, however, commerce began to develop out of the feudal system, a great revolution was set in motion. Gradually nationalities, nationalism, and in consequence the national question came into being. The first simple national policy—which cannot yet be termed national—shifted from without to within the society. Instead of being purely occasional and accidental, as heretofore, it assumed permanent and regular features. And only by this shift to *within* the society did it become *national*. The development of capital slowly shook the foundation of the existing order, and with its aid there began the consolidation of the land and great monarchies developed.

We may well ask: What interest prompted the movement which nationalized the conditions of social production? In the next chapter we shall answer this question. Before concluding this chapter, however, we wish to point out the following: the first protagonist of national ideas, the bourgeoisie (the mercantile and industrial bourgeoisie), which was so young and progressive in its day, waged an energetic struggle with the old order and created a new world. Needless to say, it could not at the same time also defend the traditional concepts. *From its very beginning nationalism has been independent of traditions.*

They who berate nationalism in general as something obsolete and reactionary, as a traditional thing, are remarkably shallow and ignorant. Nationalism is a product of the bourgeois society— it was born simultaneously with it, its reign is as old as that of the bourgeois society, and it must be reckoned with as much as any other phenomenon of bourgeois society. Speaking from the proletarian standpoint, we must therefore say that the proletariat is directly concerned with nationalism, with the national wealth, and with the territory. Since the proletariat takes part in the production, then it must also be interested in the conditions of production, and there must develop a specific proletarian type of nationalism—as is, indeed, the fact.

A generally essential condition, one of the prerequisites of the capitalistic system of production, is freedom. Commerce and industry develop only through free competition, i. e., when there is freedom to transport capital and goods and to trade with them. The worker must also be free to sell his labor power; he must be able to move about freely, for only in this manner can surplus value, the life-blood of capitalism, be created. The freedom to travel is the first and most essential of all liberties, for without it all others have no value.

Travel and transportation, naturally, depend on the territory. The prerequisite of freedom of transportation is a free territory. And this makes clear to us what interest led the bourgeoisie to engage in the struggle to make the land free. The struggle was waged first to free a specific territory, with definite boundaries. These boundaries marked off the whole territory in which a given language was spoken.

It also became necessary to emancipate the population living within this territory and to abolish the feudal barriers which covered the land like a network and obstructed the freedom of transportation. Thus the bourgeoisie created a relatively segregated social organism, freed it from serfdom, and harmonized the conditions of its production. That is why it was nationalistic. In addition, it also emancipated the whole population of the country —to be sure, with the aid of the masses. It united with all classes jointly against one class—against the lords of that period. This strengthened and encouraged all the more its militant and really progressive nationalism.

Thus the European *peoples* became *nations*.

There developed among each people a national consciousness, and the members of the nation became imbued with the feeling of kinship arising from their common historic past, or—to employ the materialistic terminology—from the common conditions of their system of production. The various peoples, who now desired to develop their national wealth, realized that such wealth indeed did exist, but that it was necessary to wrest it from the toils of the reigning feudalism. Thus they each began to love their respective territories—the homeland, the fatherland; that is to say, the common base of the conditions of production. They began to love its instruments of preservation and to cultivate the national language, and aspired to a truly national commonwealth.

After the French Revolution, however, the division within the society itself became clearly manifest. It became evident that the nation consists of different classes. And after the national wealth had been emancipated, and the controlling powers proceeded to the division thereof, the *class struggle* broke out in all its fury. The harmony and solidarity of which they formerly spoke were dispelled like smoke. The fundamental postulate, "the people", proved to be a fiction. The "homeland", "our" land, "our" language, "our" culture—all these conditions of the system of production remained a part of the *national* wealth. But they no longer appear as the *common* possession of all members of the nation. Even the basic feeling of kinship, arising on the ground of the common historic past, lost its original aura. It lost its passion, and remained a mere experience; *it became a tradition.*

The above is true as regards free nations, which oppress no one and are not themselves oppressed, i. e., nations which live under normal conditions of production. With them the feeling and consciousness of kinship has become a tradition, an historic reminiscence. And life itself has helped to further this condition. The material conditions of life, which gave rise to class antagonisms, have pushed aside this tradition and prevented it from exerting any social influence. Each class has assumed its social position, and it values a particular aspect of the national wealth—that aspect with which it is mostly concerned.

Free nations, which do not oppress others and are not oppressed themselves, lack the environment in which all national interests may merge. In other words, there is no instance in the conditions of production which finds that the common interests of all members of the nation are affected. Such nations have no dynamic "nationalism". It expresses itself only in weak sympathies, in "love for one's own", so to say. This "love" may simply mean that, *all other* conditions being equal, an individual will "help his own" more readily than "a stranger".

Among certain classes of free nations, there may, however, sometimes exist a latent sort of nationalism. But this is no more than a potential (a repressed) nationalism which may manifest itself strongly at the first opportune occasion. It must always be remembered, however, that this occasion will arise only when the national resources are affected, and at that, only the material resources. These, incidentally, must be affected in such a manner that the interests of some class are also involved, because the center of gravity of free nations lies not in their national existence—for their conditions of production are normal—but in their class structure, in the relations which are developed within the confines of the system of production itself. As long as the national interests of some class are not endangered, so long does the propaganda of nationalism serve only to dampen class consciousness; and on that consideration it is harmful.

But it goes without saying, that when the conditions of the system of production of a certain nation are in an anomalous state, its nationalism assumes an altogether different aspect.

VIII. NATIONALISM AND CLASS CONSCIOUSNESS

It must be noted in general, that all anomalies in the conditions of production affect adversely the relations of production, i. e., the class structure. It is a commonly known fact that under normal conditions of production the class antagonisms become more acute, whereas under abnormal conditions of production they abate somewhat. Normal conditions of production de-nationalize the people and dull its national consciousness, whereas abnormal conditions of production (i. e., when some part of the national possession is lacking or its organs of preservation are curtailed) harmonize the interests of various classes of the nation and heighten its national consciousness. Therefore, there is a kind of antagonism between the *class consciousness* and *national consciousness* of a given group, and the two are wont to obfuscate one another. It sometimes happens that the interests of the individuals of various classes in a nation, under abnormal conditions of production, are in reality harmonious in some respect, and yet certain irrational ideologists ignore these national interests, which are also of great significance to their own class. They attempt to blunt the national consciousness, which in this case should not be obscured because that would be harmful to the interests of their own class, too. The same effect is created by carrying on a nationalistic propaganda within a nation which is living under *normal* conditions of production, or where the propagandists will have the people believe that the common interests are broader and more harmonious than is really the case. In this latter instance nationalism blunts class consciousness and is therefore detrimental to the whole nation, because it hides the real relations between the various groups within the nation. This results in self-deceit, illusions, and social myopia.

It is always harmful to obscure the class or national consciousness of a given group, irrespective of whether this is a result of class or national demagogy. Whether it is class or national interests which are being obscured, or whether it is the real conditions of production or the relations of production which are being falsely interpreted, is immaterial, since the one attempt as well as the other is reactionary.

The ruling classes of free as well as of oppressed nations, take advantage of this fundamental contradiction between national and class consciousness, and are often inclined to carry on a hypocritical nationalistic propaganda in order to obscure the class-consciousness of those whom they oppress. But we should not be misled by this condition into believing that these ruling classes are in reality nationally inclined. The ruling classes are not national, but *nationalistic*.

All propaganda and every movement which is rooted in the character of the conditions of production of a given society is either national or nationalistic. Whenever it attempts to blunt the class and civic consciousness of the members of that society, and whenever it ignores the class structure and the antagonism between the interests of the classes, it is nationalistic. If, however, it does not obscure the class structure of the society, it is *national*.

The phrase "national spirit", all sorts of "cultural-historical essences", and all other exaggerated traditions are the best warning signals against a confusion of the two. Nationalistic speeches are always liberally dotted with them. Empty phraseology, crammed with these and similar conceptions, is not national but nationalistic.

Taking into consideration the fact that there exists a common national character which is the same for all members of the nation, a person who thinks *nationalistically* is inclined to forget on that account all the social differences between the individuals making up the nation. On the other hand, a person who thinks *nationally* —even when he recognizes the existence of a common character created in the environment of common conditions of production— realizes nevertheless, first of all, that it is rather difficult to define this national character and the national-cultural type, for they are too intangible; and secondly, that within every nationality the separate characteristics of each class appear much more acutely and can be more readily discerned.

Finally, a person who thinks *nationalistically* believes that all members of society should be nationalists; he conceives of nationalism and patriotism as a holy imperative. But a person who thinks *nationally* does not consider it "traitorous" when he discovers that certain classes of the society are wholly free of nationalism, while others understand nationalism each in their own way, in relation to their respective class interests.

IX. THE NATIONALISM OF THE GREAT LAND OWNERS

The great land owners are the class which lives from land-rent. Naturally, their income consists in part also of interest derived from their capital. But land-rent is the principal source of their income. As a result they are mainly concerned about the immobile things, about their estates. They cherish the territory only in as much as it represents a piece of land from which they can exact their rents. Their nationalism is inherently a land nationalism. It is affected only when some other neighboring people attempt to annex the soil itself; for should such conquest be achieved, the land owners would lose their source of income. The land owners are not concerned with the fact that the territory also serves other classes of their nation as a national market, and it would hardly trouble them at all should a foreign people, foreign capitalists, attempt to wrest from their own bourgeoisie the domestic market offered by the territory. However, other incidental interests oblige them to give some attention to those matters.

For the land owning class occupies a transitory position in the history of social development. This class is rapidly becoming capitalistic and it is therefore beginning to find itself in a new relationship to the national wealth and to the instruments of national preservation; the land owning class is but a remnant of the feudal system, whose death knell social progress has long since sounded. The land owners have lost their economic power, and they are losing more and more of the political power which they still retain in some countries. It is inevitable that these changes should affect their nationalism, the nature of which is utterly chauvinistic. In some backward countries, where the land owning class has to a certain extent preserved its identity, it still exerts a greater influence on the State than do other classes.

One must bear in mind, that the present-day State is a class State. The respective interests of the various groups in the State are different. Naturally then, not all groups in the society are in a position of power. The State regime is intimately associated with some one class. As far as possible, however, the State strives to gain the confidence of the whole population, irrespective of class. In order to exert its influence the state pretends to steer a middle course between all classes. It is possible for it to maintin such a position, however, only when it can raise some issue which rises above all antagonisms within the social organism. This issue is nationalism.

And wherever they still retain the political power in their hands, the big land owners do precisely that. We frequently behold the following phenomenon: the same adherents to feudalism, who formerly had no conception whatsoever of "national ideals" or "the national mission", are now the first to shout these slogans. In reality, though, they acquired this idea from their former enemy, the bourgeoisie. This phenomenon can be explained only by the fact that the land owners are forced to pretend to a position *above* all classes. In order not to awaken any dissatisfaction in the subordinated populace, they ferret out everything that has any semblance of national value and go to all extremes to preserve it, thus pulling the wool over the eyes of the populace. That also is why the big land owners are so sensitive about the national honor, and are so exaggeratedly finicky in a nationalist sense. They are, so to say, the permanent powder-barrel of nationalism, and are always ready to explode on the slightest provocation.

The nationalism of the land owning class has another characteristic; this class has preserved the whole store of traditions amassed during the feudal period. And although nationalism itself had nothing in common with traditionalism when it made its first appearance, the land owners nevertheless enmesh it in the toils of old traditions.*

In the countries where the bourgeoisie is in control, and the land owners are powerless, the traditional nationalism of the latter class manifests itself clearly, as does also the reactionary and barren nature of its tactics. Sensing their imminent doom, they strew their grievous path with not less grievous scandals. This is the type of "nationalism" we find in France. The number of scandals is an inverse index to the number of days which this class still has to live.

X. THE NATIONALISM OF THE GREAT BOURGEOISIE

As we stated previously, the great bourgeoisie is independent of traditions. We can safely say, that if it is nationalistic, its nationalism is in no way related to traditions. It is but mildly concerned about the internal national market and with the national language which prevails in this market. The great bourgeoisie has long ago transcended the narrow bounds of the national market and the national language, and now stalks head-up across the great expansive world-market. In the disposition of its wares, the great bourgeoisie is not confined to the environment of the national language, for it has no direct relations with the consumer. The consumer speaks not with the manufacturer but with the dealer. The manufacturer himself need know no other language save his mother tongue, for he can employ correspondents and agents to conduct his business with foreign firms. And the financier, the money capitalist, whose clutches are on the whole course of modern economy, has even less contact with the domestic market than has the great industrialist.

---

* Because the great land owners are in the limelight of political life, there are some observers who conclude that nationalism and traditionalism are synonomous. Such a superficial conclusion does no honor to those who believe in nationalism. Only in the case of the great land owners do nationalism and traditionalism have an identical meaning. Their nationalism is *aggressive* in foreign policy and is the chief supporter of militarism. Their nationalism is *conservative* in domestic policy and is the chief supporter of the *status quo*. These nationalists label as "anti-national" and "traitorous" every movement of the oppressed. They wish to obscure every difference between the "internal" and "external" enemy, pointing to the first as an ally of the second.

The great bourgeoisie, therefore, is not concerned over domestic national politics. It strives for the world-supremacy of its national capital. It seeks to crowd all "foreign" capital out of the world-market, so that its own profits may be the greater. For this purpose, a strong navy and a well-trained army are essential. Such "noble" matters as "the national cultural spirit" and so on seldom interest it. It is much more interested in bayonets, shrapnel, and battleships. It has but little concern for such things as language and national education. It is much more concerned with the budget of the army and navy. But in order to have its say about the latter, it must gain political power; and the real basis for political power is, of course, the territory.

*Thus, the territory and its boundaries are of value to the great bourgeoisie as a base from which to capture the world-market.**

XI. THE NATIONALISM OF THE MIDDLE-CLASS

Unlike the land owning class, the middle-class regards the territory as something more valuable than a piece of land. *The territory serves this class in the capacity of a consumers' market.* The boundaries of this market coincide with the bounds wherein the national language prevails. The immediate buyer must speak the same language as the immediate seller. Thus, it follows that the middle-class is interested in having more and more people speak its language. The nationalism of this bourgeois group draws its whole sustenance from the interests of the national market. Therefore, this element is the mainstay, though not the sole supporter, of the political suppression of foreign languages. For to this class the essence of nationalism lies in language and all that flows from language, such as traditional culture, education, and so on.

It sometimes happens that the great land owners of a certain ruling nation desire to annex the land on which an oppressed people lives. They therefore strive to assimilate these inhabitants. They assume the guise of culture crusaders, crush the language of

---

* Among the intelligentzia there are almost no ideologists who concern themselves with the formulation of a *weltanschauung* for the great bourgeoisie. Only the daily press caters to the great bourgeoisie—for the press is not too particular in its choice of chauvinistic propaganda.

the nation which they desire to assimilate, and strangle its education. The middle-class is always the readiest partner of the land owners in this noble task, for the former presumes to be the devoted "knights" of the "culture crusade". To be convinced thereof one has but to remember the assimilatory *politik* in Prussian Silesia.

The ideologists of this class employ the same phraseology as the land owners. Incidentally, they also have another similarity to the latter: they occupy the middle position between the two main classes of society; and they, too, pretend to stand above the class struggle.

In reality they fear every social upheaval, for it might signify their death warrant. They sanctify orderliness, and mortally fear revolution. They cling fast to whatever property is still in their possession, and tremble lest that too be wrested from them. They are therefore the bulwark of "law and order", and are ready to defend with fire and sword the existing order of things. In general, they are vexatious, as might be expected from an element which is on the down-grade to pauperization, and which cannot fight for its future or face it squarely. Everything that is in whatever degree unusual or strange, appears to them as rebellious, traitorous and subversive. Their poor dull wit will not permit them to rise above their drab possessiveness.

All this has provided excellent soil for various nationalistic prejudices and superstitions. The poor head of the petty bourgeoisie is filled only with "we" and "they", "native" and "alien". Incidentally, the members of this class are always at one another's throat because of mutual competition, and there is no common meeting ground whereon their class interests may converge. They are not capable of developing a *class* consciousness, and therefore their *national* self-consciousness emerges with greater vigor. This group also creates it own "ideals". But this is not the place to dwell upon them.

What is of importance to us is the fact that the middle-class, being unequivocally interested in the protection of its domestic market, indirectly supports the chauvinistic domestic and foreign policy of the land owners. · This wretched type of nationalism plays no independent role; and when it loses its strong ally, the land owning class, it will completely die out. The more rapidly this propertied class becomes declassed, and its members are distributed among the proletariat and the great bourgeoisie, the quicker will this type of nationalism become extinct.

Some elements of the middle-class and petty bourgeoisie who are concerned with the national culture—teachers, historians, writers, artists, etc.—are inclined to a peaceful form of honorable, respectable, "cultural" nationalism. They place great hope in the recognition of the right of every nation to its own self-determination. They have no desire to destroy every other nationality and do not wish to swallow anyone. In domestic politics they are liberal, frequently even radical, and they maintain the same position in international politics. And yet, they do love the "native" more than the "alien"; somehow, the traditions of their own culture are dearer to their hearts. They are not nationalistically "snobbish", but they feel that they must protect their national prestige.

The more intellectually developed and progressive elements do not even deny the class structure of society. Nevertheless, they are not concerned therewith, because in general, they loath conflict and disorder. They have only managed to preserve in a petrified state the earlier sentiment of pre-revolutionary, bourgeois nationalism, with its old national-democratic traditions.*

Until now we have considered the nationalism of the ruling classes. As we have seen, it is multi-colored. Naturally, it is difficult to distinguish between the national ideals of the landlords, of the great bourgeoisie, and those of the middle and petty bourgeoisie. It is even difficult to determine the economic line of demarcation between these classes. There are innumerable transitional forms which make one type of nationalism approximate another, and to the unexperienced eye they all seem to fuse into one whole. However, the materialistic conception of history teaches us to dis-

---

* We have already pointed out that this type of nationalism is called "spiritual" nationalism, which should not be confused, however, with the pseudo "spiritual" nationalism of the great landlords. The landlords and their allies merely shout phrases and are not concerned with the content or meaning of their spiritual fictions. Such is not the case with the middle class. This class attempts to understand its "spiritual" nationalism, though its approach is essentially dogmatic.

tinguish in all cases between the basic characteristics and their variations, and always to resolve into its original elements what may superficially appear to be one compounded whole.

XII. THE NATIONALISM OF THE PROLETARIAT ,

It is false to accept the widespread fallacy which claims that the proletariat has no relation with the national wealth and therefore also has no national feelings and interests. No class in a society is outside the conditions of production of that society. It therefore follows that the state of these conditions of production is of vital concern also to the proletariat. Let us forget the flippant and dangerous conceptions about this question usually entertained by the progressive elements. If the general base and reservoir of the conditions of production, the territory, is valuable to the land owning class for its land-resources and as a base for its political power; if this territory serves the bourgeoisie as a base for the capture of the world-market, and serves the middle-classes of society as the consumers' market; and if the organs of preservation of the national wealth have for each of the above-mentioned classes their respective worth, then *the territory also has its value for the proletariat, i. e., as a place in which to work.* The organs of preservation, too, are of special value to the proletariat.

Were the worker a thousand times over a "god in human form", as certain demagogic agitators try to convince us, he must still eat, and must therefore work. Unemployment is not a very pleasant thing for him. Even Marx recognized the fact that there exists a degree of competition among workers for the place of work when he said, "The great industry masses together in a single place a crowd of people unknown to each other. Competition divides their interests . Thus combination has always a double end, that of eliminating competition among themselves while enabling them to make a general competition against the capitalist."[6] Among certain uncultured workers, this competition

---

6 *The Poverty of Philosophy*, p. 188.

often results in physical conflict between urban workers and laborers from other communities even of the same country. More cultured workers have a higher, finer concept of competition; they will not engage in physical conflict with workers from the provinces. But when there is a great influx of immigrants from other countries who beat down the wage-scale, then the interests of even the most cultured workers are affected, and they can no longer remain indifferent.

Some individuals whose abilities to think have been stultified by partisan phraseology and vulgar agitation will protest that we are desecrating the holiest of tenets when we demonstrate the verity of our above contentions through facts. What more convincing proof is needed than the fact that Volmar's *Munchener Zeitung,* for example, is always quick to raise an alarm when Bavarian private or governmental contractors hire Italian instead of German workers. And Volmar is at the head of a great party. To be sure, he is a revisionist; but nevertheless, at the party conference in Jena, he is a very esteemed comrade. Or consider, for instance, the policy of the Australian Government as regards immigrants. It is manifestly clear that the immigration restrictions there are not in the interests of capital, but of the workers. Nor is it necessary to go into the attitude and behavior of the American proletariat toward the Chinese coolie; the horrible facts of pogroms perpetrated on Chinese workers are sufficiently well known to the reader. And is not the fact that this accursed problem is by no means alien to the proletariat further manifested by the growing interest of party leaders in the national question? The most vital way in which the national question affects the worker is through the territory as *place of employment.*

There are also other workers' interests related thereto. These are the cultural interests of language, education, and literature. All these are valuable as media for the development of class consciousness. However, class consciousness is really nurtured not so much by the "culture" as by the processes of the class struggle itself.

But the class struggle can take place only where the worker toils, i. e., where he has already occupied a certain work-place. The weaker his status at this position, the less ground he has for a systematic struggle. As long as the worker does not occupy a definite position, he can wage no struggle. It is, therefore, in his own interests to protect his position.

From whatever angle we may approach the national question to determine the scope of its existence for the proletariat, even if we should primarily approach it only by way of his cultural needs, we must always arrive finally at its material basis, i. e., at the question of the place of employment and the strategic base of struggle which the territory represents for the proletariat.

The problem of employment has not only a class aspect, but also a national aspect. Thus, the English worker must protect his place of employment not only against the profit considerations of the capitalist, but also against the immigrant worker. It follows therefore, that as long as the national work-place is not secure, the national problem overshadows the labor problem. And as long as the workers of a given nation have not yet made their place of employment secure, the problem of work is of far greater importance to them than the issues of the class struggle.

In consequence we have the following results: first, the masses which are just becoming proletarized and are looking for work are generally incapable of becoming readily class conscious, and are therefore only nationalistically inclined; secondly, the class consciousness of even the cultural proletariat is greatly obscured by its national consciousness whenever the proletariat is forced to defend its national place of employment. Thus, the constant immigration of new workers into England and the United States of America is a threat to the security of the places of employment of the English and American workers, and as a result the national consciousness of the latter is heightened, deterring the development of their class consciousness. This is one of the main reasons why the labor movements in those countries have not yet developed beyond their present trade-unionist framework.

The orthodox Marxist dogmatists have not as yet been able to explain this extraordinary backwardness of the English and American proletariat. Nor can they beg the question.

This fact does not bear on the *relations of production,* and therefore they cannot explain it. In order to explain this fact, we must analyze the *conditions* of the English and American production respectively. The national question must be considered more deeply and honestly; it is necessary once and for all to break with unfounded prejudices. We must understand that class consciousness cannot develop normally unless the national problem, in whatever form it may exist, has been solved.

Those students who ignore the role of the *conditions of production* and devote themselves exclusively to a study of the *relations of production* are not in a position to understand the national question. Therefore, the following contradictions in the capitalistic economy must forever remain for them an insoluble mystery. They cannot explain why, on the one hand, the capitalistic system appears as international, and destroys all boundaries between tribes and peoples and uproots all traditions, while on the other hand, it is itself instrumental in the intensification of the international struggle and heightens national self-consciousness. How is it possible that at the same time when the various societies are drawn economically closer together, and their respective and relative distinctions are modified, the national problem is intensified and the various national movements develop? Unless the materialist can answer this problem, he must entangle himself in a mesh of contradictions.

Kautsky made several attempts to explain this problem, but in so doing he deserted his materialistic concepts. Nevertheless, we must admit, that in a recent series of articles on the national question, he gradually approaches the theory which we have here developed. And according to this theory, the solution of the above-mentioned riddle is quite clear. If we take into consideration the fact that humanity is divided into groups of production, then we will understand that the inherent striving of capital to expand must result in friction between these relatively distinct groups. One aspect of the above mentioned contradiction is the cause; the other is the effect. This is one of the many contradictions with which modern society is burdened.

We have previously stated that the national question, and also the conversion of the various peoples into nations, is a result of the capitalistic mode of production. It might therefore be presumed that the *national struggle* must disappear together with the *class struggle*. But this conclusion would be too far-fetched.

Every serious student must consider as even more far-fetched and hazardous the contention that *national differences* will be eradicated simultaneously with the eradication of *class differences*. We do not wish to dwell on this question, for we consider it inconsequential to do so. Furthermore, no definite factual answer can be given at the present moment. As far as we are concerned, the national question is a concrete reality today, and we cannot prophesy what will be the condition a hundred years hence— whether the nations will remain intact, or whether they will fuse with one another.

XIII. SUMMARY

During the feudal period the various social groups, each of which was engaged in the struggle for existence under a different and relatively distinct complex of conditions of production, emerged as separate *peoples*. The physiognomy and character of each people have their relatively distinct qualities.

But the feudal period also gave birth to capitalism, in consequence whereof there soon appeared the following twofold material, socio-economic contradictions in the current system of production: on the one hand, because of the higher degree of their development, the forces of production were no longer compatible with the ossified feudal *relations of production;* and on the other hand, the forces of production which were affected by the development of capitalism were no longer compatible with the petrified system of the *conditions of production*. For the feudal system had disintegrated the people and their territories by the innumerable barriers erected by its baronetcies, thus hindering the development of capitalism.

As a rule, every disparity between the *forces of production* and the *relations of production* results in a social problem which can be solved only by the emancipation of the oppressed *class*. This type of contradiction, which appeared at the beginning of capitalism, was felt most severely by the bourgeoisie; and the latter, therefore, took the initiative to wipe it out. It succeeded in achieving this purpose through the French Revolution.

Every disparity of the second sort, i. e., between the *forces of production* while they are in the process of development, and the *conditions of production* which hinder this development, results in a *national* problem which can be solved only by the emancipation of the oppressed *nation*. This type of contradiction, which manifested itself at the very beginning of capitalism, was felt by all classes of the society of that day. Therefore, all oppressed classes at the time of the French Revolution were imbued with the feeling of a common nationality which was being oppressed by the "upper-strata". It was generally believed that there was a common national harmony of interests, and only the ruling classes of that period were excluded from this ostensible harmony. *Nationalism* then assumed the aspects under which we understand it today.

The development of the capitalistic economy created the basis for the feeling of kinship which we call *nationalism*. This development transformed the former *peoples* into the modern *nations*.

Nationalism, therefore, first became manifest not in the external politics of the ruling classes, but in the internal struggle of the oppressed classes. Nationalism, in the present sense of the word, was carried over to the sphere of external politics only later, when the national question made its full appearance.

Soon after the newly developed capitalism had superseded feudalism, it became evident that the expansion of its forces of production was impeded not only by the state of the conditions of production *within* the relatively separated societies, but also by the relative distinctness of the various conditions of production. Striving naturally to expand the sphere of its conditions of production, every society comes into conflict with neighboring societies which offer it resistance. Thus, the development of the capitalistic system places the *national question* in the limelight.

The root of the national question lies in the conflict between relatively distinct socio-economic organisms. The national question is manifest in international competition.

International competition is not a result of some despotic, egotistic trait of the ruling classes. Rather it is a result of the unconditional need of the capitalistic economies to expand while they are developing.

This competition develops in predisposed individuals, who are concerned thereby, certain sentiments and emotions. And although the sentiments and emotions are deeply enrooted in economic life, it seems to those people who are imbued with them that they are in no way related to the material life. They fail to see the deep economic basis of these feelings, and they therefore lose every possibility of understanding their own motives, which to them appear holy and far removed from the materialistic.

From these sentiments arise multifarious fantastic nationalistic ideologies, which are prone to obscure the national consciousness and emphasize the antagonism between the latter and class consciousness.

The capitalistic system engendered the national question not merely for the bourgeoisie alone but also for all other classes of society, since each class is in one way or another affected by this international competition. Fundamentally, the territory is of value to them all as the base of the conditions of production.

Among *free* nations who oppress no one and are not oppressed themselves, nationalism is but so much conserved energy. However, at the first opportunity this energy becomes kinetic. The *ruling classes* are the first to lose their balance. They are always imbued with the desire to capture the world market or to expand the domestic market. Once this equilibrium is destroyed, hitherto latent nationalistic feelings suddenly flare forth in an all-consuming conflagration. The nationalism which arises from the desire to expand the market is aggressive and of a consciously bellicose nature. The weapons employed are the conquest of foreign territory and the forced assimilation of national minorities.

The striving of the proletariat to expand its labor market and work-sphere cannot, however, express itself in the form of a policy of conquest. The proletariat and the proletarizing masses have no direct influence on international politics. The only means of expanding the work-sphere is the peaceful emigration to foreign lands.

The emigrating masses, which are wandering all over the world in search of work, introduce no new national policy. The migrating worker, who has been expelled from his sphere of conditions of production, feels no deep ties for his former home. And were it not for external circumstances such as the traditions· of his early education or his blood relationship with those who have remained at home, the emigrating worker would not even manifest those weak sentiments for his fatherland to which he sometimes gives expression.

The situation is quite different, however, as regards the proletariat of those countries to which the wanderers emigrate. In their case, there is manifested an endeavor to retain for themselves the work-places, and this is accompanied by an intensified national self-consciousness. In the case of the proletariat of a free nation, this latter phenomenon assumes the character of a militant defensive against the "pernicious foreigner". This is evidenced to an even greater degree by the attitude and sentiment of the proletarizing masses, because they are interested even more than the proletariat in retaining the integrity of their national work-place. We see, therefore, that as far as the proletariat is concerned, the question of emigration and immigration is fundamentally connected with the national question. Thus the localistic character of proletarian nationalism is made clear. We see, too, that in the case of free nations which are not oppressed, nationalism has multifarious forms because it depends on who is exhibiting it—the ruling class or the oppressed classes.

*   *   *

The nationalism of oppressed nationalities assumes a more peculiar form. The system of production of oppressed nationalities is always subject to abnormal conditions. The conditions of production are abnormal when, as we stated above, a nation is deprived of its territory and its organs of national preservation (such as political independence and the freedom of language and cultural development) or when it is hindered in the fullest enjoyment of these. Such abnormal conditions tend to harmonize the interests of all members of a nation. This external pressure not only lessens and dissipates the influence of the conditions of production but also hinders the development of the relations of production and the class struggle, because the normal development of the mode of production is hampered. Class antagonisms are abnormally mollified while national solidarity exerts a more potent influence.

Not only the special interests of every class are affected by this external pressure, but also every individual in the nationality feels it and understands that this pressure is of national moment. It derives from a foreign nation and is directed against his own nationality as such. Under such circumstances, the mother tongue, for example, assumes greater significance than that of a mere means to preserve the local market. When the freedom of the language is curtailed, the oppressed person becomes all the more attached thereto. In other words, the national question of an oppressed people is detached from its association with the material conditions of production. The cultural aspects assume an independent significance, and all the members of the nation become interested in *national self-determination.*

In the course of the struggle for national emancipation, however, the class structure and class psychology manifest themselves. One can usually identify the middle and petty bourgeoisie, and above all the clerical elements and land owners, as those groups of an oppressed nation which are vitally concerned with traditions. The dabblers in national education, in national literature (teachers, writers, etc.), usually garb their traditionalism in national hues. The chief protagonists of national emancipation, however, are always the progressive elements of the masses and the intelligentzia. Where these latter elements are sufficiently developed and have already freed themselves from the bonds of traditionalism, their nationalism assumes a purer character. Fundamentally the emancipation process is not nationalistic but national; and among such progressive elements of oppressed nations there develops a genuine nationalism which does not aspire to the preservation of traditions, which will not exaggerate them, which has no illusions about the ostensible oneness of the nation, which comprehends clearly the class structure of society, and which does not seek to confuse anyone's real class interests. It is the aim of this type of nationalism to achieve the real emancipation of the nation through the normalization of its conditions and relations of production.

Genuine nationalism in no way obscures class-consciousness. It manifests itself only among the progressive elements of oppressed nations. The genuine nationalism of the progressive class—of the organized revolutionary proletariat of an oppressed nation—expresses itself in the strong, clearly-defined demands embodied in its minimum program. It is the purpose of these demands to assure the nation normal conditions of production, and to assure the proletariat of a normal base for its labor and class struggle.

Once this goal has been achieved, the purpose of genuine nationalism has been realized. Instead of the former solidarity of national interests engendered by certain emancipation processes—a forced and abnormal solidarity—there now appears in a new and clear form a healthy class structure and a sound class struggle.

SECTION THREE

HISTORICAL AND DOCUMENTARY

A. LIEBERMAN: FATHER OF JEWISH
SOCIALISM[1]

F ORTY YEARS have elapsed since the Jewish socialist press made its first appearance. The Hebrew journal, *Haemet* ("Truth"), the first Jewish socialist publication, made its debut in Vienna in May, 1877. The journal and its publisher and editor, Aaron Lieberman, are among the most interesting and extraordinary phenomena of modern Jewish history. To understand the first Jewish socialist publication and the period in which it originated, we must first make a study of the man Lieberman, who truly deserves the title of "Father of Jewish Socialism".

Aaron Shmuel Lieberman (later known as Arthur Freeman, his pennames being *Bar Drora* and *Daniel Ish Chamudot*) was born about 1848 in the town of Luna in the province of Grodno, Russia. He received his education in the larger cities of Sowolke and Vilna. Independently, both he and his father (a Hebrew teacher tutoring in the homes of the well-to-do) fell under the influence of the *Haskala*.[2] Thus the young Lieberman was spared the conflict which the freethinking youth of that period had with their pious parents. In his father's home, Lieberman obtained a knowledge of the Hebrew language and literature. Throughout his life he was a fanatical devotee of Hebrew, the language of his socialist propaganda.

In accordance with the Jewish custom of those days, the future nihilist married at an early age and was already a father when he entered the Rabbinical school in Vilna. In the 70's the Rabbinical school in Vilna was a center of enlightened, liberal, and even revolutionary thought. Several pupils were aware of the socialist movement among the Russian intelligentzia; and two, Aaron Lieberman and his younger friend, Zundelovitch (born in 1854), were active socialist propagandists.

1873-78 were important years in the Russian revolutionary movement. That period marked the commencement of the interesting movement of "mingling with the people". The social-revolutionary intelligentzia learned manual trades, dressed as peasants and workers, and mingled with the masses, thereby spreading revolutionary ideas. The spiritual leader of this movement was P. Lavrov who published a fortnightly journal, *V'Period*, which was printed in London and illegally circulated in Russia. Jewish youth was not unaffected by this propaganda which gave birth to the *Chorni Peredial*[3] and the terrorist activities of the *Narodnaya Volya*.[3] Among the more prominent Jewish names actively identified with the underground movement of the 70's were the Levinthal brothers, Axelrod, Aronson, Lazare Goldenberg, Goldstein, L. Zuckerman, Jessie Helfman, and Gotz. Jewish socialist writers such as M. Vintchevsky, L. Cantor,

---

1 Written in 1917.

2 See footnote 3, p. 90.

3 Non-Marxian mass movements embracing peasants and workers which merged with other groups to form the Socialist-Revolutionary Party.

Yahalal, and M. Lilienblum appeared on the scene. The pogroms disillusioned the last three in the revolutionary ideals, and they joined the *Chibat Zion*[4] movement.

Zundelovitch and Lieberman were original. Whereas other Jewish socialists agitated among the Gentile workers or were contented merely with writing Hebrew poetry on social problems, the two young students of the Rabbinical school attempted to win the Jewish masses over to Socialism. This was a unique approach, for at that time not only Gentile, but also Jewish intellectuals negated the economic role of the Jewish masses. Jews are not fit for productive work, they claimed; they are by nature brokers, merchants, money-lenders and "parasites"—in short, an element that is not susceptible to socialist propaganda. Zundelovitch and Lieberman were more intimately acquainted with the Jewish masses. Being themselves proletarians and raised among the Jewish proletariat, they knew that the Jewish masses lived by their own toil—that the Jewish people was not a people of exploiters and parasites, but a people of exploited and oppressed workers.

They therefore devoted themselves to the dissemination of socialist propaganda among the Jewish masses. With this aim in view, Zundelovitch organized a group of young Jewish intellectuals in Vilna. But he was soon drawn into the Russian political movement and left for St. Petersburg. There he established an illegal press, fell into the clutches of the Czarist police, and was sentenced to Siberia. He was not freed until three years later, during the Revolution of 1905.

Lieberman made a timely escape from the Czarist police by fleeing abroad where he devoted the rest of his short life to spreading socialist propaganda among Jews.

Immediately after his escape Lieberman organized in Berlin the "Jewish Group of the Internationale", consisting of Jewish socialist emigres from Russia. He then left for London where he worked on Lavrov's *V'Period*. He also organized a Jewish socialist society—the first in Jewish history. The membership was a comparatively large one for that period, totalling thirty-seven, mostly workers. Lieberman was also a worker, earning his living as a lithographer.

The records of this society are to be found in the archives of the Foreign Committee of the *Bund* at Geneva. Lieberman was the secretary of the branch. The title page reads:

RECORD OF THE SOCIETY OF THE HEBREW SOCIALISTS OF LONDON

Founded Iyar 26, in the Year 5636, May 20, 1876

The record contains the program of the society, written in Hebrew as well as in Yiddish (although the minutes of sessions were in Yiddish). The first Jewish socialist program states in part:

We are convinced that the present order, which holds sway everywhere, is ruthless and unjust. The capitalists, rulers, and clergy have taken unto themselves all human rights and property and have enslaved the working masses through the power of their money.

As long as private ownership continues, economic misery shall not cease; as long as humanity is divided into nations and classes, hatred will not cease; as long as the clergy continues to sway the emotions of the people, religious hatred will continue.

The liberation of humanity can be achieved only through a basic change in the political, economic, and social relations—by uprooting

4 See footnote 9, p. 97.

the existing order and constructing in its place a new society based on socialism which will abolish the injustice and domination of capital, which will eradicate the parasites and the system of "mine" and "thine".

We Jews are an integral part of humanity and cannot be liberated except through the liberation of all humanity.

The liberation of humanity from misery and slavery can be achieved by the workers only if they unite in a struggle against their despoilers, destroy the existing order, and replace it by the reign of labor, justice, freedom, and the fraternity of mankind.

The workers of Europe and America have united in various societies to achieve their aim and are preparing for a revolution, for the establishment of the reign of labor socialism (*Socializmus Laavoda* in the Hebrew text). Therefore, we, the children of Israel, have decided to affiliate ourselves with this noble Alliance of Labor.

This program was written by Lieberman and was unanimously accepted by the society.

The society existed seven months, disbanding with Lieberman's departure from London.

During his stay in London, Lieberman published the first socialist proclamation in Hebrew. Commencing with *el shlomei bachurei yisrael* ("To the intelligent youth of Israel"), he appealed to the youth to devote their energy to the public welfare and participate in the struggle for the emancipation of the working masses of all peoples. In a biblical style he portrays the awakening of the Jewish masses and their struggle against their Jewish exploiters. The Jewish people will soon recognize their enemies and will exclaim:

Thus have your sins been visited upon us; your crimes have caused us sorrow. You have brought upon us the anger of the sword and the crash of thunder and lightning. Your sin has inflamed against us the hatred of the people; your treacherous hand has carried a blaze of religious hatred against us. Sharpened swords have been cast at us and have pierced through the bodies of thousands of our brethren. You have humiliated our people. Your deceit in trade has branded the Jewish people, the very same people whom your plundering has suppressed and tortured, to a much greater extent than all other evildoers on earth.

This proclamation was signed by the "Loyal Volunteers of the People of the House of Israel". The proclamation showed a deep love for the Jewish people and for humanity. The opening of the proclamation was: "We, the friends of the Jewish people and of all the suffering masses . . ."

After his departure from London, Lieberman settled in Vienna where he became acquainted with the conservative and nationalist publicist, Peretz Smolenskin, and for a short time was a contributor to the latter's periodical, *Hashachar* ("Dawn"). But he soon went his own way; and in May, 1876, he founded *Haemet,* the first Jewish socialist organ. Although Lieberman cloaked his writings in metaphors to escape Czarist censors, *Haemet* did not have a long life; the Vienna authorities shut it down after the third issue and arrested its editor. He was extradited by the Prussian police and was tried in Berlin with two other Russo-Jewish socialists (Hurwich and Aaronson, a brother-in-law of Eduard Bernstein).

Lieberman was sentenced to prison (according to some, for fifteen months; according to others, for nine months) and was not freed until January, 1880. All in all, Lieberman spent two years in the prison of Vienna, in continuous danger of being handed over to the Russian authorities.

Prison life affected Lieberman's mental balance. A tragic love affair in London and America, where he went after his liberation, did not help restore it. On November 18, 1880, the father of Jewish socialism committed suicide in Syracuse, New York. His last written words were: "Long live the world! He who finds only misery and pain is doomed to die. Do not accuse me ere you have put yourself in my position."

Only three small issues of *Haemet* appeared. It contained insufficient material from which to glean the *weltanschauung* of that period in general and of Aaron Lieberman in particular. We have not even a clear idea as to which articles were written by Lieberman and which by his colleagues, for Lieberman refused to publish the names of the authors with the articles. Without doubt the prospectus as well as the leading articles and notices were Lieberman's own products.

It seems that Lieberman was far from scientific socialism and Marx and Engels. Marxian literature forty years ago was little known and even less recognized. The socialism of *Haemet* has an idealistic and scholarly character. Lieberman's prospectus in *Haemet* stated:

The darkness which to this day governs the minds of the majority is the father of all evil. It has penetrated to the base of society and has shattered its foundation. Darkness has paved the road for deceit. With its aid brutal rulers have enslaved the people . . . The people knows endless pain . . . and is degenerating through ignorance. The people cannot choose between evil and good. Only truth can bring enlightenment to the human mind and distinguish good from evil.

Champions for justice are to be found among all peoples. Only our Jewish literature has lacked *emet* (truth); for since prophecy ceased among the Jewish people, our writers have ceased to take an interest in the miserable life and needs of the people.

Characteristic of Lieberman was his uncritical assumption that the Jews understood Hebrew.

The outstanding theoretical work in *Haemet* was Lieberman's "The Struggle for Existence and Its Relation to the Life of Society" (the leading article of the second number). He concluded that the struggle for existence was forcing humanity to unite into one society and that "solidarity is the best weapon in the struggle of life".

The sketches and poetry of *Haemet* are replete with socialist thoughts and sentiments. A few articles, such as the leading article in the first number, dealt with the Jews, including those of Hungary and London.

Immediately after Lieberman's death, J. A. Trivaush in his novel, *Dor Tahapuchot* ("The Confused Generation"), pictured his hero Aaron Lieberman in the role of "Frank". He knew him intimately and portrayed him as a man of inner contradictions. On one hand he was a nihilist, discrediting the past and denying the right of existence of all nations, including the Jewish; on the other hand, he was a fanatical Hebraist and lover of the Jewish people. Morris Vintchevsky, his personal friend, in his excellent "Memoirs", pictured Lieberman as stormy, paradoxical, and artistic.

A. LIEBERMAN173

The documents of the founder of Jewish socialism reveal in him a deep conflict. He denied the existence of a Jewish people, while elsewhere he expressed almost Zionist thoughts. S. L. Zitron (in *Hed Hazman*) and M. K. (in *Hashiloach*) relate that in his long discussions with Peretz Smolenskin, Lieberman "negated the historic past and dismissed the national problem". Lieberman's leading article in the first number of *Haemet,* devoted to the Jewish problem, categorically denied the existence of a Jewish people, as may be seen from the following: "We Jews do not possess a culture of our own which differentiates and isolates us from the nations among whom we live . . . Any bond which may ever have existed between us has long been torn asunder."

Thus wrote an author *who spoke to Jews in the name of Jews in the ancient Hebrew tongue* which for centuries served as the cultural tie of our scattered people!

The previously mentioned records of the London society illuminate a different characteristic of Lieberman. The minutes of the tenth meeting, held on the second of Ab, 1876, contain a motion of Lieberman that the next meeting, which would have been held on the ninth of Ab, be postponed.

This move was opposed by George Saper, who said, "We socialists are not interested in *Tisha B'Ab*. We have renounced ancient tradition . . . We are interested in the equality of humanity."

To this Lieberman replied, "At the present time *Tisha B'Ab* has the same significance for us Jewish socialists as it has for all Jews; for as long as the social revolution has not taken place, political freedom is of prime importance to every people. To the Jewish people it is of the utmost importance. On this day we lost our independence for which our people has mourned for the past 1,800 years." The society agreed to Lieberman's proposal and postponed the meeting.

Lieberman's cosmopolitanism came from the prevailing belief of the socialists of all nations that they were on the eve of the social revolution. Lieberman refused to publish advertisements in his *Haemet*. Expecting the social revolution at any moment, Lieberman avoided anything that might identify socialism with the present order. He considered both nationalism and advertising to be capitalistic phenomena which might carry a bourgeois spirit into the labor movement.

The father of Jewish socialism did not succeed in creating harmony between his deep Jewish national instinct and his carefully construed socialist philosophy.

Lieberman's picture of the Russian martyrs published by M. Vintchevsky in the *Zukunft* (1909, p. 88) was an artistic achievement. Artistic tendencies were noticeable also in Lieberman's handwriting, preserved in the archive of the *Bund* in Geneva and in the New York Public Library. These writings reveal a soul full of beauty and artistry.

Lieberman's friend, Hurwich, relates a most unique incident in *Biloia*. He tells us that Lieberman presented a most extraordinary gift to his deified teacher, Lavrov. The gift was Lieberman's own hat, with the following note: "As it is impossible for me to send you my head, I send you my hat."

Lieberman's tragic inner struggles drove him to suicide. The father of Jewish socialism died before the advent of the Russian pogroms—they might have clarified his attitude to the Jewish problem.

THE JUBILEE OF THE JEWISH LABOR
MOVEMENT[1]

IT WILL BE twenty-five years in July since the Jewish workers in
Russia went out on their first mass strike and the Jewish labor movement began to assume a more or less planned and conscious character.
This was the first important step of the Jewish labor movement not only
because of the extent and the duration of the strike (all workers in Bialystok mills were on strike for two months) but also because of its wonderful
organization. These first steps towards organization of Jewish labor date
back to 1887, exactly ten years before the rise of the *Bund.*

Broadly speaking, the Jewish labor movement is not as young as is
commonly thought. In two years we shall celebrate the fiftieth anniversary
of the first known Jewish trade union. I mean the association of women's
clothing workers in Mohilev, organized in 1864. [This association was
described by S. Tatichev in the journal, *Promishlenost i Zdorovie,* (May,
1903); by Sarah Rabinowitch ("The Organization of the Jewish Proletariat", 1903); and by S. A. Margolin in *Voskhod* (May 1906).] However, the whole period between the organization of this labor association
and the rise of the *Bund* has not yet been thoroughly investigated. For
that reason I hope the reader will bear with me while I try to acquaint him
with at least the most important events of that period.

The Jewish labor movement in Russia is fifty years younger than the
Russian labor movement, yet it has had its interesting aspects from the
very beginning. The above-mentioned women's tailors association functioned not only as a regular fraternal organization, offering financial aid
or sick and death benefits to its members, but also led the struggle of the
workers against the employers. Naturally the' employers were very much
averse to the association, which had already a great influence among the
workers, and reported it to the authorities. Consequently the leaders of
the association suffered severely at the hands of the police. The strikes
which the association waged against the employers were very important,
not only because of the number of workers involved and the size of the
plants, but also because of the nature of their demands. The great
majority of Jewish workers were employed by small industrialists. It is
no wonder that the first steps toward labor organization were made in
the manual trades rather than in the large factories.

The first traces of economic struggle in Jewish industry appear in the
seventies. In 1875 some very interesting correspondence from the south-
west section of Russia was published in *V'Period* (illegal journal of the
celebrated Russian revolutionary socialist, P. Lavrov). There we have
descriptions of some of the unorganized strikes of Jewish workers in the
tobacco factories of Vilna and other cities. Due to the "conspiracy" laws,
the exact dates of the strikes were not given nor were the letters signed.

1Written in 1916.

We know now, however, that they came from the pen of one of the first Jewish socialists, A. Zundelovitch.

One finds very little information about the Jewish weavers of Bialystok in the first issue of the illegal *Bialystok Worker*. In its leading article (April, 1899) it says in part: "Who of the older weavers does not remember the terrible strikes that took place some decades ago? The 'rebels', as they were then called, threw a scare into the manufacturers and the master weavers." The writer tells us that during those strikes the workers quite often invoked terrorism, broke factory windows, and were responsible for similar disorders. Most of the strikes were of a defensive nature. They were called to combat oppressive measures instituted by the employers such as wage cuts, lengthening of the working day, fining the workers excessively, and harsh treatment of employees.

The *Rabotchia Dielo* (Nos. 4-5, part I, p. 34) gives us a description of a huge aggressive strike. It took place during the Russo-Turkish War of 1877-1878. The manufacturers were doing a booming business filling army orders and sending exports to Roumania. The workers demanded higher wages. After a three day strike they won. All the Bialystok workers participated in the strike: Jews (about 1,500), Germans, and Poles—involving a total of 15,000 workers.

All the above conflicts, however, belong to the pre-history of the Jewish labor movement, because the element of class consciousness and planned organization was lacking. In that distant past the movement was blindly groping. Even the Mohilev association of women's tailors had a strongly religious character. Like all the associations of that period it had, for example, its own Sefer Tora (Biblical Scroll) and met in the synagogue, but employers were rigidly excluded from membership.

With regard to the economic struggle, the history of the Jewish labor movement may be divided into short periods.

(1) The early period with which we have already dealt, in which the socialist ideology and the economic struggle of the workers existed in separate spheres. Both were weak and divided, with no point of contact between them. The workers occasionally went out on strike but they had no conception at all of socialism or class struggle. The few Jewish socialists of that time (with the exception of Zundelovitch) had not yet begun to think in terms of the class struggle. Socialism had not yet found the path to the Jewish workers and the latter did not know how to proceed towards a class conscious organization. This period lasted from the sixties to about 1889.

(2) The preparation period for a broad organization started in the Russian Pale of Settlement with the general strike of the Jewish weavers in Bialystok in 1887, and with the founding of the first small strike fund in Vilna in 1888. We can therefore consider 1887 as the beginning of the organized Jewish labor movement in the Pale. In the next decade the workers and the socialists sought and found each other.

(3) The economic and political organization began with the founding of the "General Jewish Workers' Alliance of Lithuania, Poland and Russia", the *Bund,* in September, 1897, and continued until 1901-1902. A new Jewish labor movement then appeared on the scene—the Poale Zion or Socialist Zionists. The *Bund* on its part ceased to rely solely on the economic struggle of the Jewish workers and assumed an outspoken political character.

(4) The period of political splits can be divided into two sub-periods: from 1901 or 1902 to the Revolution of 1905, and from the Revolution to 1907. The fifth period begins now, and it is not up to the historian to consider it; that is left to the party spokesman and publicist.

All this concerns only the Jewish workers in Russia. In the remaining countries with Jewish communities, the course of events, naturally, was different. It is interesting to note, however, that at the time that a broad movement bearing a clear-cut mass character began in Russia, a similar manifestation appeared in other Galut countries. The first large strike of Jewish tailors in New York occurred in 1886, and in 1889 ten thousand Jewish tailors went out on strike for the first time in London. The Polish socialists began to organize the Jewish proletariat of Galicia early in the nineties. In 1894 in Amsterdam, the first general strike of Jewish diamond workers broke out and resulted in the organization of the powerful Diamond Workers Union.

Although we have treated the beginnings of Jewish labor struggles in Russia before those in other countries, the almost simultaneous rise of broad mass movements in the other large Galut centers must be kept in mind. There is good reason for this development: the eighties and nineties were a period of world-wide economic recovery which contrasted markedly with the terrible crisis of the late seventies. Parallel with this upward swing was the growth of socialism throughout the world. In America (Chicago) huge labor disorders broke out during 1886, and in Europe the Socialist International was revived in 1889. Deeply significant events also took place in Jewish life: a powerful anti-Semitic agitation developed; emigration from Russia, Galicia, and Roumania to America, England, and Holland rose tremendously. The eighties and nineties were a period of blind groping, of universal uncertainty and dissatisfaction. Due to the common need for emigration, a living bond tended to unify the Jewish masses of the different countries.

World-wide horizons spread before them, and the national idea began to manifest itself. The fruit of proletarian thought from different countries was carried over imperceptible, spiritual paths from one end of the world to the other. Socialist ideas were brought from tyrannized Russia to free England and America. Filled there with a new content, they returned through London, Koenigsberg, and Vienna to the Ghettos of Galicia and Russia. A worker who had just gone on strike in New York could exchange his new impressions with a friend who would soon be striking in Bialystok or Vilna. His head full of vague longings, the Jewish worker set out on the long road. At all points enroute, through Austria, Germany, France, England and Holland, he came in contact with comrades from all countries, weaving a spiritual thread between east and west. In that way the seed of revolutionary thought was carried to the four corners of the world. The flow of migration spread the Jewish labor movement everywhere.

It is for that reason that the years 1886 (the first mass strike in New York), 1887 (Bialystok), and 1889 (London) bring back glorious memories not only for each country with Jewish communities, but also for the whole world, wherever there are exploited and wherever a Jewish worker struggles for a better life. If the self-appointed leaders of the Jewish labor movement had even the slightest conception of their own history, they would now clebrate, throughout the world, the twenty-fifth anniversary of the Jewish class conscious proletarian struggle in Russia.

In order that the reader may see why the Bialystok strike actually had the importance I ascribe to it, I shall outline the course of its events.

During the Russo-Turkish war of 1877, wages among the weavers rose greatly because of favorable market conditions and the pressure of a successful strike. This was a golden era; they earned from 10 to 15 rubles a week. Taking into consideration the low cost of living, this was a tremendous gain. (Living quarters cost one and a half rubles a month; a pound of meat was four or five kopeks.) Naturally there had to come an end to this golden era. A host of new workers were attracted to the trade; and on top of this, the manufacturers' booming business slumped after the war. Competition between the workers and the inexperience of the new hands forced wages down to such a low level, that in 1885-1886 the weavers had to adapt themselves to a starvation wage of from one to three rubles a week, working from 14 to 16 hours a day. At the same time rent and food prices rose. The workers had no choice but to go out on strike.

The strike was only against the master weavers, because their workers received the lowest wages, much less than even the factory weavers. All the two thousand Jewish workers who were employed by master weavers walked out.

The strike was organized on the following lines. The strike committee found it impossible to stop the whole trade at once, as it would have been difficult to raise the necessary funds for the support of such a large army of strikers. They therefore carried out a piece-meal stoppage. At any one time workers from only certain workshops were to stop, and the others who remained at work were to support the strikers. The discipline was exemplary; the complicated plan worked excellently. Workshops were stopped one after the other. As one group won and returned to work, others struck. A link in this strike chain lasted only a few days at the most, and the workers won everywhere.

The walk-out began in July, 1887. The governor of Grodno himself made a trip to Bialystok. He assembled all the workers and attempted to talk them into stopping the strike, but to no avail. The strike was won in September.

The socialist intelligentzia had no relationship whatsoever with the strike. Besides, it was not carrying on any socialist agitation in Bialystok at the time. In Vilna likewise, there was still not the necessary connection between the socialist propaganda of the intellectuals on the one hand and the economic struggle of the working masses on the other. Socialist propaganda in Vilna had been carried on since 1885, but the correct approach to the workers had not been found. It was only during 1893-1894 that the mutual search for each other by both parts of the socialist movement—the intellectuals and the workers—ended.

During these early years of groping, both sides made considerable progress. In 1887 there is record of only one strike of Jewish workers in Bialystok; in 1888, four strikes; in 1892, three strikes; in 1893, seven strikes; and in 1894, nine strikes. (There were only several small strikes in Vilna and also a strike of brush makers in Vilkovisk.) Socialist agitation was already bearing some fruit, as witness the celebration of May First as early as 1892 by some Jewish workers in Vilna.

During 1893-1894 almost all the socialists perceived the necessity of leading the economic struggle of the worker so as to educate him through his daily needs. In this way the problem of bringing socialism to the working masses was finally solved. This rapprochement on the basis of the economic struggle brought new strength to the Jewish labor movement, enlarging and enriching it. For the first six or seven years the movement had almost exclusively an economic and cultural character. Only in 1900-1902 did the Jewish worker step into the political struggle.

The extent of the economic struggle in Lithuania and Poland can be seen from the following figures, which show how many Jewish workers struck during the decade 1895-1904.

Year	Number of Strikes (Jewish)	Approximate Number of Striking Jewish Workers
1895	83	4,700
1896	92	3,300
1897	150	23,800
1898	179	11,000
1899	223	18,600
1900	277	16,000
1901	453	22,000
1902	455	28,000
1903	340	41,000
1904	166	8,000
Total	2,418	176,400

If we calculate the average size of the strikes for each year, it will be seen that the largest occurred in 1897—160 men per strike. The *Bund* was organized towards the end of that year of militant struggle. Going further, we discover that the smallest strikes (averages of 58, 49, and 62 men per strike) occurred in 1900-1902. In these years the Jewish labor movement began to split; Poale Zionists appeared and the *Bund* expelled them from its organizations. This proves to us that the history of the Jewish labor parties has an interesting relationship to the development of the Jewish struggle on the economic front.

I close with the following observation: This year we have a fourfold celebration. It is 35 years since the Jewish workers spontaneously took their first, not as yet conscious step; 25 years since their first planned movement; 15 years since the founding of the first Jewish labor party, the *Bund;* and 5 years since the founding of the World Confederation of the Jewish Socialist Labor Party, Poale Zion.

1877, 1887, 1897, 1907! Four historic years in the formation of Jewish proletarian revolutionary activity. At each step the movement is ten years older; each time it is ten years riper in its consciousness; in each decade it takes a step forward to a new, broader perspective. From a chaotic state to the first spark of consciousness, and from a strong organization to world-wide unity—that is the development of the Jewish proletariat.

REMINISCENCES

*On the Occasion of the Tenth Anniversary of the Poale Zion
in Russia, 1906-1916*

THIS PURIM will mark ten years of the founding convention of the Poale Zion Party in Russia. Ten years! It is impossible to transcribe the emotions that rise up in the mind of an "old" Party worker like myself when he is reminded of that memorable event. However, let us narrate the rather dry historical facts of the small, hardly distinguishable beginnings from which the convention arose. Let us consider also those historical events which raised our weak and limited undertaking to its present high level.

Here are the facts. The convention, the jubilee of which we shall soon be celebrating, was not the "first". The Party had actually existed five years previously and during that time had called several conferences. The Poale Zion idea, the concept of organic unity between socialism and Zionism, had already attained quite a respectable age. Our idea is not much younger than socialism proper. It was originally formulated by that celebrated German socialist and member of the First International, Moses Hess. A more concrete and modern form of Socialist Zionism was first propounded by our comrade, Nachman Syrkin, who is justly considered in our movement as its spiritual father.

Nachman Syrkin first developed his new and militant concept in his speeches and articles on the Jewish question. His lectures were delivered to Russian Jewish youths studying abroad, and his articles were published in *Das Deutsche Wort* in Vienna. Syrkin's propaganda continued from 1898 to 1901. Its first tangible result was the organization of a group of "Socialist Zionists". Under its auspices in Berlin, in May, 1901, Syrkin issued his widely circulated Russian pamphlet, "An Appeal to the Jewish Youth". This was the first official manifesto of Poale Zionism, even though it did not bear that precise name.

Syrkin's ideas were developed independently, having little connection with the forgotten philosophy of Moses Hess. Similarly, in Russia proper, there arose an independent Socialist Zionist movement which had no relationship to Syrkin's propaganda abroad. The first group of socialist, class conscious Poale Zionists in Russia was formed in November, 1900, in Yekaterinoslav. Its founders were the writer of these lines and Simon Dobin, who later went over to the *Seimists* Party[1] and there earned a reputation for being a clever and wholesome Jewish writer.

You will permit me to say a little more about this first organization. From September, 1900, to May, 1901, the writer, who belonged to the Russian Social-Democratic Party in Yekaterinoslav, delivered a series of papers on Socialist Zionism to an educational club of intelligent young

---

1 See footnote 8, p. 97.

proletarians.[2] It consisted of about one hundred and fifty members. Dr. Shmarya Levin, who was then the government recognized Rabbi in Yekaterinoslav, delivered a series of lectures to the same club against the new idea. The lengthy and highly intelligent discussions, in which other prominent Zionist leaders participated (they were all against uniting Zionism and socialism), resulted in the club accepting the new viewpoint and calling itself the "Zionist Socialist Labor Alliance". Its first public appearance was in the organization of a self-defense group during the small pogrom of Pesach, 1901. Its second appearance was during the strike of men's tailors, during Succot of the same year. That was the first strike of Jewish workers in this big city.

All these things are being disclosed now for the first time. The facts show, above all, that the first Jewish self-defense group was organized by the Poale Zion two and a half years before the Jewish Socialist *Bund* (in Homel, September, 1903).

Let us now rapidly scan the history of the movement from 1901 to 1906.

The name "Poale Zion" was first adopted by a club in Minsk in 1899,[3] under the leadership of A. Litwin (the now well-known American Jewish writer), Berger, and Rubentchik, after the same group had denied the value of the class struggle in the Galut. They are the precursors of the so-called "Minsker Poale Zion" which united with the Socialist Territorialists in 1907. A socialist club with the name "Poale Zion" was formed in Odessa in 1902 under the influence of Yekaterinoslav and Poltava. Soon the whole of western Russia had scattered groups and

---

2 In his article, "At the Cradle of Socialist Zionism", in the New York *Die Warheit* of March 13th, 1916, Borochov relates the following:

I was then a member of the Russian Social-Democratic Party and worked under the supervision of the Yekaterinoslav branch which published the illegal *Yuzhni Rabotchi* ("The Southern Worker"). Regarding the other members of the S. D. committee, I remember the Christian, Pazniakoff, who was expelled from the theological seminary for his atheism; the Georgian, Schaki; and also a Jew by the name of Taratuta.

Pazniakoff (a man of great erudition) and I used to imbibe freely of Karl Marx and Richard Avenarius. Both of us were only lads of nineteen, but we knew Marx's *Capital* by heart. We agitated among the workers—Christians as well as Jewish—and distributed illegal pamphlets.

My duty was to read Bogdanov's popular book, *Principles of Political Economy*, with the workers, explaining it to them in simple words and by concrete illustrations. I do not remember what made me change my ideas. It must have been after a chance joint meeting of Jewish and Christian workers that the truth of Socialist Zionism dawned on me. The committee then discovered that I had a bad influence on the workers—I was teaching them to think for themselves. I was accordingly expelled from the Russian Social-Democratic Party.

Years later Pazniakoff again became a devout Christian mystic, and he completely severed himself from socialism. Taratuta became a terrorist anarchist and fell in an armed struggle with a regiment of Cossacks. I do not know what happened to Schaki, the Georgian.

What can an expelled Russian Social-Democrat do when he becomes a Zionist "unbeliever"? I joined a large educational club of Jewish students and made them the first Poale Zionists in Russia. Menachem Mendel Ussishkin, head of the Yekaterinoslav Zionist region, was a man of steel and iron. He boasted of living at the corner of "Iron" and "Stiff-necked" streets. (The streets were really named that way.) Ussishkin sternly and categorically declared, "I will not tolerate such new-fangled ideas!" Dr. Shmarya Levin was also against our socialist endeavors and in his fine and cultured manner attempted to influence us through friendly argumentation. He came personally to the same educational club and delivered a series of lectures against Socialist Zionism.

Youth, however, did not follow its elders, and the club adopted my motion to call itself the "Zionist Socialist Labor Alliance".

3 Borochov errs in the date. The Minsk Poale Zion was organized in 1897.

organizations accepting the new tendency. In 1902 they issued their own illegal organ in Russian.

An interesting organization of socialist Poale Zionists arose in Vitebsk around 1903. Its theorist was Hirsch Z., a man of outstanding intellect who had a most tragic fàte. (His pupil Chashin is now a well-known Party worker.)[4] From Vitebsk, Poale Zionism penetrated into *Bund* territory in 1903-5 and spread over Lithuania and Poland.

In 1903 the movement was united with its spiritual father, Dr. Nachman Syrkin, through his paper, *Hamon* ("The Masses"). A year later there was formed the *Vozrozhdenye* group, which issued an interesting paper. This group later led to an unfortunate split within the party.

Many splits tore our youthful movement to pieces in the years 1904 to 1906. The Uganda issue awakened territorial tendencies in many of the young organizations. Even that early fighter for Socialist Zionism, Nachman Syrkin, was for a long time carried away by the current. The territorialist sections seceded in January, 1905, at their first convention in Odessa, wherein they named themselves the "Zionist Socialist Labor Party" (the "S. S."). In August of the same year followed a second split, forced by the *Vozrozhdenye* group which formed the party. They rejected Palestine together with all Zionist work.

At the Kiev conference of the pro-Palestine Poale Zion in July, 1905, the Jewish Social-Democratic Party Poale Zion was constituted. Shortly after, it sent forty-seven delegates to the Sixth Zionist Congress in Basle. Following the congress, most of the delegates assembled in Zurich and chose a Central Committee. But the *Seimist* influence was already being felt, and the Central Committee did not have a chance to see the light of day. In December, 1905, the split was completed at a highly dramatic conference in Berdichev. Two organizational conferences were held almost simultaneously; ours in Poltava and the *Seimists'* in Kiev.

Thus came that great historical event of our movement, the "All-Russian Organizational Convention of the Jewish Social-Democratic Labor Party Poale Zion", which finally put an end to all splits. It is the tenth anniversary of this Convention that we are now preparing to celebrate.[5]

The conference began on Purim eve (February, 1906) in Poltava, in the presence of thirty delegates. Meetings were held under cover in the small room of a Jewish bakery on the outskirts of the city. For seven days and nights we sat and slept there, not taking a step outside for fear the Czarist police would notice us. The profoundest theoretical questions and the most difficult organizational problems were courageously and enthusiastically dealt with in that uncomfortable environment. Finally the police did notice us, and we had to transfer ourselves hurriedly to a hotel in the center of the city.

Our "retreat" took place in perfect order, so that the enemy was unable to capture any prisoners of war.[6] Our small army quite peacefully

---

4 Chashin turned communist after the war

5 In his article, "Ten Years of Jewish Socialism", in *Die Warheit*, December 5, 1915, Borochov states that the Party then had 16,000 dues paying members.

6 In *Die Warheit* of March 13, 1916, Borochov relates: "To this day seven pounds of our dynamite lie buried in the courtyard of the bakery where we met for the first seven days. An additional twenty pounds, together with seven finished bombs, were found later when comrade B. Z. R. and myself were arrested. The Poltava committee was holding this for the emergency of a pogrom or uprising."

continued its deliberations in the hotel which we had forcibly captured by sternly warning the proprietor not to accept any other guests. But the police discovered us even in our new abode, and two prisoners fell into their none-too-gentle hands; but the minutes and other documents were carried to safety in time. We hastily finished the most important organizational work, elected the first Central Committee, and appointed a commission to draw up the Party platform.

The commission hid itself in a small town in the province of Poltava immediately after the police had surprised us in the hotel. There again ferreted out by the Czarist minions, we transferred ourselves to Simferopol, once more leaving two prisoners in the clutches of the government.

The result of the commission's deliberations was the ideological strengthening of our Party. One of the resolutions of the conference was to establish the "World Poale Zion Alliance".

In the course of these ten years, the Russian Poale Zion has played an important role in the world movement. Our Party in Palestine is to some extent the product of the Russian Party. The same comrades who organized the movement in Russia participated in establishing and leading the Party in Palestine. Russia systematically contributed editors to the Party periodicals in Austria, America, England, Palestine and Argentina. Russia was for a long period the foundry in which Poale Zionist thought was molten and cast for the whole world.

The secessionists, the S. S. and the *Seimists,* who in the beginning far surpassed the Poale Zion both numerically and intellectually, quickly disappeared. Their influence over the Jewish community soon evaporated, because everything that was vital in their platforms was already in the program of the Poale Zion. We continued to grow in numbers and still more in influence.

The day is not far off when the Poale Zion will assume the leadership of the whole Jewish working class. That will be history's judgment of the small, secret conference in the hot and dusty bakery where we were in constant fear of the police.

OUR PLATFORM

I.

THE NATIONAL problem arises because the development of the forces of production of a nationality conflicts with the state of conditions of production.[1] The most prevalent national conflict is the result of the development of the forces of production within one country clashing with the conditions in foreign countries. The most general prerequisite of the development of the forces of production is the territory in which the group lives. The territory comprises all the internal conditions of production; it is the ultimate source and governs all outside influences. A territory is the positive base of a distinct, independent national life.

Expatriated peoples lack this positive base. In the course of their adaptation to the natural and historic environment of the nations among whom they dwell, they tend to lose their distinctive national traits and to merge with the surrounding social *milieu*. That such peoples nevertheless exist as distinct national entities demonstrates that objective forces do not permit them to adapt themselves to the surrounding social *milieu* or, at best, hinder the process of their adaptation. Two diametrically opposed forces operate in the life of landless peoples: (1) the urge to *assimilate*, which is a result of the desire of the group to adapt itself to the environment, and (2) the tendency to *isolate* the group and make it inaccessable to the environmental pressure.

The second factor (isolation) operates as a negative element in the national development of expatriated peoples.

The national cohesion of territorial groups is based upon their national wealth, that is, upon their territories and the material conditions of production therein. A territorial nation possesses its own national economy within which the development of the forces of production takes place, and thus it constitutes a complete economic unit. In the course of its development, a nation's forces of production may be hampered by the resistance of adverse conditions. The nation is then faced by a conflict which arises from the need to expand the field of opportunities which determines its production. This necessitates the invasion of foreign territories. In such a case, the national policies assume an aggressive character. When, however, the forces of production of a given group suffer from the intrusion of foreign economic interests, that group is faced by a national conflict which arises from the need of guarding the integrity of its national territory. The policies of such a nation are defensive (protective) in character.

The *class struggle* is the concrete expression of the social conflicts which arise because the development of the forces of production disturbs the mode of economic relations of production. The *national struggle*, however, is an expression of the conflict between the developing forces of production and the existing conditions of production. But whereas social conflicts,

---
1 See p. 140.

183

such as the class struggle, take place within the socio-economic organism, national conflicts transcend the bounds of the territorial economic unit. Of course we are not speaking of completely isolated economic units, for such do not exist. But we do have to recognize the existence of *relatively* independent economic units. The increasing economic interdependence of the capitalistic system makes it possible for us to speak of even a world economy.

There is a marked distinction between national and social conflicts. The class struggle—the concrete expression of social conflicts—grows out of the economic exploitation of one class by another. Competition within the bounds of a definite group is of importance only to the individuals concerned and does not provoke any social conflicts; competition between the individuals of a social group is a social phenomenon but not a social problem. National struggles, however, grow out of competition between national groups; and the exploitation of one national group by another is merely an incidental phenomenon which creates no crucial social problem. Only in one case does national exploitation attain the importance of an acute social problem, namely, when two national groups live together in one economic unit but constitute two distinct classes. Such a relationship exists in India, for instance, where the British residents form the class of bureaucrats and capitalists while the natives form the class of peasants and workers.

From a social point of view, national competition under capitalism is very different from individual competition. Individual competition aids in the development of the forces of production, sharpens the inner contradictions, and undermines the bases of the capitalistic society. National competition, however, is a hindrance to individual competition and acts in the same manner as a monopoly. In Czarist Russia, for example, the Jew could have held his ground in competition with the individual Russian; but since this was an economic struggle between two national groups, the Russian majority was in a position to eliminate the competition of the Jewish minority. National competition, like any factor which tends to paralyze the freedom of individual competition, hampers the development of a capitalistic economy and defers its rise and ultimate decline. National competition is not merely a struggle between two groups; it is an endeavor of one national group to seize the material possessions of another national group and to replace the latter minority along all economic lines.

Effective national competition is possible only within the national economic territory. No nation can compete successfully unless it has a strategic base. When national competition takes place between a nation living on its own territory and one that is expatriated, the territorial nation endeavors to expel the expatriated one and to deprive it of the use of its economic resources. But since the expatriated nation has no basic possessions of its own, it cannot exist unless it is allowed to use the material possessions of the majority nation.

In order to penetrate the economic sphere of the native population, the expatriated nationality endeavors to adapt itself to the conditions prevailing in its new home. The native inhabitants, however, do not allow their economic strongholds to pass into the hands of newly arrived immigrants. The new immigrant groups are therefore forced to become "useful" by turning to economic fields as yet unoccupied. They are tolerated as long as they are active in economic functions which no one has previously assumed. But when the development of the forces of production has reached a stage wherein the native population can itself perform those same economic functions, the foreign nationality becomes "superfluous", and a movement is begun to rid the country of its "foreigners". Since the "foreigners" have no national material possessions to use in the competitive struggle with the native population, they are forced to yield their economic positions, thereby losing their livelihood. In short, the landless nationality can more or less withstand exploitation, bad as it may be; but as soon as exploitation is replaced by national competition, the landless nationality loses its economic position.

At no time is the foreign group allowed to enter into agriculture and other basic industries. Even when it is being exploited, the foreign group is tolerated only in commerce and in the last levels of production.[2] As soon as the native population is ready to occupy those positions, the foreign nationality is entirely isolated from any possibilities of access to the economy of the land in which it lives. A national struggle thus comes into being.

The Jews are the classic example of an expatriated group.[3] The Jewish nation in the Galut has no material possessions of its own, and it is helpless in the national competitive struggle.

In our analysis of the Jewish problem we must bear in mind the fact that the national struggle is closely allied with the social. There is no struggle which is equally in the interest of all the classes of a nation. Every class has national interests differing from the national interests of other classes. National movements do not transcend class divisions; they merely represent the interests of one of several classes within the nation. A national conflict develops not because the development of the forces of production of the whole nation conflicts with the conditions of production, but rather because the developing needs of one or more classes clash with the conditions of production of its national group. Hence the great variety of types of nationalism and national ideologies.

Since the Jewish nation has no peasantry, our analysis of its national problem deals with urban classes: the upper, middle, and petty bourgeoisie; the masses who are being proletarized; and the proletariat.

The upper bourgeoisie, because it is not confined to the home market, is not national in any true sense, but highly cosmopolitan. The Jewish bourgeoisie finds its interests best served by assimilation; and were it not for the "poor *Ostjuden*",[4] the Jewish upper bourgeoisie would not be disturbed by the Jewish problem. The continuous stream of immigration of East European Jews and frequent pogroms remind the upper bourgeoisie of Western Europe only too often of the miserable lot of their brethren.

---

2 See p. 65.

3 There are some aspects of Borochovism the truth of which is denied by some students of history. Ezekiel Kaufman, for instance, considers Borochov's classification of the Jews as one of the expatriated, landless nations as wrong. The Jews, he claims, are the only landless nation; therefore, their case must be considered as unique. He challenges Borochov's assumption of the impossibility for a minority to gain positions in the basic industries and points out cases in history as evidence. He denies that the Jews entered European economy after it had assumed a definite shape and therefore came to occupy secondary positions. He maintains that the Jews were pushed, during the early medieval period, out of agriculture and certain branches of industry and commerce by special efforts of the Christian society, which were directed only against the Jews and which interfered in an artificial way with the natural economic tendencies. The basic problem in Jewish life of the Galut, he maintains, is not the isolation and crowding of the Jews in certain industries but their competition with the non-Jews situated in the same economic class.

4 East European Jews.

The East European Jewish bourgeoisie is, of course, more directly affected by the status of Jewry. The West European upper bourgeoisie, however, considers the entire problem to be a gratuitous and unpleasant burden. And yet it cannot find a safe retreat away from our East European masses. Since the Jewish upper bourgeoisie would like above all else to lose its individuality and be assimilated completely by the native bourgeoisie, it is very much affected by anti-Semitism. It fears everything which tends to spread anti-Semitism. If anti-Semitism were the hobby of only a few psychopathic and feeble-minded individuals, it would not be dangerous. But anti-Semitism is very popular among the masses, and very frequently its propaganda is tied up closely with the social unrest of the lowest elements of the working class. This creates a dangerous cumulation of Judaeophobia.

Anti-Semitism is becoming a dangerous political movement. Anti-Semitism flourishes because of the national competition between the Jewish and non-Jewish petty bourgeoisie and between the Jewish and non-Jewish proletarized and unemployed masses. Anti-Semitism menaces both the poor helpless Jews and the all-powerful Rothschilds. The latter, however, understand very well where the source of trouble lies: the poverty-ridden Jewish masses are at fault. The Jewish plutocracy abhors these masses, but anti-Semitism reminds it of its kinship to them. Two souls reside within the breast of the Jewish upper bourgeoisie—the soul of a proud European and the soul of an unwilling guardian of his Eastern coreligionists. Were there no anti-Semitism, the misery and poverty of the Jewish emigrants would be of little concern to the Jewish upper bourgeoisie. It is impossible, however, to leave them in some West European city (on their way to a place of refuge) in the care of the local government, for that would arouse anti-Semitic ire. Therefore, in spite of themselves and despite their efforts to ignore the Jewish problem, the Jewish aristocrats must turn philanthropists. They must provide shelter for the Jewish emigrants and must make collections for pogrom-ridden Jewry. Everywhere the Jewish upper bourgeoisie is engaged in the search for a solution to the Jewish problem and a means of being delivered of the Jewish masses. This is the sole form in which the Jewish problem presents itself to the Jewish upper bourgeoisie.

The middle bourgeoisie is bound more closely to the Jewish masses. In general, the economic interests of a middle and petty bourgeoisie depend on the market which the mass of the people affords, which market is coextensive with the national language and cultural institutions. Therefore, in the case of territorial nations, the middle and petty bourgeoisie is the chief supporter of all types of "cultural" nationalism. Since this section of the Jewish bourgeoisie has no territory and market, it falls under the influence of assimilatory forces. On the other hand, because of the intense national competition in which the middle and lower bourgeoisie is involved, the isolating factor of anti-Semitism is felt in every branch of activity. Anti-Semitism is at the root of all the discriminatory laws against Jews in politically backward countries and of the social boycott in the bourgeois-democratic countries. The boycott, which is becoming more organized and more intensive, overtakes the Jewish bourgeoisie everywhere: in trade, in industry, in social life, and even in the press. With the growth of capitalism there is a corresponding growth of political democracy on the one hand, and of national competition on the other. Those who see in the growth of political democracy the elimination of discriminatory laws against the Jews and the corresponding lessening of the acute form of Judaeophobia (such as pogroms) see merely one side of the process.

They fail to recognize the continual sharpening of national competition in bourgeois society, the growth of which is parallel with that of democracy. This process strengthens the hostility and makes for a stronger and more efficiently organized boycott against the Jews. The Jewish middle and petty bourgeoisie, with no territory and no market of its own, is powerless against this menace. In the white-collar class the discrimination against the Jewish physician, engineer, and journalist forces them to face the Jewish problem. Jewish misery is closer to them than to the upper bourgeoisie. Their nationalism, however, is of a specifically middle and petty bourgeois character. Lacking any means of support in their struggle for a market, they tend to speak of an independent political existence and of a Jewish state where they would play a leading political role. They feel the effects of state anti-Semitism very strongly and therefore strive to protect Jewish civil and national rights. Since they are directly affected by the poverty and degeneration of the Jewish masses, they tend to advocate a Jewish national policy.

But as long as they succeed in retaining their middle class position, as long as the boycott and the isolation brought about by anti-Semitism have not yet undermined their material well-being, the center of gravity of their political interests continues to be in the Galut. Their personal needs remain outside the Jewish national sphere, for the conflict between their economic interests and the conditions of production restricting Jewish life has not yet reached a peak. In other words, as long as the Jewish middle bourgeoisie retains its economic position it is relatively unconcerned with the Jewish problem. True, the Jewish problem is a cause of certain discomforts to the middle class, but the class is not sufficiently hard pressed to desire a radical change in its condition. Its energy can be utilized to a certain extent in behalf of the rehabilitation of Jewish life, but the middle class as a whole can never be the base for a movement of Jewish emancipation.

II.

For the purpose of this discussion we may consider the Jewish petty bourgeoisie and the proletarized masses as one group. As a result of historical circumstances, this group constitutes a large majority of the Jewish people. To us proletarian Zionists this class is doubly significant. In the first place, the Jewish proletariat has become socially differentiated from the larger group only recently. (To understand the Jewish proletariat it is necessary to analyze properly the petty bourgeoisie, which still serves as its reservoir of manpower.) Secondly, the heterogeneous mass of emigrating petty bourgeoisie and proletarians-to-be is the main source of the human material for the future Jewish rehabilitation.

National competition, which is characterized by economic isolation and government boycott, both organized and unorganized, weighs heavily on the back of the Jewish petty bourgeoisie. The Jewish petty bourgeoisie suffers much more acutely than does the petty bourgeoisie of any other nation and is forced to enter the ranks of the proletariat. However, the extent to which Jews can become members of the established working class is quite insufficient. Capitalistic economy requires a large reserve of unemployed labor. To this reserve the Jewish petty bourgeoisie supplies a larger percentage of its number than does the petty bourgeoisie of other peoples.

Should we divide world production into two groups, one of which is engaged in creating the means of production and the other in producing consumers' goods, we would find that Jewish capital is invested mainly in the production of consumers' goods. Because of the effects of national rivalry among the masses who are in search of jobs, Jewish labor finds employment almost exclusively at the hands of the small Jewish industrialist. Hatred of Jews on the part of non-Jewish employers and non-Jewish workers practically excludes Jewish labor from non-Jewish work-shops.

Aside from the intentional boycott, both organized and unorganized, there are other factors which contribute toward the inability of the Jewish worker to face the competition of the non-Jewish worker. The Jewish proletarized elements are mainly city-bred, while their non-Jewish rivals hail from an agricultural environment. The latter have a number of advantages over the former. They are stronger physically, and their standard of living is lower. The Jewish worker, steeped in the traditions of a non-worker's life, requires much more comfort and luxury; therefore he adapts himself more quickly to the class conflict and enters the struggle with his employer more readily than the non-Jewish worker. In addition, for a number of historical reasons, the Jewish worker is not as well prepared technically as the non-Jewish city-bred worker. These factors, however, are insignificant in comparison with that of national competition between the Jewish and non-Jewish worker. National competition is found even in the well-developed capitalistic countries, such as America, England, and South Africa—wherever the Jewish immigrants encounter masses of non-Jewish immigrants who are better adapted to obtain employment. As a result Jewish labor gains employment mainly from the Jewish middle bourgeoisie.

As soon as the national conflicts and national competition grow intense, a conscious anti-Jewish boycott is undertaken which results in immigration restrictions. In both England and America there is ample evidence of a growth of anti-Semitism with all its reactionary characteristics and consequences. Since Jewish capital becomes the sole employer of Jewish labor, the growing need for proletarization among the Jewish masses cannot be satisfied.

Jewish capital is mainly invested in the production of consumers' goods. This type of production is usually characterized by seasonal employment, sweatshop conditions, and piece-work. The exclusion of Jewish labor from the heavy industries is so prevalent that non-Jewish workers consider them as their own special field of employment. The encounters between the Jewish and non-Jewish workers at Bialystok are ample proof of this state of affairs.

The national problem of the declining Jewish petty bourgeoisie consists in its search for a market which should free it from the horrible economic isolation which characterizes it at present.

In the case of this group, the national problem is very acute. To solve it, the Jewish petty bourgeoisie is forced to abandon its native lands and to migrate to new countries, but even there it finds no satisfactory solution. Misery overtakes the bourgeoisie; poverty is its lot in the new country. It therefore enters the labor market and is transformed into a part of the working masses. In the labor market, too, it must face national competition. Consequently, the proletarized Jewish petty bourgeoisie can penetrate only the final levels of production. Thus there arises a national struggle based on need and the impossibility of satisfying the need.

The national question of the petty bourgeoisie, then, is the quest for a national market and the conservation of the associated cultural institutions such as the language, national education, etc. Concretely, the problem of the Jewish petty bourgeoisie is that of emigration: the quest of an expatriated nation for a place of economic security.

The Jewish problem migrates with the Jews. Thus a universal Jewish problem is created which involves not only Jewish philanthropists but also the political powers of the civilized nations.

In general the existence of an impoverished petty bourgeoisie constitutes a great danger. This element represents the decaying remnants of a previous economic order. They are socially and psychologically disorganized and constitute a "mob" whose activities will be characterized mainly by chaos and reaction. Wherever they are given a chance to engage independently in the solution of a social problem, they inevitably produce undesirable and chaotic results. The progressive forces within a democratic country must always be on the alert lest these elements cause irreparable damage. But these "dregs of the capitalistic order" also participate in the quest for a solution of the Jewish problem. Pogroms and other primitive forms of reaction—these are their method of solving the Jewish problem. This "solution" succeeds only in poisoning the entire surrounding political life. This mob is the same everywhere: in Baku and in London, in Kishinev and in New York, in New Orleans and in Berlin, in Tokyo and in Melbourne, in San Francisco and in Vienna. Everywhere its method is identical: pogroms and violence. It kills Jews in Russia, massacres Armenians in Caucasia, and lynches Negroes in America. This mob is the mainstay of all political charlatans and of all the reactionary forces of a moribund social order. These excesses which the dying regime sponsors are a permanent menace to law and order in democratic countries. But they are inevitable as long as migrations of petty bourgeois and proletarian masses continue and as long as national competition exists between them and the corresponding Jewish classes. It is significant that these anti-social methods of solving the Jewish problem are employed by the most reactionary elements of society under the leadership of representatives of the middle bourgeoisie and the chauvinistic intelligentzia. The democratic governments, however, cannot afford such chaotic methods for the solution of any problem. For these interfere with the law and order which are so necessary for the proper development of capitalism. Open violence and public scandals are not in the interests of the ruling bourgeoisie. Both the bourgeoisie and the revolutionary proletariat are equally interested in a peaceful and systematic solution of the various problems, including the Jewish problem.

How then is the solution of the problem to be achieved? Those factors which tend to intensify the conflict did not exist in the feudal countries where Jews had been living for a long time. The complete social isolation of the Jews and the migrations common to Jews and non-Jews alike are of recent appearance and are closely bound up with the development of capitalism. Under these circumstances it is futile to resort to assimilation as a solution. It may sound paradoxical, but it is true nevertheless, that in the Middle Ages the prospects for assimilation were not as utopian as they are under the present order. In the Middle Ages the isolation of the Jew was not as fundamental as it is at the present time. The Jews, though excluded from the basic economic processes of life, nevertheless had some economic foundation. They fulfilled a function which accelerated the development of the system of production of that society and were thus "useful". The then existing civilized world was their national market. Later, as capitalism developed, the Jews were eliminated, and wholesale expulsion took place. But this was not typical of every country where Jews lived and did not occur in all places at the same time.

Only in the first epoch of the newly developed industrial capitalism did the assimilating factor operate strongly in Jewish life.

It was then that the industrial revolution caused the walls of the Ghetto to collapse, and a wide field of free competition was opened to the Jews. The epoch of the decisive struggle between capitalism and feudalism was the golden era of Jewish assimilation. But this era of free competition which characterized the rise of capitalism was superseded by national competition. Then assimilation gave way to isolation.

All assimilationists are essentially utopianists, for all the forces operating within Jewish life point in a diametrically opposed direction. Intensified national competition does not stimulate Jews to assimilate; on the contrary, it strengthens the bounds of national solidarity. It unites all the scattered parts of the Jewish nation into one isolated unit. Along with the development of the inner national forces, national competition evokes universal interest in the solution of the Jewish problem.

All the processes operating within Jewish life arise from national competition against the Jews and are influenced by Jewish migration. Therefore, to obtain a correct perspective of the development and dynamics of Jewish life, it is necessary to make a thorough investigation of the tendencies of Jewish migration.

Emigration alone does not solve the Jewish problem. It leaves the Jew helpless in a strange country. For that reason Jewish immigration and any other national immigration tend toward compact settlements. This concentration alleviates the process of adaptation to the newly found environment, but at the same time it accelerates the rise of national competition in the countries into which the Jews have recently immigrated. If so large a number of Jewish immigrants had not settled in New York, Philadelphia, and Chicago, it is doubtful whether national competition against them would have come into existence; but the existence of the Jews as such would have become impossible. The outward contradictions of Jewish immigration—the clash between the habits brought along from the old country and the conditions in the new country—necessitate concentration.

Such concentration, however, contains a double contradiction. Mass concentration aims at facilitating the process of adaptation to the new environment, but it results in the segregation of the newly arrived group and hinders the process of adaptation. Upon his arrival, the immigrant seeks to enter the first levels of production. Through their concentration in the large cities, the Jews retain their former economic traditions and are condemned to the final levels of production—the manufacturing of consumers' goods. Thus the need of the Jews to develop their forces of production and to become proletarized remains unsatisfied.

The contradictions inherent in this process lead to decentralization of the concentrated mass of immigrants. Jewry settles in more or less compact masses not in one place, but in many, thus aggravating the problem. Instead of remaining localized, the contradictions appear in numerous places. The Jewish problem thus becomes more acute and evolves into a world problem.

As a result of these two fundamental contradictions, the Jewish petty bourgeoisie and working masses are confronted by two needs. The impossibility of penetrating into the higher levels of production creates the need for concentrated immigration into an undeveloped country. Instead of being limited to the final levels of the production as is the case in all other countries, the Jews could in a short time assume the leading position in the economy of the new land. Jewish migration must be transformed from immigration into colonization. This means a territorial solution of the Jewish problem.

In order that the Jewish immigration may be diverted to colonization of undeveloped countries, it is not sufficient that the colonization merely should be useful to the Jews. It is also necessary that the immigration to the previous centers become more difficult. This, as a matter of fact, is taking place. Because of national competition, immigration into the well-developed capitalistic countries is being limited. At the same time, the need for Jewish emigration is steadily becoming greater; and it can no longer be satisfied by the old centers of absorption. New lands must be found, and the emigrants increasingly tend to go to semi-agricultural countries.

To avoid decentralization, there is need for organizational forces which would unite the Jewish masses and which would introduce system into the spontaneous processes of migration. Left alone, Jewish migration will continue to be a confused and scattering process. A new and conscious element is required. The Jewish emigrating masses must be organized, and their movements, directed. That is the task of the conscious Jewish proletariat.

The scheme of the dynamics of Jewish life operates as follows: (1) emigration of the petty bourgeoisie who turn to proletarization, (2) concentration of Jewish immigration, and (3) organized regulation of this immigration. The first two factors are the products of the spontaneous processes operating in Jewish life; the last, however, is introduced by the organized Jewish proletariat.

Capitalistic economy has reached the stage where no revolutionary changes are possible without the participation of the working masses and especially of the organized sections of the proletariat. The emancipation of the Jewish people either will be brought about by Jewish labor, or it will not be attained at all. But the labor movement has only one weapon at its command: the class struggle. The class struggle must assume a political character if it is to lead to a better future.

Proletarian Zionism is possible only if its aims can be achieved through the class struggle; Zionism can be realized only if protelarian Zionism can be realized.

III.

Proletarian Zionism is a complex product of Jewish proletarian thought. After eliminating all factors that are incidental, temporary, or local, and aberrations that inevitably complicate every fundamental social process, we could find an unusually strict consistency in the development of the Poale Zion. As in the case of every social movement, the evolution of Jewish proletarian thought is the result of a wide gap between the needs of the masses and possibility of satisfying these needs. The main factors that give rise to this gap operate in two directions: (1) the *social* conflict between the developing forces of production of the Jewish proletariat and the economic relationships in which it lives, and (2) the *national* conflict between the developing forces of production of the Jewish proletariat and the sum total of the conditions of production.

The Jewish proletariat therefore faces two tremendous tasks: the abolition of the capitalistic system and the elimination of national oppression. The social conflict is invariably clearer and much closer to the proletariat than the national conflict. The social conflict is embodied in the personal relations between the employer and the employee. The fact that the capitalistic economy makes the worker *de facto* master over the operation of the means of production gives the worker at once a powerful weapon of struggle. The obvious exploitation of the worker and the possibility of his laying down his tools and gaining concessions thereby present the economic side of the social conflict in bold relief. For this reason the worker grasps this phase of the conflict in the very early stages of its development.

The political aspect of this conflict is much more complicated and therefore harder to analyze and comprehend. The determining factors are more remote from the worker, and his encounter with them takes place at a relatively advanced stage of the economic struggle.

As a result of the law of economy which operates in organic and social mechanics (a direct consequence of the more general law of conservation of energy), every gap between need and provision seeks its abridgement first of all within the framework of the conditions that caused the gap. Only gradually there matures the realization of the necessity to change the conditions. The emphasis of the struggle then shifts to new and more remote spheres. At the beginning of its struggle, the proletariat strives to attain liberation by means of the economic conflict. Only at a later and more advanced stage does this struggle assume a political nature. The Jewish proletariat passed very rapidly through both stages of development of the social conflict. The economic struggle very easily transformed itself into a political struggle because of the harsh conditions prevailing under the Czarist regime.

The national conflict is infinitely more complex than the social conflict. In the case of the national struggle the personal relations between the oppressed and oppressor do not play such an important role. In spite of the personal character of national encounters, it is clear at first sight that national oppression is of an impersonal nature. The objective and impersonal characteristics of class exploitation appear to the proletariat only at a late stage in the development of proletarian thought. National oppression, on the other hand, immediately makes its impersonal nature manifest to the observer. The oppressed Jew is not faced by a particular individual non-Jew who is directly responsible for his sufferings. It is very clear to him that a whole social group oppresses him. The Jew finds it difficult to analyze his social relations to this group, especially in the early period of the conflict. In addition, the mutual national relationships do not provide the oppressed group with any weapons for its struggle.

The stages in the development of national conflicts are therefore more numerous than those of social conflicts. The Jewish worker first of all tried to solve his national problem under the same conditions which had given rise to the problem. Gradually, however, he arrived at the revolutionary solution—the need for a radical change in the conditions of his national existence.

We can now understand why some Jewish proletarian parties offer a highly advanced analysis of the social conflict but are very backward in their interpretation of the national problem. Such parties may have a large following, but that only proves that the national conflict is not sufficiently advanced for the true analysis to win support. Such backward programs are doomed to extinction with the development of the national conflict.

It is not at all surprising to see such proletarian parties existing among Jews, especially when we remember that the Jewish problem is probably the most complicated of all. To find a correct solution requires the expenditure of much energy. It is for this reason that the initial response of the Jewish proletarian parties to the national problem is often primitive and reactionary.

The proletariat must be considered from two different angles. In the first place, the proletariat produces the social wealth; in the second place, it constitutes a class which carries on its own struggles with the non-proletarian classes. The worker, as a worker, is interested only in the raising of his wage level and in the general improvement of his conditions of work. For this purpose the worker needs, first of all, a secure place of work. As long as the worker still has to compete with others in the search for employment, he is part and parcel to the proletarizing masses and has not assumed as yet a definite proletarian class physiognomy. The worker becomes a full-fledged proletarian only after he has acquired the feeling of security in his place of work; only then is he ready to take up the struggle against capital for the betterment of his condition. His place of work becomes a strategic base for his struggle, in contrast to what it had been formerly—a *casus belli* among the workers themselves. At this stage of development there emerges proletarian solidarity. Of course, workers' solidarity is not an absolute guarantee against competition for employment. On the contrary, the danger of dismissal is always imminent; every now and then the worker has to be able to defend his place in the face of competition of his fellow worker. He again emerges as a potential member of the unemployed, with the interests which were peculiar to his former status during the transitional period of proletarization. Thus in dilatory fashion, sometimes falling, sometimes halting, often retreating, the proletarian slowly emerges purified by the sufferings of his bitter struggle for work and bread. The road travelled by the proletarian in the formation of his class consciousness is long and hard.

The worker who is bound by his economic insecurity to the work place, so that he cannot use it as a strategic base, is not in a position to carry on independent political action and can play no historic role. He is not master of his own fate. But when we speak of the proletariat as a class, we must exclude the competition for employment among the workers and imply only the unconditional class solidarity in the struggle against capital. The worker is concerned with the place of work only insofar as he has not succeeded in entirely severing his relations with the proletarizing masses to which he formerly belonged and into which he may be thrust again at some future time. The interests of the proletariat as a class are related only to the strategic base—to those conditions under which it carries on its struggle against the bourgeoisie. In summary, the development of the forces of production of the masses who are forced to proletarization compels them to find a place of work; the development of the forces of production of the proletariat demands a normal strategic base for an effective class struggle. The striving for a strategic base is neither less materialistic nor less idealistic that the struggle for a place of work; but the former concerns an entire stratum of society, while the latter is merely in the interest of individuals or groups. In the sphere of interests connected with the search for a work place, there arises not only a personal but also a national competition. The achievement of a strategic base eliminates both. Without a work place it is impossible to carry on a struggle; and as long as any group of workers is subject to national competition, it cannot carry on the class struggle successfully. Its strategic base is bound to remain weak.

Thus although the proletariat as a class is ideologically not concerned with national competition, national competition may nevertheless have an indirect but important bearing on its interests. With the petty bourgeoisie and the proletarizing masses, this competition expresses itself concretely in the form of a national struggle. In the case of the proletariat, the competition assumes the form of a national problem. The national problem looms before the proletariat as well as before all the classes of the nation. If the development of the forces of production of the proletariat (i. e., of its class struggle) is hampered by the abnormal conditions of its strategic base, then there arises before it the national problem. The national consciousness of the proletariat awakens.

In some classes which retain a caste character, national consciousness and class consciousness exist and function independently of each other. For example, the feudal lords of Russia are "genuine Russian patriots" as well as members of the nobility. As Russians they have the "welfare of the nation" at heart, but as nobility they are ready to exploit the nation for their own ends. The middle and petty bourgeoisie and the impoverished masses characteristically have their class consciousness obliterated by their national consciousness. Class consciousness is, so to speak, excommunicated as a threat to "national unity". These above classes are, then, *nationalistic*. Only with the proletariat is the national problem closely allied with the same strategic base, with the same imperatives of the class struggle upon which is built its class consciousness.

One characteristic of the relationship between class consciousness and national consciousness should be noted. Because the national interests of the proletariat have little in common with the national struggle of the other classes, proletarian nationalism is not aggressive. The nationalism of the proletariat is thoroughly negative; it fades away as soon as the need for normalizing the strategic base is gone. That does not imply, however, a lack of positive content. No other class is as capable of providing a real national program such as the proletariat offers.

There are all sorts of misunderstandings with regard to the nationalism of the proletariat. Some who fail to see the positive content consider proletarian nationalism reactionary. Others, who see clearly the causes which have given rise to it, are apologetic; they consider a Jewish national program to be a tragic necessity. "Unfortunately, we are forced to carry through a national program. We would like to assimilate, but we are forced to remain Jews"—such for example is the tone of the propaganda of the S. S.

But these errors are merely the result of immature thought. The proletariat welcomes everything which aids in the development of its forces of production and opposes everything which hampers that development. Therefore the obfuscation of class consciousness and of national consciousness are equally odious to the proletariat. The proletarian is not ashamed of the tasks which are incumbent upon him as a class conscious worker, and he is equally unashamed of his national obligations. With pride we declare, "We are Social Democrats, and we are Jews." Our national consciousness is negative in that it is emancipatory in character. If we were the proletariat of a free nation, which neither oppresses nor

OUR PLATFORM   195

is oppressed, we would not be interested in any problems of national life. Even now, when under the pressure of national conflicts we have acquired national consciousness, spiritual culture concerns us less than social and economic problems. Ours is a realistic nationalism, free from any "spiritual" admixture.

For the Jewish proletariat the national problem arises because the development of its forces of production disturbs the conditions of its strategic base. The strategic base of the Jewish worker is unsatisfactory both politically and economically. The economic struggle of the Jewish worker is successful during the busy season when his employers are forced to yield under pressure in order not to lose valuable time. Once the season is over, the employers are in a position to take back all the concessions which they had previously granted. At the beginning of the new season, the fruits of the economic struggle have vanished; and the worker once more has to take up the struggle in order to regain the same uncertain victory. The Jewish strategic base is even less satisfactory politically. Since the Jewish worker is employed almost wholly in the production of consumers' goods and performs no important function in any of the primary levels of production, he does not hold in his grasp even a single fundamental thread of the economy of the land in which he lives. Thus his influence upon the general mode of life is very limited. He is incapable of paralyzing the economic organism in a single stroke as can the railroad or other workers who are more advantageously situated in the economic structure. The Jewish worker is not exploited by *gross Kapital;* his exploiter is the small capitalist whose role in production is negligible. When the Jewish worker does go on strike against the industry which exploits him, he does not appreciably disturb the equilibrium of the country. He is not even strong enough to obtain his just demands without the support of the other more fortunate workers of the surrounding nationalities. He cannot obtain even the most minor concession when his national needs do not coincide with those of workers of another nationality. This helplessness engenders within him the sense of proletarian solidarity and brings him closer to revolutionary ideals. As a matter of fact, class antagonisms within Jewish life are comparatively minor. In the first place, the concentration of capital is small. Then, too, the Jewish middle class, which is oppressed even more than the middle class of any other oppressed nationality (such as the Armenian, etc.), constitutes itself as an opposition group. Politically it offers the proletariat some support, unreliable though it may be. Under these conditions, the Jewish proletariat is doomed to trail behind the mighty political labor movements of the country.

The Jewish proletariat is in need of revolution more than any other. It is hoping most ardently for the good which is expected to come with the growth of democracy in society. The terrible national oppression; the exploitation on the part of petty Jewish capitalists; and the comparatively high cultural level and restlessness of the city-bred Jewish proletarian, the son of the "people of the book"—these generate an overwhelming revolutionary energy and an exalted spirit of self-sacrifice. This revolutionary zeal, hampered by the limitations of the strategic base, very frequently assumes grotesque forms. A disease of surplus energy is the tragedy of the Jewish proletariat, and is the source of its sufferings. A chained Prometheus who in helpless rage tears the feathers of the vulture that preys on him—that is the symbol of the Jewish proletariat.

IV.

In its efforts to solve the problems connected with the national conflict, the Jewish proletariat has undergone definite stages of thought and activity. Its reactions have become steadily more complex, more coordinated, and more revolutionary. At first the Jewish worker attempted to solve his national problem in the framework of the conditions that had given rise to it. Only at a later stage did he realize the need for a radical change in the conditions themselves. Each one of the stages through which the proletariat passed was of significance, for each was anticipating the following, more revolutionary stage. It is the Jewish proletariat that has developed the most coordinated program for the solution of the national problem, namely, the program of the Jewish Social-Democratic Workers Party, Poale Zion.

Our ultimate aim, our maximum program, is socialism—the socialization of the means of production. The only way to achieve socialism is through the class struggle of the Jews within the ranks of world-wide Social-Democracy. On this we shall not dwell.

Our immediate aim, our minimum program, is Zionism. The necessity for a territory in the case of the Jews results from the unsatisfactory economic strategic base of the Jewish proletariat. The anomalous state of the Jewish people will disappear as soon as the conditions of production prevailing in Jewish life are done away with. Only when the Jews find themselves in the primary levels of production will their proletariat hold in its hands the fate of the economy of the country. When Jews participate in those sectors of economic life wherein the social fabric of the whole country is woven, then will the organization of the Jewish proletariat become free and not reliant on the proletariat of the neighboring peoples. The Jewish workers' class struggle will no longer be directed against a powerless bourgeoisie, as in Galut, but against a mighty bourgeoisie which organizes the production of the country. The class struggle will enable the proletariat to wield the necessary social, economic, and political influence.

Our point of departure is the development of the class struggle of the Jewish proletariat. Our point of view excludes a general program of the Jewish people *as a whole*. The anomalies of the *entire* Jewish nation are of interest to us only as an objective explanation of the contradictions in the life of the Jewish proletariat. The subjective motivation of our program flows solely from the class interests of the Jewish proletariat. We defend our own interests, that is, the interests of the Jewish worker. We also defend our cultural needs and economic needs, wherever we are. We fight for the political, the national, and the ordinary human rights of the Jewish worker. For that reason we also advance national demands along with the general demands of the Social-Democratic minimum program. The national demands enter automatically into our minimum program.

We will consider the Jewish question fully solved and its anomalies wholly removed (insofar as it is possible within the framework of bourgeois society) only when territorial autonomy for the Jewish people shall have been attained and the entire nation shall constitute a relatively unified national economic organism.

But colonizing a territory is a prolonged process, during which we must also defend our needs in the Galut. We must assume that a large part of the Jewish people, including a part of the proletariat, will always remain in the Galut as an ordinary national minority. For that reason we include in our program, along with territorial demands, the demand for the maximum protection of our national needs in the Galut. Explicitly, this means national political autonomy for the Jews in all Galut lands.

National autonomy is not a radical solution of the Jewish problem and, therefore, cannot remove the anomalies of the Jewish economic strategic base. However, it provides the Jewish proletariat with the necessary political forms. It serves to place the proletariat in the political arena face to face with the Jewish bourgeoisie. But even if it is incapable of making a radical change and cannot give the Jewish proletariat an efficient weapon in the struggle against the prevailing form of capitalism, we must still remember that national political autonomy is the maximum obtainable in the Galut. The shortcomings of national political autonomy emanate from the abnormal conditions of Galut life.

National political autonomy, even with all the democratic guarantees possible, remains only a mere palliative. Without territorial autonomy it will not lessen the national oppression of the Jewish people, will not change the Jewish social structure, and will not set great forces in motion. Jews, however, will be granted a normal representation which will serve to make an end to shameful backdoor politics. It will be a powerful unifying force among the Jewish masses; it will provide the Jewish nationality with a proper financial apparatus; and what is most important, it will provide them with a political education, will teach them even in the Galut to create and shape their own destiny.

This achievement is small in comparison with what can be obtained in an autonomous territory, but it is important when compared with what exists at present. We know how limited our civil equality will be in practice; yet we demand legal civil equality. We know that our national equality in the Galut will in reality be very circumscribed; nevertheless, we demand full national equality without any legal limitations. Life itself will see to it that we do not gain too much, so we must do everything within our power to get the optimum out of national equality.

An examination of the growth of democracy will reveal the stages in the attainment of national political autonomy. Just as socialism will result from processes implicit in the concentration of capital and will be established by means of the class struggle, just as the fall of autocracy will result from processes inherent in the capitalistic development of Russian society and will be precipitated by the class struggle—just so will the realization of national political autonomy result from processes inherent in the development of society along nationality lines and will come about through the class struggle of the proletariat and its allies. However, our most important national demand is territorial autonomy. It is being realized by means of processes inherent in Jewish immigration. In the course of its migration, the Jewish people does not degenerate, nor does it resurrect itself; it merely transforms itself.

V.

The most general law governing migration in the capitalistic era is the following: *the direction of migratory labor depends upon the direction of migratory capital.* This law was propounded by Marx. In order to deduce the real facts concerning general and Jewish migration, it will be necessary to describe the social relationships between the entrepreneur and the laborer.

Language is the medium of contact, constituting a national bond. In small-scale industries, the entrepreneur and the laborers are in close propinquity; for there the entrepreneur not only organizes and distributes the jobs, but frequently also works shoulder to shoulder with the employees. Mutual understanding of questions pertaining to the functioning of the industry thus develops another national bond. But in large industrial establishments, a complex hierarchy of managers and officials separates the entrepreneur capitalist from the laborers. Therefore, in large-scale production there is no necessary national tie between entrepreneur and worker.

Similarly, in the field of distribution the language is merely a means of communication between the seller and the buyer. The wholesale merchant is separated from the consumer by brokers and other intermediaries. To him, therefore, language and other national ties are of little significance. The retailer, however, is closely allied with the consumer by language and national customs. Large industry and business are international, while petty industry (and a part of middle industry as well) bears a clearly defined national character. The latter's sphere of activities is determined by the national market, and its sphere of exploitation reaches only the workers within the national boundaries. (As far as Jewish industry is concerned, this particular analysis has to be modified; for the Jews find themselves in a foreign economy. They do not use their national language in business but generally assume the language of the land. However, wherever they live in compact masses, Jews do not assume the foreign language very readily.) The petty merchant is very close to the consumer and is therefore liable to national boycott, but the large capitalist can very easily hide his nationality under a hierarchy of intermediaries.

This fundamental fact—the existence of national ties between the entrepreneur, worker, and consumer in petty industry, and the absence of them in large industry—is even more obvious during the migration of capital and labor. *Capital and labor of petty industry always migrate together and retain their national character in their new domicile.*

The migration of labor is never directed to countries where there exists a large labor reserve in the peasantry. Countries such as Germany, France, and Italy will never be countries of immigration as long as their capitalistic development follows the present trend.

In determining the direction of migration we must also consider the differences between the level of economic development and the level of cultural and political development. In the European democratic countries, all parts of the population enjoy the benefits of a high cultural and political level of life, regardless of sharp economic differences. If we want to apply to the phenomenon of mass migration the law according to which migration tends in the direction of least resistance, we must determine the resistances and all the factors connected with them. We then arrive at the following important conclusions. Of two countries acceptable for immigration, that country which promises the higher economic level affords the line of least resistance. Of two countries with identical economic levels, that country which promises the higher cultural and political level affords the line of least resistance.

The causes of emigration may lie in a prolonged economic depression or oppression. In the capitalistic era, the proletarizing masses emigrate because of persistent economic pressure. The landless peasant masses migrate to new countries, where pools of unused capital accumulate because of the absence of reserve labor forces. Accumulation of capital is possible only in places where there are good prospects for its development. The cultural and political standards of a country are of great importance in determining the influx of capital. For that reason the ruined peasant population of Europe will not migrate into politically backward countries. *The migration of European peasantry is tending and will continue in the direction of the democratic countries of the New World.*

The outstanding national character of the lower middle class is evident in the process of immigration. The peasants concentrate into national blocs in their newly found homes. Italians, Germans, and other nationalities each make up independent settlements. Along with the Italian peasants, who constitute a mass of small consumers, there immigrate also Italian petty merchants, artisans, and professionals. This is also the case with every national group of immigrants.

Only international investment capital, the transfer of which gives direction to immigration, is perfectly free of any national character. (One other group bears no national character in immigration. It includes the dregs of society, such as professional thieves, white slave traffickers, and gamblers. International hooliganism knows no nation or fatherland. Its favorite centers of immigration are the harbor cities, the gold and diamond districts, and all places where it is possible to fish in troubled waters.)

Of an entirely different character is the immigration of the urban petty industrial population. In the case of this element, the migration of wage-labor depends on the small capitalist. The urban petty industrial population follows the entrepreneurs of its nation. No matter how acute the need for proletarization grows to be, it will not be filled unless conditions force the petty capitalist to emigrate. On the surface, it would seem that economic ruin is sufficient to cause the emigration of small capitalists. This, however, is erroneous; for a ruined capitalist loses his class status. In order for capitalists to emigrate, there must be a constant economic threat or continual persecution. In the case of Jewish emigration, pogroms, civil persecution, and general insecurity play a decisive role. If the new country of refuge is economically suitable, if Jewish capital may be utilized to advantage and production enhanced, emigration of the impoverished masses increases and the success of the first pioneers of Jewish capital brings additional numbers of Jewish entrepreneurs and workers. Mass immigration is thus precipitated and gains impetus from new pogroms and persecutions. (It must be noted, too, that for petty capital the cultural and political development of the country is of much less significance than it is for large capitalistic ventures.)

Until recently, international capital was directed to the newly developing countries. The large inflow of capital into those countries accelerated the development of the forces of production, exploited natural resources, and created a demand for labor. For that reason, an intensive migration of the proletarizing peasantry of many nations has been directed toward the new countries. Since a developing economy ruled by international capital created a need for consumers' and service goods, there was room for Jewish immigration. Jews followed the general stream of world migration.

This situation was the case until recently. Lately, new tendencies began to appear. The natural resources, for the development of which a great deal of capital has been expended, became limited. Wage reductions became common, and capitalists' profits diminished. International capital began to look for new investment channels and turned to financing agricultural projects. At the same time, workers who had been too compactly settled were unable to find employment. Thus a break occurred in world immigration, and even larger groups of immigrants turned to agrarian countries.

It is necessary to point out two characteristics of agricultural colonization in undeveloped countries. These characteristics arise from the fact that colonization takes place upon the initiative of government institutions which encourage loans in order to improve conditions in the grain trade and to provide live stock and machinery on a long term credit basis. Italian, German, and Slavic peasants, who formerly immigrated into the United States, Australia, and South Africa as unskilled workers, at present go to Argentina, Brazil, and Canada where they become independent homesteaders on government lands, with an inventory for which they can pay on the installment plan. Even though these homesteaders appear to be independent, they nevertheless find themselves in the clutches of investment capital. Because of long term credit, loans from international financiers do not seem so oppressive and do not ruin the farmers. In agrarian countries the farmers cannot grow products to meet their household needs; they must grow crops for the market. They must pay their debts and must therefore exchange their products for money. The new countries dump large quantities of grain on the world market, and the resulting competition eliminates those elements which cannot maintain the proper standard of farming. On the other hand, long term credit helps the farmer to entrench himself in his holdings and keeps him from proletarization. In countries which are predominantly agricultural there is no place for individual large farms because of the lack of laborers. Instead of offering one's services to the landowner, one has the opportunity to acquire land for oneself. Even the intensification of agriculture does not tend to ruin the farmer, because the farmers cooperate in the introduction of machines, new methods of fertilization, and land irrigation. In this, the government is of great help. Along with the farmer of a particular nationality, there enter into the land petty merchants of the same nationality who satisfy the limited needs of the farming population.

From what has been said, it is possible to draw important conclusions concerning the tendencies of Jewish migration. Since the stream of world migration has turned in another direction, Jewish migration must also find new channels. But are predominantly agricultural countries adapted to Jewish immigration?

To answer this question we must first distinguish between spontaneous immigration and planned colonization.

It is clear that spontaneous, unregulated Jewish immigration cannot direct itself to new countries in order to serve commercial and industrial functions or to take up agriculture. The former task is impossible, because in those countries there is no place for petty capital. Small-scale production and petty commerce do not reach the world market. If the Jewish masses do not find a local market for their products there, they have no good reason for immigrating into such countries. It is true that the Jews can make a determined attempt to engage in farming, but such attempts are doomed to failure. Jewish farmers would have to compete in the world market and would surely lose. As city-bred people, the Jews are unable to compete with Italian and other peasants who have an agricultural background. The geographical location is unimportant. Jewish workers may live in Africa and the Italians in America—they will still compete in the world market. For this reason, all attempts at Jewish land colonization to date have been a failure and have borne merely a philanthropic character.

Equally unsuccessful will be the attempts at planned colonization in such lands. The organization of such colonization must, from its very inception, assume the character of a large-scale financial enterprise. It will have to compete in the world market and will swiftly be led to bankruptcy. If, on the other hand, it should attempt to engage in large-scale manufacturing, it will fail either because of comparatively low productivity or because of the relatively higher price of Jewish labor.

Territorialism, if it is to continue to be a revolutionary movement within the Jewish people, must find support in the spontaneous processes of Jewish life. Territorialism does not signify a mere spontaneous migration of Jews, but a spontaneously concentrated immigration. The analysis of territorialism may be considered as complete only when one can point to the land for immigration. Territorialism apart from a particular territory is utopian.

The above determined laws with regard to the processes of immigration and emigration have led us to the conclusion that Jewish immigration is being excluded from countries of wide land colonization and from countries of large industrial investments. The world-wide stream of immigration increasingly tends toward agricultural countries which offer free land to immigrants. The Jews, in the era of capitalistic competition, cannot at once turn to farming. The economic activities of the Jewish immigrants tend to lose their industrial and commercial character and to be transferred from the final levels of the process of production to the primary levels—to the basic industries and farming. This transfer, however, cannot occur at once.

For that reason, Jewish migration differs from the general stream of migration and must seek for itself entirely different channels. Everything that tends to isolate Jewish life helps to make Jews more nationally conscious. Jewish immigration assumes a national character, and this spirit finds expression in the spread of a national ideology of emigration.

The need for emigration of the Jewish nation is merely one of the forces leading to its rehabilitation. When planned immigration will assume a national character, it will fuse with our other aspirations for rebirth. Abstract territorialism is an incomplete ideology of national emancipation; the whole and synthetic form is Zionism.

Jewish immigration is slowly tending to divert itself to a country where petty Jewish capital and labor may be utilized in such forms of production as will serve as a transition from an urban to an agricultural economy and from the production of consumers' goods to more basic forms of industry. The country into which Jews will immigrate will not be highly industrial nor predominantly agricultural, but rather semi-agricultural. Jews alone will migrate there, separated from the general stream of immigration. The country will have no attraction for immigrants from other nations.

This land will be the only one available to the Jews; and of all countries available for immigrants of all lands, this country will provide the line of greatest resistance. It will be a country of low cultural and political development. Big capital will hardly find use for itself there, while Jewish petty and middle capital will find a market for its products in both this country and its environs. *The land of spontaneously concentrated Jewish immigration will be Palestine.*

The immigration of the Jews into Palestine will differ considerably from their previous wanderings. Formerly, they had to adapt themselves to the needs of the native population; their primary function was to satisfy the native consumers' needs or, as in the case of the United States, the needs of a mixed population which consisted more of immigrants than of natives.

In Palestine, Jewish immigrants for the first time not only will aim to satisfy the needs of the native population, but will also produce for the external market of the surrounding countries of the Mediterranean, and in time even for the world market. Until now, Jews have always been dependent upon the native populations in the lands of the Galut. The organization of Jewish labor was not self-sufficient but was determined by the nature of the relationships that existed among the native population. The Jewish welfare in the Galut was always dependent upon the "usefulness" of the Jews to the ruling nationality. The needs of the natives, their ability to pay, and the rivalry between Jewish merchants and professionals and the corresponding groups of the native population— all of these factors helped bring about a narrowed field for Jewish economy in the Galut. Aside from these limitations the Jews, both in their old places of residence and in the new lands of immigration, began to be displaced and become pauperized; they became superfluous. Compulsory isolation became their fate; national oppression and persecutions took place. The chief cause for this one-sided dependence of the Jews on the native population lay in the expatriation of the Jewish people.

With the migration into Palestine the situation will change radically. The welfare and functions of Jewish immigrants in Palestine will depend not on the native population but on the foreign market, which will for a long time be able to absorb the products of Palestine because of the favorable location of the Mediterranean. Jewish labor will encounter national competition neither on the part of the native population nor on the part of the new immigrants. In Palestine, the Jews will perform the functions which serve as a transition from the production of consumers' goods to the creation of the means of production.

As to the question of how many Jewish immigrants Palestine can absorb, it is easy to see that the absorptive capacity of the land depends on the degree of capitalistic development in the neighboring countries.

If, for instance, Egypt becomes a land with increasing exports, it is evident that the imports to Egypt will grow as well. Since the Jewish settlers in Palestine will be interested in the neighboring foreign market, large-scale capitalistic enterprises will develop among the Jews. The tendencies of Jewish immigration will be affected by those of the world market insofar as they affect the southeastern shores of the Mediterranean Sea. We do not assert that Jewish immigration into Palestine will always progress uniformly; from time to time it may fluctuate. Also, because of economic crises or political complications, there may be a temporary exodus from Palestine. *But the general tendency will undoubtedly be a continual growth of Jewish immigration into Palestine.* Those who think that such a radical transformation of Jewish life as territorialism implies can occur without a bitter struggle, without cruelty and injustices, without suffering for innocent and guilty alike, are utopianists. Such revolutions are not recorded in ink with high sounding phrases; they are written in sweat, tears, and blood.

We have investigated the tendency towards the concentration of Jewish immigration and towards the formation of a relatively economically independent Jewish community in Palestine. The masses of the Jews in the Galut, who do not take a far-seeing view of their emigration needs, will join in our Zionist endeavors because of their immediate needs. The greater the interest of the surrounding nations in the radical solution of the Jewish problem and the greater the national consciousness and organization of the Jews in the Galut in response to oppression and isolation, the more energetically will organized Zionism impress itself upon this spontaneous process and the more desirable will its results be.

The broadening and consolidation of Jewish economic and cultural positions in Palestine will proceed at a rapid pace along with the above mentioned processes. Parallel with the growth of economic independence will come the growth of political independence. The ideal of political autonomy for the Jews will be consummated by *political territorial autonomy in Palestine.*

Political territorial autonomy in Palestine is the ultimate aim of Zionism. For proletarian Zionists, this is also a step toward socialism.

VI.

Because proletarian Zionism has recognized the *spontaneous concentration of Jewish immigration into Palestine,* it has completely shaken off all former utopian concepts with regard to the realization of territorial autonomy.

Immigration to Palestine rises above those measures with which utopianists usually approach the question of Palestine. Some of us may revere Palestine as our former fatherland. Others may consider Palestine a proper center of immigration because of its geographic proximity to centers of Jewish population. Still others may imagine that the ideology of the movement, of national emancipation, includes a special preference for Palestine. Others, on the other hand, may believe that Zionism is guided by purely practical calculations. All these differences of opinion have no bearing on our analysis.

Our Palestinism is not a matter of principle, because it has nothing to do with old traditions. Nor is our Palestinism purely practical; for we do not recognize the existence of other fit territories to choose from. The trend of thought of the practical adherents of Palestine is as follows: a territory is needed; Palestine is a possible territory; it is the best territory under the circumstances; therefore, Palestine. Our line of thought, however, is: there are migratory processes inherent in the Jewish life; Palestine is the future land for the spontaneous waves of immigration; consequently we will have territorial autonomy in Palestine. The practical adherents of Palestine assert that theoretically they are territorialists, while practically they are for Palestine. With us, however, theoretical territorialism is not to be distinguished from concrete territorialism;

for concentrated Jewish immigration will direct itself toward Palestine and not toward any other territory. We do not claim that Palestine is the sole or best territory; we merely indicate that Palestine is the territory where territorial autonomy will be obtained. Our Palestinism is neither theoretical nor practical, but rather predictive.

Thus we have liquidated the "search for a territory". This task we entrusted to the inherent processes of Jewish immigration. Our task is not to find a territory, but to obtain territorial political autonomy in Palestine.

The general task of the territorialist movement is to regulate the spontaneous processes, especially the immigration processes, which lead finally to territorial autonomy. As a matter of fact, we have two territorial movements: bourgeois Zionism and proletarian Zionism. What then is the role of each in Jewish life?

In every spontaneous process, it is necessary to distinguish between two factors, even though the distinction is difficult: creative factors and liberating factors.

The development and accumulation of the forces of production, the creation of new combinations of material forces, the growth of capitalism— these are the creative factors in the evolution of modern society. The creation of free conditions for the development of the productive forces, the growth of democracy—these are the liberating factors of modern social evolution. Both the creative and the liberating factors are spontaneous, even though they both are subject to regulation.

The bourgeoisie regulates the creative factors of the spontaneous process; the proletariat regulates the liberating factors. The development of capitalism is being carried on by the bourgeoisie; but it is the struggles of the proletariat that bring about the growth of democracy.

The sphere of activity of the bourgeoisie cannot be precisely delimited from the sphere of activity of the proletariat. The bourgeoisie is partly interested in the growth of democracy and aids in the process, but its role is insignificant in comparison with that of the proletariat. On the other hand, in whatever concerns the development of the forces of production and the capitalistic evolution of society, the organizing role belongs to the bourgeoisie. Although the proletariat is interested in the development of the forces of production, its sphere of activity lies outside of it, and it puts forth no particular demands therein. When the dictatorship of the proletariat shall have been attained, labor will organize all work. Until then, the proletariat does not interfere, as a class, in the regulation of the creative factors. Thus, it is not the task of the proletariat to be concerned with digging canals or building railroads. Here the proletariat puts forth no demands, because these are the creative factors of capitalistic evolution. But whenever it does interfere in the technical organization of the work, it is for the sake of obtaining better working and living conditions. In the case of colonization, one finds an identical situation. Colonization methods are not the concern of the proletariat in the capitalistic era; for they are a part of the creative area of capitalistic activity, a part of the organization of production. The proletariat, however, may demand some regulation of the property relationships and other legal arrangements in the colonies; for these are in its proper sphere—the liberating one.

When we pass to those spontaneous processes in which territorialism is realized, we must again distinguish between creative and liberating factors and thus clarify the respective roles of the bourgeoisie and of the proletariat.

The creative elements in the process consist in the accumulation of capital and labor in Palestine, in the exploitation of the natural resources of the land, in technological development, and in the general development of the forces of production. To regulate all these is chiefly the task of bourgeois Zionism. Immigration into Palestine must be properly guided, and colonization must be supervised.

To regulate the spontaneous Jewish immigration into Palestine means to facilitate the entry of capital and labor and to utilize those forces in the most economical and rational manner possible. This must be the realistic direction of the activity of the Zionist Congress.

The Jewish proletariat lives in the Galut, and there it struggles for its daily needs. Among these needs is the freedom of immigration into Palestine—the inviolability of the right of entry there. Objective processes lead the Jewish proletariat to Palestine, and in Palestine it must struggle bitterly. It would be easier to attain freedom in Palestine if life in the Galut were more bearable; and the stronger our political power in Palestine, the more respected will our rights be in Galut. This is an integration of Galut and Zion. The maximum we can obtain in the Galut is national political autonomy. In Palestine, however, the maximum is territorial and political autonomy. Which we shall obtain first does not matter. National political autonomy in the Galut is not only one of the means by which territorial autonomy in Palestine can be obtained, but is also an independent goal. These are two aims that are united by the historic process which unfolds itself simultaneously in all its breadth in Galut and in Palestine.

Utopianism always suffers because it strives to ignore historical processes. Utopianism wishes by means of human endeavor to create something not inherent in social life. Fatalism, on the other hand, assumes that the effective participation of human will is impossible with regard to these historical processes, and thus it drifts passively with the stream. Utopianism knows of no historical processes. The utopianists fear to mention the phrase "historical processes"; for they see in the so-called historical process fatalism and passivity. The fatalists, on the other hand, fear the conscious interference with the historical process as a dangerous artificiality. The fatalists forget that history is made by men who follow definite and conscious aims. Utopianists forget that the results of human activity coincide with human aims and purposes only when those aims and purposes are well adapted to the historical necessities of social life.

We ask, "What role can our will, our consciousness, play in the historical processes of Jewish life?" To the conscious interference of human will there must be added another factor, that of organization. Organization is not a mere sum of individual efforts, but rather a collective social force. Along with the historical social tendencies we must introduce planning. To regulate historical processes means to facilitate and accelerate their progress, to conserve social energy, and to obtain the optimum results from the labor put forth.